Chicken Soup
for the Soul.

My Clever,
Curious,
Caring Cat

Chicken Soup for the Soul: My Clever, Curious, Caring Cat
101 Tales of Feline Friendship
Amy Newmark

Published by Chicken Soup for the Soul, LLC www.chickensoup.com
Copyright ©2021 by Chicken Soup for the Soul, LLC. All Rights Reserved.

The publisher gratefully acknowledges the many publishers and individuals who granted Chicken Soup for the Soul permission to reprint the cited material.

Front cover and interior photos: Maine Coon cat courtesy of istockphoto.com/GlobalP (©GlobalP), cat with blue eyes courtesy of istockphoto.com/Irina Vasilevskaia (Irina Vasilevskaia), cat hanging from logo courtesy of istockphoto.com/Astakhova (©Astakhova)
Back cover and interior photos: British Longhair cat courtesy of istockphoto.com/feedough(©feedough), cat in box courtesy of istockphoto.com/esolla (©esolla), cat looking up courtesy of istockphoto.com/Sonsedska (©Sonsedska)
Photo of Amy Newmark courtesy of Susan Morrow at SwickPix

Cover and Interior by Daniel Zaccari

Distributed to the booktrade by Simon & Schuster. SAN: 200-2442

Publisher's Cataloging-In-Publication Data
(Prepared by The Donohue Group, Inc.)

Names: Newmark, Amy, compiler.
Title: Chicken soup for the soul : my clever, curious, caring cat : 101 tales of feline friendship / [compiled by] Amy Newmark.
Other Titles: My clever, curious, caring cat : 101 tales of feline friendship
Description: [Cos Cob, Connecticut] : Chicken Soup for the Soul, LLC, [2021]
Identifiers: ISBN 9781611590791 (print) | ISBN 9781611593198 (ebook)
Subjects: LCSH: Cats--Literary collections. | Cats--Anecdotes. | Human-animal relationships--Literary collections. | Human-animal relationships--Anecdotes. | LCGFT: Anecdotes.
Classification: LCC SF445.5 .C45 2021 (print) | LCC SF445.5 (ebook) | DDC 636.8002--dc23
Library of Congress Control Number: 2021939453

PRINTED IN THE UNITED STATES OF AMERICA
on acid∞free paper

25 24 23 22 21   01 02 03 04 05 06 07 08 09 10

My Clever, Curious, Caring Cat

101 Tales of Feline Friendship

Amy Newmark

Chicken Soup for the Soul, LLC
Cos Cob, CT

Changing lives one story at a time®
www.chickensoup.com

Table of Contents

❶

~Who's in Charge Here?~

❷

~Four-Legged Therapists~

❸

~Cat Sense~

❹

~Miracles Happen~

❺
~Life Lessons from the Cat~

❻
~Cat-astrophes~

❼
~We Are Family~

❽
~I Knead You~

❾
~My Very Good, Very Bad Cat~

Chapter
1

Who's in Charge Here?

The Cat That Saved Dogs

Cats will outsmart dogs every time.
~John Grogan

The Pit Bull lunged at Molly, and my hand fluttered to my chest. What if the dog hurt her? The little twelve-year-old cat was a final link to my sister who'd passed away years earlier.

Like my sister, Molly was petite and independent, taking in stride whatever life threw at her. But even a sassy feline was no match for the snarling brute standing before her. Or so I thought. Turns out, I was wrong.

While Brandi, my neighbor, fumbled for a leash to pull the dog away, Molly refused to budge. She didn't run or arch her back in fear as some cats do. She stood her ground, her cool green eyes unwavering.

The dog's growl became a whimper, and his brow furrowed in bewilderment at this fearsome feline.

I heaved a sigh of relief. If anything had happened to her, I would've been heartbroken. A dozen years earlier, Nancy had selected the gray-and-white kitten for me from a litter born on the farm where she and my brother-in-law lived.

"What should I name her?" I'd asked.

"Why not Molly?" she suggested. So, Molly it was.

Over the years, the little cat grew dearer to me. Like my sister, the cat was surprisingly tough. Before cancer took its toll on my sister, she taught school for many years. Though barely five feet tall, she could control a classroom with one glance from her clear blue eyes.

My thoughts returned to the present as Brandi gasped in admiration. "That Molly is something. I'm going to use her to train all our rescue dogs. They're more adoptable if they're cat-friendly."

Brandi led a rescue group that saved dogs from our local shelter and placed them in homes where foster families socialized the animals until they were adopted into "forever homes."

Soon, every dog Brandi rescued encountered a stare-down from Molly. After the "trainees" left, the unflappable cat would twitch her tail and sashay about her business.

In time, my husband and I also fostered dozens of dogs, and every pooch learned to get along with cats before heading to their adopters' homes.

On the rescue group's website, all the pups that stayed in our home, as well as those Brandi fostered, earned the "cat-friendly" badge next to their names. Prospective adopters were often skeptical, so I'd use my phone to make videos of the pooches lying quietly as Molly strutted past. Sometimes, she even snuggled next to them in their beds.

Brandi has since moved, and we don't keep many pups these days. But during the time we were actively fostering, Molly "trained" about forty canines, helping them make the transition from unmannered shelter dogs to gentle pets bound for loving homes.

Some adopters update us regularly, sending pictures of canines we cared for, living the good life in their new homes. The photos often include cats lounging nearby, and they make me smile. Many dogs were tiny puppies while in our care. They have many years ahead to experience the love of families who were willing to take in a rescue as long as the newcomer could get along with cats already in the household. A few were elderly dogs in need of homes to live out their final years, and being cat-friendly increased their adoptability. Either way, my brave kitty had a hand, or paw, in all those happy endings.

At fourteen, Molly is still going strong and continues to be a daily reminder of my courageous sister, who could face down a room full of unruly kids or the specter of cancer, just as the cat she named doesn't back down from anything.

— Beth Gooch —

Cat on a Mission

People that don't like cats haven't met the right one yet.
~Deborah A. Edwards

In 1995, I was twenty-two and working as a 911 dispatcher. Late one evening, one of the county paramedics came in carrying a young gray-and-white cat. He was trying to find a home for him because his family was relocating to an apartment that didn't allow pets. Still grieving the loss of my beloved cat Rudy about a year before, I wanted to adopt a new kitty, but my father was dead set against it. Since I still lived with my parents, I respected his decision, but on this particular night I simply could not resist the longhaired ball of fur that came into the office looking for a new home. I knew Dad would be angry, but I also knew he secretly liked cats and felt certain that I could convince him to let me keep him.

Well, I was wrong! When I came trudging in with the cat later that evening, Dad was furious. Before I knew it, we were engaged in one of the worst arguments I can ever recall. Dad was a kind and loving man, but he could rattle the rafters when anger got the best of him. Bringing home another wayward cat that night rubbed him the wrong way. We shouted back and forth for at least a half-hour before he finally caved in with the stipulation that I would be solely responsible for his feeding, cleaning, and vet bills. He wanted nothing to do with him. I agreed but still proceeded to stomp and pout down the hall to my bedroom like a child, fuming, mumbling, and carrying the cat in my arms.

As I lay in bed, still huffing, puffing, and sniffling while petting him, I decided to name him Simon. Before long, I found myself talking to him because, well, I had no one else to talk to. As I gently stroked his ears and listened to him purr, I told him that we would have to find a way to make Dad warm up to him.

"You know," I said. "You're going to have to go out there and butter him up if you want to stay."

In the past, my dad had always protested first about the many strays or homeless cats my sister and I brought home, but he had also been the first to get attached to them. This time, however, I wasn't sure this would be the case. After a while, I headed back to the living room, with Simon right behind me. What happened next is almost impossible to believe. If both my mother and I hadn't witnessed it, I'm not even sure *we* would believe it!

Simon ran down the hall, passing me altogether, and headed straight for Dad, who was relaxing in his recliner watching television. He leapt right onto his lap, only to have Dad shove him off. He stood there for a moment, switching his tail back and forth, and then leapt right up again. Again, Dad shoved him off, his eyes rolling. Simon immediately jumped onto his lap a third time, only to be shoved off again, this time with a lengthy stream of curse words. With that, Simon went around to the side of the chair, stood on his back legs and, placing his front paws on the arm of it, just stared at Dad for a moment.

"Go on, GET!" Dad growled as he shooed him away. At this, Simon went around to the back of the chair and jumped up onto Dad's shoulders. This time, Dad just pretended to ignore him, hoping he would take the hint and leave him alone. Simon, however, seemed dead set on endearing himself to Dad, so he persisted. Mom and I just sat there watching in disbelief as the cat proceeded to climb up and park himself right on top of Dad's head! To this day, I still chuckle at the memory of him sitting up there. Dad's eyes rolled upward, and he scowled as he looked up at Simon, who had stretched his head downward and begun nudging him with his cold nose.

"You're not gonna leave me alone, are you?" Dad asked, as Simon continued to sit patiently on top of his noggin. Finally, with a submissive sigh, Dad announced, "Fine, you can stay!"

With that, Simon hopped down and headed straight for my lap, where he curled up comfortably and purred loudly, almost as if to say, "Mission accomplished!"

From that day on, Dad and Simon were the best of friends. Even after I got married two years later and moved out of state, their bond never wavered. Anytime Mom and Dad came to visit, Simon would make a beeline for Dad's lap. To say that Simon had successfully buttered up Dad would be a massive understatement. I think Dad became more attached to Simon than he had to any other cat we had adopted. By the time he reached adulthood, Simon had grown into a beautiful cat who clearly bore the characteristics of a Maine Coon breed with his pointed features, luxurious fur, and very large frame. I have a picture of Dad sitting in our blue recliner with Simon on his lap, which he practically covered altogether.

Dad passed away in 2000, and Simon died four years later. I like to think of them as being together in heaven, with Dad relaxing in a recliner and Simon curled up on his lap (or perhaps on his head), just like always.

— Linda Yencha Nichols —

Pookie

*Pets are humanizing. They remind us we have
an obligation and responsibility to preserve
and nurture and care for all life.*
~James Cromwell

I found him on my doorstep one day in late summer, nearly eight years ago. He regarded me fearfully as I walked up the garden path toward him. As I drew closer, he crouched with muscles taut, ready to take flight. I stopped and waited for him to make his next move. I talked to him in what I hoped were soothing tones, but as soon as I started to move toward him again, he sprang up and vanished into the bushes surrounding the front of the house.

The following day, the little cat was there again, lying on the doorstep, but still with the don't-come-near-me look on his face. This time, however, instead of a hurried flight into the bushes, he got up slowly, stretched, and walked around the side of the house in quite a dignified manner. I decided to leave a saucer of milk on the doorstep in case he was hungry and let him go his own way. After all, I thought, he might live in the neighborhood and just be paying me a visit. The next day, the saucer was empty.

Over the next few days, he spent more and more time hanging around the house until it became obvious that he was a stray. The saucer of milk was replaced by a bowl of cat food, and he became a regular visitor, morning and evening. Although he looked fully grown, probably about a year old, he was small and very pretty. He had long gray fur, and all four feet were tipped with white. As far as I could see, his eyes were a smoky blue, but I could never get close enough to tell. When it became clear that he intended to stay, I named him Pookie — short for Pussy Cat, the name my mother had affectionately given to all our cats. In spite of repeated attempts to befriend him, he never came close enough for me to touch.

I love cats, as I do all animals. They were always part of my childhood. I would gladly have given Pookie a permanent home, but unfortunately that wasn't possible. We had four rescue dogs, one of whom was a dedicated cat-hater who would have happily killed any feline she could catch. So, I put "Cat Found" notices up in the neighborhood and a short piece in the local newspaper, all to no avail. Taking him to the crowded Humane Society, where I was sure he would be euthanized, was out of the question. So, I resigned myself to coping with an outdoor cat.

Autumn came and went. The weather turned to snow and ice, and Pookie was as aloof and evasive as ever, running from me if I got too close but always present at mealtimes. One day, I opened the front door to retrieve the morning paper and was shocked to see a little bundle of gray fur lying motionless on the walk. At first, as I bent to touch him, I thought that Pookie was dead. Then a faint cry, barely audible, reassured me that he was still alive, although badly injured. I hurried into the house and locked up all the dogs. Then I returned to carry his frozen little body into the kitchen. I saw congealed blood on his head and neck, and fresh blood oozed from his mouth. I wrapped him in a warm blanket and sponged the blood off his face and body, realizing for the first time how thin he was despite several weeks of nourishing food. As soon as my vet's office was open, I rushed him there immediately.

As the vet sutured Pookie's wounds and administered antibiotics, he said this looked like a typical cat fight where a large male had beaten up a weaker cat that he found in his territory. He said he would keep Pookie overnight, and if he was doing well, he would send him home with me in the morning.

All I could offer Pookie in the way of shelter during his recovery was a glassed-in, unheated porch where everything was liable to freeze in winter. So, before he came home, I found a sturdy box that I wrapped securely in a blanket with only a small covered opening at the front. Another woolly blanket lay on a heating pad inside and made a warm nest for him.

He tolerated treatment of his wounds, lustily ate the food I brought him, and used a litter box when he was strong enough to walk. But, to my surprise and disappointment, he remained aloof, never showing any particular pleasure when I petted him. I found this very strange. I couldn't remember a time when I hadn't been able to win the affection and trust of an animal. Even pet rats from childhood had bonded closer to me than this little cat.

While he was recovering, I managed to find a no-kill cat shelter about thirty miles from my home. When I contacted them, the owners said they were willing to have my erstwhile stray join their "happy cats." So, when Pookie was fully recovered, a nice lady appeared with a portable cage, and he was borne away without giving me a second glance.

I often wondered what happened to my little protégé, and one day I called the shelter and asked if he had settled in and was happy. I was surprised to hear that he had been adopted a few weeks after he arrived at the shelter. If I was really interested, someone could call the adoptees and check on him.

Apparently, an elderly couple had chosen Pookie because he reminded them of a beloved cat they'd had previously, who had died of old age. Then I had another surprise. The three of them had bonded instantly, and Pookie was a cherished member of the family who loved to sit on their laps and sleep on their bed at night. I could hardly believe what I was hearing!

A trifle ruefully, I thought of the times I had held Pookie in my arms as he recovered from his wounds, stroking him tenderly as he lay inert on my lap. Never once was there the remotest rumble of acceptance, that deep purring sound like the idling of an old automobile or any rhythmic pummeling of contented little paws on my knees. Though I had hoped to win his affection, I didn't. But caring and doing the right thing were reward enough.

— Monica Agnew Kinnaman —

Mother Kitten

The smart cat doesn't let on that he is.
~H.G. Frommer

The kitten came to live with us uninvited. She was born to a very wild and precocious feline that roamed the neighborhood's back yards. Not being a cat person, my self-appointed role was to capture her and hand her over to the vet.

With some concern, our family seemed to accept the fact that this kitten might continue her mother's reproductive cycle. Occasionally, I spoke soft, affectionate words to this adorable fur ball as she ran and jumped the fence to escape from me.

Then, after a three-day weekend trip away from home, we walked into the living room and found the untamable kitten at the glass patio door. She peeked in while gently holding a newborn in her mouth.

Completely perplexed, I slid aside the heavy door as she pranced in and dropped the tiny thing at my feet. Then a second and third kitten were left for us. My husband Carl and I looked at each other and wondered why this uncatchable animal was willing to suddenly trust humans with her precious young.

We found a cardboard box, lined it with an old towel, set it right inside the glass door, and put the three newborns in their new abode. From that day on, our new cat was called Mother Kitten because we had no idea that she was old enough to become a mother.

While we were willing to welcome her into the Cordell household, she preferred the outdoors. Fortunately, Mother Kitten did prove to be excellent at her new responsibilities. They required her to set aside all her fear of people. It was amazing to have a somewhat wild animal choose to trust us.

In the beginning, there were boundaries between our three children and the huggable kittens. The children were not allowed to touch the cute visitors for a while as we attempted to honor the need for this mother to face her fear.

We found it to be so cool when Mother Kitten would come to the back door and stare through it until someone let her in. She would step into the small cardboard enclosure with her kittens, lie down, and nurse her young while she cleaned them. It seems she had an exceptional body clock that told her when to attend to them.

After about a week, I began to touch the kittens sparingly, hoping it would not stop their mother from caring for them. They flourished and grew into completely tame animals. After a while, Mother Kitten allowed me to touch her cautiously, but it was still months before I could pet her, even though she had allowed all of us to handle the kittens. Eventually, we were able to get her into a carrier and take to the vet for neutering.

My husband worked the 6:00 P.M. and 10:00 P.M. newscasts at the local NBC-TV affiliate. Carl came home between 11:00 P.M. and midnight. One evening, when he arrived, he found the sliding glass door unlocked and slightly open. In the morning, with an ounce of gentle frustration, he confronted me, suggesting that it was irresponsible for me to leave the back door unlocked and open.

I did not hesitate to correct him and informed him that I didn't leave the door unlocked or open. Carl shared that it was not the first time it had happened, and he was concerned for our safety. While I acknowledged his concern, I curtly informed him that I did not like being falsely accused.

He asked, "Well, then, if not you, who left the door open?"

I sarcastically responded, "It must have been Mother Kitten."

Carl tried to hold back his laughter, but it bubbled out as he dropped the issue.

The next evening, Carl was at the kitchen counter when Mother

Kitten executed her surprising nightly escape. She clawed her way up the heavy, light-blocking curtains, planted her chin on the lock, and forced it down to the unlocked position. Then she maneuvered her nose-pushing to create a small space between the wall and the door handle. Finally, Mother Kitten dropped to the floor and forced her eight-pound body through. We could sense her bravado, her "Ha, don't cage me in" attitude.

By the way, she never learned to close the door behind herself. And there was never another false accusation directed at me about that patio door.

— Toni Cordell —

Cat Versus Dog

*Cats are absolute individuals, with their own ideas
about everything, including the people they own.*
~John Dingman

The red cat sat just beyond the electric fence bordering our yard every day, close enough to tantalize but far enough to torment with no fear of reprisal. When she got bored with our dog's barking and racing back and forth, she sauntered off, her tail flicking in victory.

Every night, she slunk through our front garden, leaving her scent on stones and flowers so he would know she'd invaded his turf. Every morning, he would investigate the trail of his worst nightmare: the cat that would not obey. He would then lounge in the sunshine, establishing rightful ownership of his domain.

Several times a month, the red cat would hunt for mice and chipmunks in the stone walls surrounding our property. Our dog would race to battle his nemesis, barking in fury at her invasion. The red cat would leap lightly to the top of the wall and gaze down at him while he seethed.

On a day that will never be forgotten by anyone, our electric fence was turned off by accident. When the cat sashayed in front of the dog, he chased her. He dashed over the usual boundaries and kept going. She fled for the safety of our garage, and he followed her inside. Panicked, she raced out of the garage and into the back yard with our dog right on her heels.

Our neighbor swept our dog up in his arms, laughing until tears ran down his face. No one and nothing had ever bested that cat until then. Our dog savored his triumph over the cat. For several weeks, the red cat left our dog in peace, but then she resumed her campaign of terror.

The week after our dog died, the cat changed up her daily torment regimen. She sat in the front garden for a while. When no dog appeared for the routine chase, she performed a luxuriant, thorough grooming. She paused now and then to stare at the window from which he used to watch the world.

For weeks, the red cat haunted our front garden and the stone wall — her reliable places to incite mayhem. Eventually, her visits dwindled to occasional jaunts to chase her prey and glance at the window.

One day, when I was yanking invasive ivy off the stone wall, I felt something watching me. I turned to find the cat gazing at me from a safe distance. I said hello to her and went back to work. The next time I turned around, she had crossed the property line and sat closer to me.

These days, the red cat sleeps under our Jeep when the day is cold and the car is still warm from running errands. She hunkers under the pines and basks on the sun-warmed pavers in front of our house.

On Thanksgiving, I was writing at my desk when I felt eyes on me. The red cat was sitting motionless at the top of the steps; her gaze felt like an invitation to come out and say hello.

If he could see her now, my dog would go out of his mind.

Me?

I go out to greet my friend.

— Louise M. Foerster —

Top Cat

*The problem with cats is that they get the same exact
look whether they see a moth or an ax murderer.*
~Paula Poundstone

My orange Somali cat, Milo, takes his job as "top cat" seriously. Sometimes, he scouts out the back room, the one we rarely use. Sometimes, he watches for prehistoric creatures that happen to stalk past our windows. Other times, he just naps or spends his time hassling his feline housemate, Sharry (rhymes with starry). Regardless of what the days bring, Milo never seems to find life boring.

Yesterday, I watched as he meandered past the bathroom. Suddenly, his hair bristled, and he stopped in his tracks. An unknown, strange-looking object lay right in front of the bathtub! Milo immediately assumed a predator's stance, his furry feet moving back and forth like tiny pistons as though he'd attack that strange "thing" at any moment.

Slowly, Milo crept toward the potential enemy and almost scratched a hole in the floor trying to make himself look smaller. The enemy didn't move — ha! It was probably frozen with fear!

Milo might have thought he was invisible as he crouched to watch the bushy object, but in our small bathroom he stood out like Big Bird hiding in a flock of sparrows!

Top Cat crept closer, but the object didn't move a hair. Was it watching him, too? The Somali's ears pitched forward and back, forward and back. He listened for the slightest sound. None. Oh, enough already!

He could wait no longer. With a lunge, Milo landed on top of his prey.

It still didn't move — and by now Milo realized that it never would. "It" was a dustpan/brush combo that now lay in two pieces, oblivious to the energy being exerted around it. The dustpan and brush were part of my weekly cleaning routine and hadn't been put away yet.

Poor Milo lost a week's worth of energy before realizing that "it" wasn't dangerous after all! Still, he'd done his job. That's what top cats do. If cats ever shrug, that's what Milo did that day. Whether he felt embarrassed about being tricked by a dustpan brush, we'll never know. Satisfied that all was well on afternoon patrol, he turned on his heels and went to take a nap.

Housemate Sharry gave him a look that plainly said, "Fool cat." I made up for her lack of respect by praising my hero to the highest heavens. Milo had done some of his best work, and I was proud. Nothing is going to threaten our domain as long as this family's top cat is on duty!

After all, that's Milo's job.

— Louisa Godissart McQuillen —

The Thief

I have noticed that what cats most appreciate in
a human being is not the ability to produce food,
which they take for granted, but his or her
entertainment value.
~Geoffrey Household

The midday sun shined softly through the chintz curtains as my mom sat up from her nap and yawned. Her stooped shoulders hid her once sturdy, five-foot-seven-inch frame. A shuffling gait replaced the staccato of her heels. The once-blond curls now were iron gray. The green eyes stared vacantly, and the crinkle of laugh lines stilled. She swung her legs over the side of the bed and started to whimper.

"Mom, what's wrong?" I asked.

"I'm hungry!"

"But you just had lunch. Your favorite, a BLT."

She had always loved the crisp, smoky flavor of the bacon married with a fresh tomato and cool lettuce. "No, I didn't. I haven't eaten all day. You're so mean. You never feed me. Where's the other girl, the blond one? At least she brings me snacks. I'm hungry," she insisted.

"Okay, okay. I'll fix you another. Sissy will be here later, Mom."

As I headed back to the kitchen, our black-and-white Maine Coon cat, Briar, slipped into the bright room. I returned quickly with another BLT. Briar's jet-black tail curled in a question mark as he wound his way around Mom's long legs. Briar raised one big white paw, jumped on the bed, and rolled over, exposing his pink belly.

"Hello, my baby," Mom cooed. He mewed, looking for a belly rub. She obliged, leaning into him. "My sweet boy." He scrunched around on the bed, and she smiled. I placed the tray on her lap as she sat up.

"Demanding little bugger, isn't he?" I said.

Briar crouched closer to Mom, his pink nose twitching in anticipation.

"Oh, no. Don't let him do that!" I pleaded from the doorway as he snatched half the sandwich from her plate, wrestling the bacon from between the white bread slices.

"Oh," Mom giggled. "I guess I'm finished." She chortled as she set aside the tray.

I hadn't heard that sound in quite a while, so I laughed too while Briar munched on his prize. My mother's vacant stare disappeared for a short time as she laughed.

Briar got down, having dragged the other half of the sandwich with him. "No, you don't, little man," I called. He continued munching, ignoring my commands to stop while Mom laughed heartily.

Still giggling, she said, "Oh, let him have it. Poor baby must be starved." He scampered out of the room, dragging the bacon along.

I cleaned up the remnants of the sandwich and said, "Oh, why not?" Mom smiled. "Thank you, dear."

"Do you need anything else, Mom?"

"Another sandwich would be nice."

"Sure, I'll see what I can do," I said, resigned to the task. I nearly tripped over Briar lounging satisfied in the kitchen doorway.

"Thank you, little man, for making her laugh. But let her have the frigging sandwich this time, please." Ignoring me, he started his bath and waited.

— M. Maureen Skahan —

A Bowl of Water

Cats do not have to be shown how to have a good time,
for they are unfailingly ingenious in that respect.
~James Mason

Claus and his sister Lavie were four and a half months old when they joined our family. The kittens made themselves at home and fell in love with their humans (our sons) right away.

We soon learned each kitten had its own quirks. While Lavie needed constant attention and fussing over, Claus was as laidback as they come. We all envied his disposition.

When it came to meals, Lavie couldn't wait to devour her food and treats, while Claus couldn't wait to hit his water bowl. Bursting with glee, Claus would drink, flinging water everywhere. Perhaps it was the shape of his head or the way he slurped with the same affectionate licks he used on his sister's face, but each time he imbibed, Claus ended up with water droplets in the middle of his forehead. In the sunshine or light, the cluster of tiny water beads sparkled against his dark face like twinkling stars. Our sons found it hilarious, and it became known as the "goof galaxy," but I thought it was breathtaking!

Over the years, we'd had many cats, but we'd never had one who viewed water as a treat. Not only did Claus love to drink, but the sight or sound of even the tiniest drop of water seemed to mesmerize him.

When I'd do laundry, I'd find Claus chilling on top of the washing machine, grooving to the rush of water pouring through the pipes and swishing through the cycles. If someone had recently showered, Claus loved sitting in the tub, watching the last drips from the faucet. He frequented the bathroom sink where he enjoyed dipping his paw in the puddles left in the basin.

Throughout the years, I yearned to hold Claus, but he never allowed me to pick him up, and he hated being touched. When I dished out catnip to the cats, I'd sneak one quick stroke down Claus's back, but that was it. Any other time I tried, Claus freaked out and scampered away, his beautiful blue eyes filled with terror.

One day, while I was washing dishes, Claus sauntered over, plopped at my feet, and started crying. "What do you want, Claus?" He blinked at me and continued meowing. "Want some water?" Claus's eyes grew huge. On hot days, I'd often set an extra water bowl on the great-room floor, but Claus had never begged me for water until now.

With great anticipation, Claus watched me open the cupboard, grab a bowl, and fill it. All the while, he stood on his hind legs meowing. He got so excited that he almost tripped me as he swooshed around my feet, but I finally made it to the rug without spilling a drop. I watched Claus drink in ecstasy and smiled. I'd found a way into his heart.

Soon after, Claus appointed me his private water servant. It wasn't long before he had me trained to drop whatever I was doing and follow him so that I could refresh his water several times each day, even when the bowl was full.

Much to my family's dismay, in addition to Claus's upstairs water dish and great-room bowl, I placed more water containers throughout our cabin, which resulted in colorful expletives each time one of us tripped over an unexpected container and dumped the water.

Claus had found his heaven on earth. He spent many hours meditating at his water bowl, with an expression of pure bliss on his face. Many times, we'd find him with his head resting on the edge of the bowl, sound asleep.

Of course, Claus didn't spend all his time worshiping water. He adored his humans and loved hanging out with them. And, unlike Lavie, Claus never missed one of our family activities.

Although famous for his goofy water antics, last year we especially appreciated Claus's mellow presence as our family trudged through the first year of the pandemic. After that, Claus celebrated the new year with us. Several weeks later, Claus broke our hearts and Lavie's when he died at the much-too-young age of ten.

Each time I think of him, I get tears in my eyes. Claus left a huge hole in our lives. It's hard to believe he's gone. It seems strange not to see his water bowls strewn about, and there's no longer anything to trip over but our own feet.

While Claus never changed his mind about me touching or holding him, I am grateful for the special relationship we shared. I loved filling his world with happiness, and in return his presence enriched my life in so many ways. Each day, Claus reminded me that true joy can be found in the simple things in life — even a bowl of water.

— Jill Burns —

Where's the Snooze Button?

Cats do care. For example, they know instinctively
what time we have to be at work in the morning,
and they wake us up twenty minutes before
the alarm goes off.
~Michael Nelson

Of all the cats I've loved, not one ever came equipped with a snooze button. More accurate than my alarm clock, each cat employed his or her unique method for waking me each morning.

Sammy Claws, my first cat, meowed in my face at the top of his lungs. If I ignored him, he'd push my eyelid open with his paw and bellow even louder, as if to say, "I know you're in there!"

Mandi, the Calico who joined us during Sammy's reign, used a more subtle approach. She marched on me like a foot soldier. If that didn't bring the desired result, she'd pounce on my stomach. She and Sammy often tag-teamed me.

Sebastian and his sister Squeakette adopted me after Sammy and Mandi passed on.

Sebastian would let me sleep until 6:30, and then he'd lick my face with his sandpaper tongue. When that failed, he unlatched the hook-and-eye screen in the bedroom window of our 1920s bungalow.

A quick glance back at me seemed to say, "Don't get up. I'll see what the neighbors are having for breakfast. I smell bacon."

The image of him darting across the busy street propelled me out of bed. I scrambled out the door in my pajamas to catch him.

As I brought him inside and set him down, he headed straight for the window again. Dry cat food sprinkled into his bowl deflected his proposed adventure. Missions accomplished, both his and mine.

After my husband replaced all the locks on the window screens, Sebastian passed the figurative baton to his sister. Squeakette taught herself how to work the touch lamp. Tapping her nose on the rim of the stained-glass shade, she created a strobe-light effect to pull me out of dreamland.

On... bright... brighter... off.

She paused after each sequence to stare at me and then repeated the action.

On... bright... brighter... off.

This routine continued until I crawled out of bed to feed this clever brother-and-sister squad.

Tabby sisters Pixie and Feathers followed Sebastian and Squeakette. Pixie's earsplitting meow at the first light of dawn could've replaced the reveille bugle in a boot camp. If I didn't respond, she nibbled on my hand or arm as if to say, "Feed me now, or I will eat YOU!" I explained to friends and family that the tiny punctures were merely marks of ownership.

If Pixie's efforts failed, Feathers would take over and run her paws down the window blinds, as if playing a harp. That was no melody she produced. Of course, feeding her rewarded the bad behavior, but her claws scraping the blinds sent shivers up my spine to my teeth.

I checked every cat that entered our home and our hearts. The snooze button wasn't there. But I found it in the form of my husband's soft voice saying, "Want me to feed the cats, dear?"

I'd nod, roll over... and smile.

— Janet Ramsdell Rockey —

Diva's Shrine

*Thank you... for gracing my life with your
lovely presence, for adding the sweet measure
of your soul to my existence.*
~Richard Matheson

The captain's chair
where Cupcake slept
will be the place
these things are kept:

a *Daily Times*
she lay across;
the catnip mouse
she liked to toss;
a twist tie, chewed;
canned tuna meat;
lamb baby food
she loved to eat;
a kitty fountain,
trickling rain —
(her water dish
was much too plain);
the collar she
refused to wear
(because it didn't

match her hair!);
a picture of
a hound, her friend,
whose nose she cuffed
until the end;
a bathrobe — (No,
it didn't fit!
But she was fond
of pawing it!);
some gravel from
the fish's bowl.
(She ate the fish...
the stones she stole.)

We'll think these things
are dear and fine
when Cupcake's gone.
They'll be her shrine.

—Liana Mahoney—

Super Taster

Dogs eat. Cats dine.
~Ann Taylor

The first two pets my wife and I had were two female kittens, sisters we named Nip and Nap. Both were short-haired tabbies. Nip was mostly gray with a touch of white on her chest and Nap was tiger striped.

They both liked food with a strong aroma, preferring the tuna we ate to the tuna that came as cat food, because they could smell our tuna when we were serving it. If Nip and Nap smelled something you were eating and they wanted in on the fun, they'd hit your leg with a paw until you got the message that they were demanding a taste.

The aroma didn't necessarily drive both of them to the table at the same time, however. Sometimes the scent of a certain food only appealed to one and not the other.

Nip, for example, was more of a meat eater and got very excited the first time she smelled pastrami. For the rest of her life, Nip always strolled over to the table for some hot pastrami every time we served it. Another dish that got Nip's senses going was fried chicken. She loved it, including the crust.

Nap was a big whipped-cream fan, which had nothing to do with getting a whiff of the smooth treat. We discovered her attraction to this whipped delicacy when I left an ice cream sundae on the table, unattended, and Nap, still a kitten, jumped up for a taste of the dessert. That was before she'd learned her table manners, but after that we would give her a little whipped cream whenever we had it in the house for holidays and special occasions. The whipped cream would often get on her nose and she'd walk away from her bowl to a quiet corner to deftly clean off her face with a paw. Whipped cream must have agreed with her because she lived to the ripe old age of nineteen, and she never stopped craving it. A dairy enthusiast, Nap also liked cheese — various kinds — and eggs, too.

Nip never went after whipped cream or cheese. She was more of a carnivorous type. The only cat food Nip and Nap both loved was mackerel. The mackerel came in a can and had a pungent odor. My wife and I could hardly stay in the kitchen when we opened a can of mackerel for them, but both cats came running. For them, it was like ambrosia. We, on the other hand, had to get the empty can in the outdoor garbage right away and wash the cats' food bowls as soon as they finished eating.

Aside from that, Nip and Nap both preferred people food to cat food throughout their lives. They were always hanging around the table when something smelled good.

But Nip had an absolute favorite — hot dogs. She didn't eat much of a hot dog. A small piece, cut up in a bowl, would do it for her, yet she did relish them. But not just any hot dog would do. She liked a particular brand — kosher, no less — and if I didn't buy that brand she wouldn't eat it no matter what. When we cooked other brands, she would race into the kitchen and she'd nag us for a piece, the fragrance promising a taste of heaven. But when we put it in her bowl and she got a good whiff of it, she'd simply turn around and ignore what, for her, was nothing more than a cheap imitation.

And she wouldn't just walk away. She'd have this down-in-the-dumps, dour look on her face. She was showing sheer disappointment, even disgust, that you'd tried a bait-and-switch stunt, tantalizing her with something scrumptious and then offering something that didn't meet her standards.

Even though these hot dogs tasted pretty good to me, Nip would have none of it. So I always went out of my way to buy the brand of hot dog she liked.

When Nip and Nap got a bit older, a butcher shop opened near us and happened to carry the brand of hot dogs Nip liked. Through the years, I always bought my hot dogs there and Nip was very happy.

When you get hot dogs from a butcher, they are not prepackaged with a brand name. They come loose, wrapped in butcher paper, and are very fresh. One time, however, on a busy holiday weekend, I purchased some meat from the butcher, hot dogs included. That night I made some of the hot dogs I'd just purchased and put Nip's portion in her bowl.

One sniff and she walked away in a huff. I thought she might be ill. I tasted no difference in the hot dog. The next morning, I called the butcher and asked him what brand of hot dogs he'd given me. He said that, because of the holiday, he'd run out of the brand I always bought but he'd given me a brand that was equally good.

"Honestly," the butcher said. "I don't know how you could even tell the difference."

I told him I couldn't tell the difference, but my cat certainly could. After a brief silence, he said, "Your cat? Your cat knew I gave you a different brand of hot dogs?"

"That's right," I said. "My cat knew it. Picked up on it right away. She loves the particular brand of hot dogs I always buy from you. She won't eat another brand, no matter what. Well, she wouldn't eat these hot dogs I just got from you yesterday, so I knew you didn't give me the brand I always order."

"This is your cat we've talking about," the butcher said, "who eats the hot dogs?"

"Well, not all of them," I said. "But she does eat the hot dogs and she'll only eat a certain brand."

A bit bewildered, the shop owner said, "And this cat knew these hot dogs were a different brand by…?"

"Smell," I said. "You see, I put a piece of hot dog in her bowl and she sniffs it. If it doesn't smell like the one she likes, she won't eat it. Won't even try it. It's that simple, and that's what happened. If you saw how disappointed she gets when it's the wrong brand, you'd understand."

"Yeah, I'm sure I would," the meat man said sarcastically. "Look, is there anything else you buy from me that the cat eats? I wouldn't want to disappoint your cat again."

"No, just the hot dogs," I said.

"Well," the butcher said, "the good news is I'm getting more of the hot dogs your cat likes later today. Come down—I'll give you some for her on the house. By the way, I'm just curious. Does the cat use mustard on the hot dog?"

"That's ridiculous," I said. "Who ever heard of a cat eating mustard—even on a hot dog?"

"You're right," he quipped. "I don't know what I was thinking."

— Robert Grayson —

Four-Legged Therapists

12

The Story of Patches

Our perfect companions never
have fewer than four feet.
~Colette

His name was Ol' Hap. He lived on the street. I knew him well and always stopped to talk to him. He had come back from World War II shell-shocked, and sometimes his mind would wander.

This particular day was bright and sunny. As I made my way down the street, I saw Ol' Hap coming in the opposite direction. He was carrying something in his arms.

As he approached, I saw that Hap had a small kitten... a tortoise-shell. "Where did you find him, Hap?" I inquired.

"He found me," Hap answered. "I was sitting on the curb over on Walnut Street by the park. I was dozing when, all of a sudden, this little fella crawled into my lap."

Hap gave me a big grin, showing his stubbly teeth. "I tried to shoo him away, but he just kept following me. I guess he's mine now."

I was surprised. I had never heard Hap talk so much.

Hap and I walked down the street, him holding the kitten like it was the most precious thing in the world. He tipped his brown bag up to his lips and took a long drag of the whiskey he always carried. Even so, he was as close to sober as I'd ever seen him.

"Are you going to keep him?" I asked.

"May as well," he replied. "He's scruffy, dirty, and smells bad just like me. He has no collar, and I think he's a stray. Like me, no one to care about him."

"How are you going to feed him, Hap? He needs lots of nourishment. He's skin and bones."

"Such a shame." Hap rubbed the kitten's head, and it seemed to cuddle closer to him. "I don't know how I'm going to feed him, but I'll find a way."

"He needs a name if you're going to keep him, Hap. That way, he will learn to listen to you. Not that cats are all good listeners."

"This one is. I've only had him a few hours, and already he listens. Mmm! What to call him." He lifted the cat so he could see right into his eyes. Then he looked him over. "Patches? That's what I'll call him. Yep, Patches."

Hap and I parted at the next corner and went our separate ways. I didn't see Hap for a couple of weeks, which was unusual because I usually saw him almost every day. When I did run into him again, I was going into the small grocery store on the corner. Just as I reached for the door, Ol' Hap came out, carrying the kitten and a bag.

"What do you have there, Hap?" I said, surprised to see him here.

"Why, it's Patches. Don't you remember?"

"Oh, I remember Patches. I wondered what you had in the bag."

"Why, I have kitten food, a loaf of bread, and some deli meat. I have to keep the two of us fed," he stated.

"You don't usually have money for food, Hap. Glad you had enough to buy this stuff."

"Well," he said, "I figured it this way. Not eating isn't good. I decided to give up whiskey and take care of Patches here." He set down the bag and scratched the kitten's head.

"Wonderful!" I exclaimed. "God bless you, Hap."

Over the next ten years, I watched Hap and Patches. They were happy, and Hap never drank again. I couldn't believe the transformation. I will never forget Hap and Patches, the miracle cat.

— Mary M. Alward —

13

My Four Furry Guardian Angels

Who hath a better friend than a cat?
~William Hardwin

In 1995, my life was in shambles. Long-standing and severe physical pain was compounded by my primary relationship being on the rocks. The icing on this awful cake was the imminent loss of my home and financial security. The best thing I had going for me was the four cats who lived with me.

The five of us had been together for years. The cats were two pairs of litter mates: Whitefoot, a longhaired tuxedo male, and his longhaired calico sister, Nia; Cotton, a snow-white male Maine Coon mix, and his brother, Safford, a silver tabby. They had all been with me since they were tiny.

Whitefoot and Safford co-existed under the same roof, but Safford was always terrified of the very mellow Whitefoot. They often hissed and snarled at one another. Whitefoot was fine with Safford's brother, Cotton; they snuggled together at the foot of my bed every night. Nia got along well with everyone; she and Safford usually slept under the blanket with me.

One morning, all my sorrows came to a head. My health was failing, making ends meet was a constant struggle, and my love life seemed to be irreparably broken. I saw no bright future before me — just more pain, heartbreak, and poverty. I decided that it was simply too difficult to continue living.

My home at the time was in a very isolated location with no phone service or I might have called for help. I was too despondent to make the long drive on rough dirt roads to the nearest public phone and then perhaps reach only voicemail.

I had concocted what I thought was a foolproof plan to end my life with minimal pain. I would walk far out into the wilderness and slice open my carotid artery with a razor-sharp knife. By the time anyone realized I was gone, scavengers would have consumed my bodily remains.

I felt bad about deserting the cats, but I believed friends would take them in and care for them. I would leave extra litter boxes and enough kibble and water to keep them alive until someone realized that I wasn't around, probably within a week or so, and come inside to see my final written words.

In my deeply depressed state, the task of writing a suicide note seemed a monumental effort. I was going to need a nap first. And so it was that I climbed into bed in the mid-afternoon, thinking that when I awoke, I would write what needed to be written, bid farewell to the cats, and then head out into the forest for the last time. That was my firm intention.

The fact that you're reading this story obviously means I didn't carry out my plan. What saved me was nothing short of miraculous. As I started drifting to sleep on what was to have been my last day of this earthly life, I felt a wet nose poking at my face. Nia was asking me to lift the covers so she could access her favorite sleeping spot. Safford soon followed, and the two cats snuggled together against my belly. Then a very odd thing happened: Whitefoot and Cotton also got under the covers. Neither of them had ever done so before, even individually. For the two enemies, Whitefoot and Safford, to lie so close to one another in complete peace was without precedent.

The pile of cats under my blanket purred in unison as if to say, "We love you. We need you. Please don't leave us." Had angelic spirits possessed them to come together and make me rethink what I was about to do? At that point, I realized how selfish it would be to bring potentially life-shattering trauma to these furry children by disappearing and never coming back — especially after they had so lovingly set aside their differences to lift my spirits.

On rising from that nap, I spent a long time just hanging out with my four-footed family members and thanking them for bringing me out of my dark mood. Remarkably, Whitefoot and Safford remained friendly with one another from that day forward.

I wouldn't recognize for a while that this event was a turning point in my life. One long-term result was that I co-founded a non-profit, cat-rescue organization that continues to this day.

Although Nia, Whitefoot, Cotton and Safford are long gone, I've continued caring for as many four-legged angels as I can manage. At times, I've had as many as eighteen living with me. Currently, there are a dozen wonderful cats in my house. I feel enormously blessed by their presence and trust in me.

Next time you're feeling low, remember this: Cats make wonderful friends. Why not visit your nearest animal shelter and see who's waiting for you there? The life you save could end up saving yours.

— Suzu Bell —

Breaking Past Fear

The memories and paw print of a beloved cat
remains in our heart and soul forever.
~Author Unknown

The photograph on the rescue website haunted me. An emaciated black-and-brown tabby slouched on the sidewalk, leaning against a brick wall. Her head hung in dejection; she looked ready to collapse from exhaustion in the hot sun.

Barb, a friend and a seasoned rescuer, had posted the picture, looking for a foster.

I had no right taking on a new responsibility at this time in my life. We had just put my mother into hospice, which required that I stop advocating for her and prepare to let her go. I drove almost daily to her home to supervise her care and maximize whatever amount of time I had left with her. Meanwhile, I already had one diabetic cat and another in renal failure. My hands were full.

The tabby turned out to be very old, feral — and blind. Unable to find food and water, she only weighed three and a half pounds when she was rescued. The veterinarian who first examined her uttered she was just a whisper of a cat. Her name became Whisper.

Barb begged me to take Whisper since I was good with crotchety, old cats. Against my better judgment, I agreed to meet the desperate creature. I couldn't bear to leave her in her cage in Barb's garage, so I brought her home. Barb said she was a hospice cat — a prognosis I felt compelled to defy.

As a licensed veterinary nurse who took in senior and special-needs cats, I anticipated what her needs would be from a practical standpoint. I settled her on a comfy bed in a floor-level alcove with no door, providing her a safe place while she adjusted. I tapped her water bowl, rattled her food dish, and gently shook the litter box so she would know where to find them. She hunkered down, listening. She never hissed, but she also never purred.

A week later, I returned to the vet with Whisper to test her blood pressure. It was too high, as I suspected. If it had been caught earlier, her blindness might have been reversed. We started her on medication, and eventually she would be able to make out light and shadows.

The first few months that I had Whisper, I was gone most days taking care of my mother. I didn't spend much time with the wee soul. She spooked easily. Like a psychic sponge, she knew when I was tense and would attack me. I felt like I was merely warehousing the aged kitty and considered returning her to Barb. Barb wisely told me to keep trying. The truth was that no one else wanted her.

As I became more immersed in my mother's physical and mental deterioration, it left me depressed and spent. Meanwhile, Whisper began to gain weight. She was a survivor, although she still wanted to have little to do with me.

One day, I decided to take care of myself for once. I loaded my kayak into the car and headed to the nearby river. A fresh breeze danced over the water as I rowed. A mallard paddled along beside me, an egret swooped by, and I saw a swan spread her wings like an angel. Two red-eared sliders watched my progress from their perch on a semi-submerged log. Their old-soul eyes cheered me on as I made my journey.

I came home after a couple of hours of air and sun, exhausted and refreshed at the same time. Whisper responded positively, greeting me with rubs and a purr. I realized this little kitty had a healing influence on me by reinforcing my better behavior.

I squeezed in more time for "my babies." I watched Whisper slowly emerge from her room to explore my house. It seemed to smooth the way if I got down to her level, so I crawled on the floor of the living room with her, guiding her. Now close to seven pounds, she had a new confidence that warmed my heart.

Six months later, Mom passed away. The end of my mother's life was comfortable, and I took solace in knowing I had facilitated a gentle transition for her. My steps got lighter with the release of my psychic load, and I went to the river as often as I could before the winter rains began.

Soon, while Whisper had come out of hiding, I discovered it was me who was now being reclusive. I wanted to get back to work but felt like a fish out of water in my old veterinary field, having been away from it for five years. I didn't know how to move forward, and I was afraid. Did I still have the skills needed to do my job?

Finally, a veterinarian friend of mine asked me to help out with a neuter-and-spay clinic she was running, and I accepted the opportunity. If Whisper could conquer her fears and navigate in her new world, so could I. The twelve-hour clinic was a huge success, and all the animals did well despite my fatigue. I was thrilled that I was able to manage such a massive project. I felt like Whisper had shown me that you're never too old to start over.

Rather unexpectedly, Whisper started to lose weight. An ultrasound confirmed she had intestinal cancer. We tried chemotherapy, but the cancer progressed. This proved to be unbeatable. As she had been in the beginning, Whisper was back in hospice.

One night, she climbed into my lap and curled up. I saw the effort she made; her face showed her exhaustion. With tears streaming, I bent down to kiss her. I thanked Whisper for her strength and inspiration over the last year and a half. I gave her permission to go. She rubbed her cheeks against mine, and within hours she quietly slipped away.

I drove to the river a few days later. Winter was upon us. The current was swift, and the water level was high. I walked along the shoreline, fighting back tears. The river represented the flow of life, and I paused to watch it race past. My time with Whisper had been too short, but she had gotten me back to my source through her persistence and courage. Who had tamed whom? I have a little, blind whisper of a tabby to thank for pulling me through a rough time.

— Terilynn Mitchell —

Breakfast at Frank's

Breakfast is everything. The beginning,
the first thing. It is the mouthful that is the
commitment to a new day, a continuing life.
~A.A. Gill

Frank was a quiet, little cat, but he always had his paw on the pulse of the family. When the household was happy, he spent his days serenely napping on the big burgundy ottoman. When someone was down, he hopped into their lap to watch Animal Planet, eyes alert in the tabby face framed by a gray M.

M for Mindful. Ministering.

He knew how the house worked — what time I ran the fiendish vacuum cleaner and what time we ate our meals. He knew when to disappear and when to show up, but because he especially understood the importance of a great breakfast, he was always on time.

Mornings, when the alarm rang, if he wasn't still dozing between Bill and me, he'd meet me at the door, chatting nonchalantly all the way to the kitchen about how much he hoped that this morning wasn't Mixed Grille day because he'd rather breakfast on something else. He didn't exactly threaten, but he let it be known that if it did happen to be Mixed Grille day, well, he just might have to run into the woods and rustle up a quick mouse. Life was too short, he thought, to ever, under any circumstances, eat Mixed Grille.

Frank loved my family, especially my sister, Allison. She and I had a chaotic childhood. Though it had made us close, neither of us had come out of it unscathed. We all deal with chaos in different ways. Allison dealt with hers with food — or the lack thereof. The only thing that ever made her feel like she had any control over her life was to stop eating entirely, which she eventually did. By the time she called me in Montana, she was very ill.

"Mom won't come," she said over the phone. "I need her. I asked her, but she won't come. She says she can't leave her cat. Her cat! She's choosing her cat over me!" I could hear the pain in her voice and the fear that if she didn't get help from someone — anyone — she might possibly not make it. "Please come, Les."

A few weeks later, Bill and I were staying at Allison's. We'd left Frank back home since someone had to hold down the fort so the other two cats, Jellybean and Rocky, didn't burn down the house. He took on the responsibility gladly. Merrily. He just loved minding things.

Bill and I stayed at my sister's for two weeks, and it didn't take us long to realize just how sick she was. Alarmingly underweight, when she did eat, she fell asleep immediately. Nothing I did seemed to make her gain any weight or any ground. Mostly, however, her emotions kept her from progressing. Though she fully understood how sick she was, at times she just couldn't make herself eat, and we realized she needed professional help if she were to recover.

Allison went into therapy, but the going was slow. Finally, she came to stay with us, and she fell under Frank's protection the minute she arrived. Frank loved her, and she hadn't been there long when he first suggested they have breakfast together.

He'd been out under the moon, patrolling the woods as was his habit. I was in the kitchen making our breakfast and chatting with him when Allison came in to join us — me for coffee and Frank for hopefully-not-Mixed-Grille.

"Good morning," I said cheerfully. "And how did you sleep?"

She didn't answer, just unfolded a tissue to reveal the limp body of a little mouse.

"Oh, yuk! That wasn't in the house, was it?"

"No," she said. "Pretty sure Frank brought it in through the cat flap."

I frowned, and she continued. "It was outside my door when I woke up this morning, lying there like a gift."

I had heard of cats doing things like that — taking offerings to people they liked — but Frank had never done that for anyone, not in all his many years. Not once.

"How... nice," I said with a laugh.

"It actually is, yes. I must look like I need a good breakfast, and I'm sure he would have made me one except, you know, no access to sausages and no opposable thumbs."

Frank looked up at her earnestly. The M over his eyes now stood for something more significant, like Medic, or Merciful, or even Motherly.

My sister did recover. She has a happier life now and a better idea of how to manage the scary feelings she internalized as a kid. I like to think that Frank helped her on that road by pointing out that sometimes the very first step to happiness is as simple as eating breakfast with a good friend.

—Leslie C. Schneider—

Mamma Mia

Kittens are angels with whiskers.
~Alexis Flora Hope

"It's kitten season. We've reached capacity," my daughter-in-law, Mandi, said. "They need a place to stay, out of the shelter, free from the noise and disease. Foster homes give them the best chance of survival."

Then Mandi asked me to consider a tuxedo cat named Mamma Mia and her five kittens: Sky, Sophie, Rosie, Harry, and Sam. You guessed it, all named after characters in the Broadway musical, *Mamma Mia.*

"How long would I have them?" I asked.

"When the kittens are two pounds, you bring them back to be spayed and neutered. Then they'll be placed on the adoption floor. Think about it. No pressure."

I was eager to support Mandi in her new job and, to be honest, score some mother-in-law points. Yet my thoughts raced.

Could I say goodbye? Handle more loss? Mandi has a gift. She can love and let go. Perfect for a shelter employee. I love and hang on. And on.

I had recently released three foster daughters back to their biological family. I was fragile. Physically. Emotionally. Spiritually. I had never wanted to be a foster mother. I'm an adoptive mother. I know how to adopt—a love and relationship that is forever and always. Fostering was like asking for heartbreak, signing up for grief. But this sibling group found us when they needed a home, so my husband and I said yes.

But, like a revolving door, the girls left my home as quickly as they had come. Releasing them back to their biological family, one at a time, was a mix of grief and relief for me.

I wondered if I could put boundaries around my heart with these animals better than I did with the girls. I knew I'd fall in love with each one.

Nevertheless, I said yes.

Like many mother cats who are brought to shelters, Mamma Mia was borderline feral. She wouldn't let me touch her. The closest I could get was when she nursed her kittens. Yet, I hung back. I wanted to keep her stress level low. I knew how important relaxation was for me as I nursed my babies. I figured the same was true of the animal kingdom. I marveled at her instinctive nature to nurse and bathe each kitten with a tenderness she could give but not receive.

Mamma Mia did her job well. The kittens thrived and grew. They allowed me to touch, cuddle and play with them. I felt a sense of satisfaction knowing they would receive the human contact necessary for success in their adoptive homes.

But what about the mamma? It's easy to love a kitten. You simply can't watch them play and not smile. But who wants an adult cat who doesn't give you the time of day? Mamma Mia wasn't just shy or aloof. She was scared to death. Just as I didn't know the extent of the trauma my foster children had experienced, I had no idea what Mamma Mia had endured. She'd just go back to the shelter and wait with the other adult cats.

A week into fostering, I was beginning to get the hang of nurturing these kitties. I had a routine down: feed, clean litter, and play, twice daily. While cuddling one of the kittens, I noticed some scabs on its nose. I examined several others and found little spots here and there on their faces and ears. I called Mandi.

"It's ringworm," she said. "We see it all the time. If you want to bring them back, we can treat it, but I can also give you a list of products to try."

Our house went into ringworm lockdown. I used ointments and sprays, and wiped down every whisker and surface, but to no avail.

The ringworm was winning. And when my husband found a spot on his leg, the ringworm declared victory.

"Bring them in," Mandi said. "We've had so much rain and humidity this spring, the ringworm is off the charts. We have a trailer set up to treat it."

I felt like a foster failure.

Then came the dilemma—how to get six cats into the crate they'd arrived in. And how, oh how, would I catch Mamma Mia? I had one idea and only one: get each kitten into the crate and hope their distress calls would lure their mamma close enough for me to make the catch. It worked.

I'll never forget walking the cat family out to my SUV on that hot and humid Sunday. I put their crate in the back, collapsed behind the wheel, and blasted the AC. The kittens were crying. Mamma Mia was crying. And before I knew it, I was crying. Really, I was sobbing. Weeping from a place so deep, that I knew my time with these kittens and their mamma wasn't a waste. It wasn't a failure. It was a gift to me and to them. Just like my foster children, I had kept them safe for as long as I could. I taught them to receive love in the time I had them. And they allowed me to grieve from a place in my soul, which brought much needed healing.

Through the summer months, I kept my eye on the shelter news and saw each kitten adopted. In the fall, I noticed Mamma Mia was moved to a shelter across state lines. That would not do for this mamma cat who'd loved her kittens so well. So, on a cool day in September, I hopped in my SUV, drove an hour, and brought her home. It took many months of a regular daily routine, but Mamma Mia, renamed Tilly Mints, eventually felt safe in my lap. Now, every evening we enjoy "Tilly Time" in her favorite hangout, my office. We mammas understand one another's story.

—Carolyn Byers Ruch—

17

City Kitties

*Of all the things God created, from sunrises
to rainbows, to black holes and humor,
cats are the most fascinating to me.*
~Jarod Kintz

"Look! Kitty Kitty is over there!"

"He's coming over. And there's Kitty's Sibling."

Kitty's Sibling doesn't like to come out for petting.

I live in a small apartment, so I don't have room for a cat. Instead, I am left with a menagerie of neighborhood cats to get my feline fix.

Kitty Kitty reminds me of my first pet, Coogie. Cat breeds are elusive to me, but this cat has a gray/brown body with some white mixed in. Kitty's Sibling is the same, just a bit bigger and much shyer. But they both enjoy the cans of food left out by the neighbors. They always pop out of a semi-abandoned house, usually in the cooler months.

A few blocks away, there is a cat I've named Bodega Kitty that hangs out at the corner store in the Washington Heights neighborhood of New York City. She looks like Kitty Kitty and Kitty's Sibling, except that she has bright blue eyes, almost like a Husky. Bodega Kitty likes to hang out behind the outdoor ice machine under the glow of the neon signs in the window. When she wants inside, she will walk in front of the sensor for the automatic door, wait for it to open, and then enter.

Closer to the apartment is Grey Kitty, a skinnier version of a British Shorthair. I don't know what kind of messes Grey Kitty gets into, as he is always very fluffy, sometimes with dirt or bits of fuzz in his hair. Grey Kitty answers to "meow meow" but will frequently run and hide under one of the parked cars on the street.

Across from Grey Kitty's domain is the residence of Highbridge Kitty. Highbridge Kitty will often be near the benches by the recreation center in front of the pool that makes an appearance in the movie *In the Heights*. The pool also used to be part of the Croton Aqueduct system that brought water down into the city for many of the residents. Highbridge Kitty loves being petted but blends in with the squirrels when she doesn't feel like being social. During the pandemic, Highbridge Kitty was often there, waiting for gloved hands to scratch behind her ears.

Walking behind the pool, one can follow the path that Edgar Allen Poe would take on his many walks to and from his home in the Bronx across the High Bridge. On this path lives Bronx Kitty. Bronx Kitty is all black with white feet, a bit of white around the eyes, and white whiskers. Bronx Kitty enjoys playing in the scrub next to the bridge and will come running at a "meow meow." Once you begin petting him, Bronx Kitty is like glue. If you try to leave, he will walk in front of you, tripping you up. Claiming you as his person, he will rub against your legs and follow you partway over the bridge. If you stop and turn around, he will follow until a curious dog or electric bike scares him back into the scrub.

The menagerie of cats always came to life in the cold months. I have since moved away from that neighborhood, without a chance to see all my neighborhood pets one last time. But they belong to the neighborhood that feeds and pets them in my place. And now I have a chance in my new neighborhood to find a new group of furry friends to give strange and literal nicknames.

— Kayla Fedeson —

18

Cats to the Rescue

*It is impossible to keep a straight face
in the presence of one or more kittens.*
~Cynthia E. Varnado

was an inordinately shy third grader and didn't make friends easily. My teacher, Mr. Doocy, called my mother and explained that
I hadn't spoken a single word in class, and we were more than
halfway through the school year. Even as a third grader, I knew
this was unusual. I watched with envy the uninhibited interaction of
my classmates.

Mom tried to excuse my behavior as something that I would
outgrow. But Mr. Doocy would not be deterred. He asked Mom if
I had something at home that I liked. He said he would arrange a
show-and-tell for the class if I brought it to school.

Playing right into Mr. Doocy's hands, Mom told him about my
cat who'd had a litter of kittens about three weeks earlier. I was crazy
about those kittens.

Bingo! Mr. Doocy suggested I bring the kittens to school the next
day. I suppose Mom was hoping to dissuade him when she explained
that I would have to bring the mother cat along with the six kittens
because they were too young to be separated from their mother. She
probably thought this would put an end to the plan. But Mr. Doocy
said that was fine.

I normally walked to school, but my mother drove me the next
morning along with a big brown cardboard box. I staggered toward

the classroom under the heavy load.

In no time, the chorus of kittens drew curious classmates to the mysterious box. Their eyes lit up in wonder when they caught sight of my tiny treasures. My little heart thumped against my chest as pride swelled within me. I had never felt so important in my entire nine years of life!

Mr. Doocy instructed me to sit on the steps outside the classroom so everyone could get a good look inside the container.

"Can I hold one?" a little girl squealed with excitement. Then all the other children chimed in like a choir, begging to hold one of the kittens.

"Yes," I said, "but only for a minute. It will make them sick if they're passed around too much. And the momma cat won't be happy when she realizes her babies are missing."

Soon, the school bell rang, but no one budged—not even Mr. Doocy. He allowed us to sit there until each student had a turn holding the kittens. Then, he escorted me to the front of the classroom and waited for the students to sit down. When everyone was silent, he glanced my way, nodding his approval, and I began to tell the students about the six tiny felines and their mother. It never occurred to me that they were all staring at me or I was talking in front of the class. The only things on my mind were my furry, little friends.

My heart swelled with pride and a newfound confidence that I could not have imagined before my sweet cats rescued me. For the rest of the day and the days that followed, I proudly sat among my classmates with a new sense of worth and importance.

I never would have imagined the transformation a cat and her kittens could bring to a girl who most likely suffered from selective mutism, a disorder that would not be diagnosed in me for years to come.

—Vikki Burke—

19

Nobody Ever Owns a Cat

Cats are designated friends.
~Norman Corwin

"**M**om." I hesitated. "Jacqui saw the cutest little kittens at the feed store today. Maybe we should think about adopting one."

I treaded lightly since my mother had never owned a cat. When she was growing up, most families in the neighborhood didn't have house cats like people do today. Instead, the neighbors would throw out leftovers for the strays or sometimes set out a special treat. Cats more or less belonged to the entire community.

When my brothers and I were young, Mom always told us nobody ever owns a cat. Thus, we were never allowed to have one. Although I wasn't able to grasp the meaning of her words at the time, I'm assuming the expression came about because cats are considered to be quite disloyal when compared to other pets, especially dogs.

It had been a year since I'd moved into my mother's house to care for her after she suffered a disabling stroke, so I wanted to respect her independence while at the same time encourage her to branch out and experience the most she could from her altered lifestyle.

Since I knew she was not fully onboard with cat ownership, I promised Mom that I would accept all the responsibility. This would be my cat, and she could simply enjoy its company.

Upon her consent, we headed to the feed store immediately and brought home the most adorable, little orange female tabby. Jacqui was thrilled for us and insisted on buying Pumpkin all the necessary supplies, including a variety of kitten toys. I had a feeling this was going to be a very spoiled cat.

Pumpkin settled in very quickly, and Mom was thoroughly amused by her clever antics, especially when I was the victim.

The frisky munchkin learned to leap through the air with the grace of a ballerina, usually landing on something that would most certainly get a rise out of me, while Mom giggled with unabashed amusement.

Even more exciting for Mom were the times (usually during one of my favorite shows) when Pumpkin would jump up and turn off the light switch that powered our TV. It usually took several minutes to reboot the satellite receiver, annoying me to the max.

Pumpkin must have been privy to the promise I made to Mom because she's always viewed me as her designated servant and acknowledges me only when she is hungry, thirsty, or wants her litter box cleaned. Her favorite way of getting my attention is by jumping on my keyboard and blocking my view of the computer screen. That always works for her because I have to stop what I am doing to remove her.

The little princess is much too prissy to chase mice. She's never caught a single mouse in the twelve years we've had her with us. Rather, her idea of exercising is posing for photoshoots, and I'm expected to act as her personal photographer. I must admit, however, that I enjoy the photoshoots as much if not more than Pumpkin.

A holiday never passes without us capturing photos of the fascinating feline dressed and posed to fit the occasion: an Easter bunny in a pretty spring dress, a scary Halloween monster, or a reindeer in a colorful Christmas sweater.

Nowadays, she's a little too heavy to leap gracefully through the air like in her early years. We no longer have to worry about her jumping up and clicking light switches or having to shift to avoid being clipped by a flying feline.

But, throughout the years, Pumpkin has been a faithful caregiver for Mom, who often becomes agitated in the evenings. The gentle, empathetic cat senses her anxiety and strives to offer comfort by jumping up on her lap to purr softly.

Never wanting to be far from her side, Pumpkin sprawls out on the back of Mom's recliner throughout most of the day and snuggles up beside her ninety-nine-year-old confidante in bed every night. They are a match made in heaven.

When I go in to get my mother up in the mornings, I can't help but pause and stare at the two of them as they lie sleeping side by side. A little smile crosses my face when I think back to Mom's words: "Nobody ever owns a cat."

—Connie Kaseweter Pullen—

Fun and Games

*We don't stop playing because we grow old;
we grow old because we stop playing.*
~George Bernard Shaw

t is Saturday after Thanksgiving 2020, the year of the COVID-19 pandemic. Lately, I've been feeling old.

My husband Bart and I are fortunate. We've been healthy. We both work remotely from home, grateful for daily work that provides structure to our days. Our three adult sons — Paz, Seth, and Gideon — are healthy and in good relationships. We phone or Zoom as often as we can. Still, it has been a year of loss and the fear of loss. We feel vulnerable, both past sixty-five, our ages placing us at higher risk.

This year, two of our four cats died. The house feels hollow without their snuggles, their habits we knew so well. We haven't hugged our sons in months. Our oldest lives abroad; we haven't seen him since January 2020, just before the pandemic hit. I keep a photo of that visit on our mantel to remind us of the last time we were all together. We don't know when we'll be able to travel again.

Every day is "Blursday," lacking the punctuation of going out, movies, restaurants, concerts, in-person worship, in-person gym, the highlights of weekend getaways. I never considered myself an anxious person, but this invisible enemy, lurking in breath, has hurt so many people. Life seems heavy. We need a lift.

After the deaths of Sky and Singh, our remaining two Siamese cats seem to need a lift, too. Three-year-old Mooji is all muscle. He jumps up onto the kitchen counter with a very human "Oomph," dropping his favorite shiny pipe cleaner in front of me, begging me to play fetch. At seventeen and arthritic, Chi doesn't have the energy to keep up with him.

Mooji needs someone closer to his age, someone to play with. And so it happens that on Saturday after our quiet Thanksgiving for two, Bart and I wait with growing excitement outside The Sanctuary at Haafsville to adopt a rescue kitten.

The rescue volunteer, in her hospital mask, opens the door. We had emailed them about Harriet, an eight-week-old tabby kitten with white markings, but first she hands me Harvest, a ten-week-old tabby with a warm golden tint. Harvest lays her fuzzy head on my chest as if she already knows where she belongs.

On the way home, I text our youngest, who lives nearby. *On our way. Cuteness aboard.* Gideon is already waiting on our screened-in porch when we arrive. We zip the cat carrier open. Harriet steps out, looks around, immediately notices a dried-up leaf on the porch floor and starts playing with it. She chirps. Harvest tiptoes out behind her, taking it all in with wide "Why me?" eyes.

"You got *two*?" Gideon cries.

We beam.

We know from experience how to introduce a new pet to our cats: very carefully. Harriet and Harvest are confined in a separate room for the first few weeks. They meet the older cats only briefly at first, with the kittens inside the carrier so the older cats can sniff them. There is some inevitable hissing.

Gradually, over the next few weeks, they begin to feel like a family.

Play brings them together. First, it's Go Fish with the fishing-pole toy. We wave it with a whoosh from Mooji to Harvest, from Harvest to Harriet. Harvest follows it with her keen eyes. Then she cautiously takes a swat. Mooji observes, his head whiplashing back and forth, until he can't stand it anymore and grabs the toy. He gets a piece of it with his claw, but it flies away. Confused by the whole endeavor, Harriet tackles Harvest instead of the toy.

The kittens chase the cursor on the computer screen or the animated bird on TV. They're thrilled when paper drops out of the printer. They enjoy shredding tissue and jumping into Amazon boxes. Harvest displays "laser focus" with the laser pointer, following its every shift, batting it with her paws.

Even our "elder statesman," Chi, finds a way to play with the little ones. While relaxing on the couch, he flicks the tip of his tail, enticing the kittens with his own built-in fishing-pole game.

Their play brings light and laughter to our Groundhog Day routine. I don't know what play means to a kitten, but I imagine, as with human children, play is learning, instinctive, rewarding. Joyful.

On New Year's, we enjoy a brief, socially distanced, masked celebration with two of our sons and their partners in separate corners of the living room with all the windows open. The sweet scent of ham and potatoes fills the house, but much of the holiday trimmings are missing. We'd skipped the Christmas tree due to both the pandemic and kittens. There'd been no large holiday gathering around our dining-room table as in past years. We can't even congregate in the kitchen to cook and chat together because we would be too close.

No matter. Here we are, (masked) face to (masked) face, at last. Like the scent of home cooking, like the music playing, I feel in my senses the sweetness of in-person contact. I hope I never take this for granted.

Seth and Laura toss a pipe cleaner for Mooji to fetch. The kittens watch, fascinated. Chi plays cheerleader on the sidelines. Gideon and Eliza wave the fishing pole. Harvest chases it left and right, around in circles, until she falls over, dizzy. Six adults watch, entranced by this living funny-cat video.

Embracing play in the middle of a grim year of loss and anxiety, we'd scooped up into our arms two soft, little balls of hope. They ping-pong around our house, joyfully playing and making six adults laugh like children.

— Faith Paulsen —

Feline Relief

*If there were to be a universal sound depicting peace,
I would surely vote for the purr.*
~Barbara L. Diamond

My shoulders ached with pain; the weight of the world lay them down.
By seven o'clock in the evening, my smile was definitely a frown.
What a day at work, twists and turns not seen before.
I slumped as I dragged myself to my back door.
Upon entering, I was met with large eyes all aglow.
Paws came pattering and purring, soft and low.
Tail swishing, ecstatically, with happy chirps to greet.
My darling little fur ball, my cat, wrapped around my feet.
In one fell swoop, I held him close. Head-butts my love replied.
The thoughts and the worries of twelve long hours slunk away and died.
His purr played a sonata I knew so well, those notes.
He rumbled out his happiness from the depths of his fluffy throat.
He followed me as I made dinner, sat at the end of my warm bath.
Watched me eat the ice cream that I kept in my emotional stash.
Moment by moment, his company, his presence of pure love and light,
blessed in me a calm as I pet his back that night.
Courage from soft fur, snug on my chest for bed.
The comfort of my wise, little cat as I lay down my weary head.

— Esther Tucker —

22

No Place Like Tahiti

I have lived with several Zen masters —
all of them cats.
~Eckhart Tolle

"Can I get a cat?" my oldest son, Keith, asked enthusiastically. The question generated immediate anxiety. In my twenty-nine years of married life, our family had somehow managed to avoid pet ownership. I've always loved animals, but I was keenly aware of the fact that I would be the one saddled with the responsibility. I could already taste the pet hair in my morning coffee. "I will not be this animal's caregiver," I declared in my meanest mom voice.

"I'll take care of it," Keith promised. "You won't have to do a thing."

I stared blankly into the face of my young adult son. He was looking for a home to purchase and had contacted a realtor. Assuming the cat would be a temporary house guest, I responded the only way any peace-loving, intelligent mom would: "Go ask your father."

My husband isn't a fan of pets inside the house. For some strange reason, he doesn't want the furniture destroyed or the carpet torn to pieces. Imagine my complete shock when my husband actually said "Yes."

With permission granted, Keith headed off to the shelter where the cat he had already selected awaited his arrival. Tahiti was a grey torbie tabby. She had a small face that gave the impression she was still a kitten although she was almost two years old. Splotches of orange gave her a unique coat that reminded the shelter staff of the Tahitian beachline. That's how Tahiti got her name.

The flyer that contained Tahiti's information said that her life began in a home with too many other kitties. When the rescue team picked her up from the crowded house, she was a frightened young mother with three tiny kittens of her own. Tahiti raised her kittens in a foster home where she became socialized, but after she had done her job as a mom she was returned to the shelter. Nine long months later, Keith brought her home.

It was a cold day in January when she arrived. The shelter sent her with a familiar blanket and Keith was told to keep her in a room isolated from the rest of the house for a few days.

Soon, it was time to explore the house and Tahiti seemed excited. She cautiously ventured into the hallway with her tail swishing slowly back and forth. Our house must have seemed like a mansion to an animal that size, especially one that had lived in a cage for so long. There was a labyrinth of stairs, furniture, and potted plants to inspect, and as she settled in, every room became her own. She chose a different spot each day to nap and when she wasn't napping, she followed me around everywhere I went. We became fast friends and I secretly dreaded the day when she and Keith would move to a home of their own.

About five months after Keith began looking for a house, a listing appeared that seemed to meet his needs. He asked if I would go with him to look at the property and as we pulled into the driveway, a scrawny orange cat sauntered down the sidewalk and quickly disappeared into the tall grass just beyond a barbed-wire fence.

The house was everything Keith had been looking for and he was anxious to make an offer. As we were getting ready to leave, I jokingly asked Keith's realtor, "Does the cat come with the house?"

"I think the cat is a stray," she answered unexcitedly. Her tone suggested that we should somehow be annoyed by the stray cat, but, little did she know I was absolutely elated. Maybe Keith would be content to leave Tahiti with me if he had a new cat to care for. The possibility stirred an immediate spark of excitement until I glanced over at my son.

"That's okay," Keith cheerfully responded. "I already have a cat."

As the weeks passed and the closing date approached, I watched solemnly as the packing process began and I tried not to think about how quiet the house would be without my son and his cat.

That evening Keith looked at Tahiti, who was resting comfortably on the back of the living-room sofa. She had adjusted well and was obviously content with her current living situation. Turning to look at me, his expression was somber. "She really seems to like you better than anyone else," he said softly. "I'll leave her here if you want me to."

No words could have been sweeter.

It was a sunny Monday morning when I received a call from my family physician. I had been waiting for the call and I knew it was coming. Tahiti was curled up beside me on the couch and wasn't at all disturbed by the ringing of my phone. "The pathology report indicates the biopsy is positive for carcinoma," my doctor reported in a gentle voice.

A diagnosis of breast cancer meant that the next year of my life would be tumultuous. It began with surgery, followed by chemo, radiation, and reconstruction. Every day was an arduous challenge, but when I woke up each morning Tahiti was there. She curled up on my lap and purred as I prayed.

How can a pet have such a profound effect on the human soul? There is nothing in this world that generates greater immediate comfort than holding a purring cat.

Seeming to know when I was at my worst, Tahiti found me and stayed with me. I could feel my blood pressure decrease as she purred, and my mind drifted back to Keith's first plea for a pet. "I will not be this animal's caregiver," I remembered saying. I couldn't argue with that statement. I hadn't been Tahiti's caregiver — because she had loyally and tenderly become mine.

— Melinda Pritzel —

Chapter 3

Cat Sense

Nine Lives, Nine Lessons

Cats know how to obtain food without labor, shelter
without confinement, and love without penalties.
~W.L. George

Any place is a comfortable place
to sleep if you're flexible enough.

The size of your opponent doesn't matter
if you've got the gall to keep fighting.

Bathe yourself every day
because appearances do matter.

Climbing your way to the top of the ladder on your own is easy;
it's the getting down on your own that's the hard part.

If you're having a bad day,
take a nap.

If someone invades your personal space, and it makes you uncomfortable,
don't hesitate to sink your claws in them until they back up.

Stretching every day is good for the soul and the bones, so stay limber.
That's the key to staying mellow and relaxed.

But, also, be bold enough to look death in the face and tell it to come
back later.
That's the key to gaining nine lives.

If at first no one's listening, repeat yourself louder this time
because your voice deserves to be heard.

—Kate Hodnett—

Cat Scan

Blessed are those who love cats,
for they shall never be lonely.
~Author Unknown

was working as a night nurse in a nursing home. One night at 11:00, I noticed that the first-floor patients' lights were still on. This was strange because the usual bedtime was 8:30 P.M.

I went to investigate. Everyone's light suddenly went out. I thought something funny was going on. I was turning to leave when I heard, "Meow, meow." At first, I thought it was a trick, but as clear as night, I heard again, "Meow, meow."

As it turned out, the residents had adopted a stray cat who had come in the front door. They had worked out a lottery system for who would keep the cat each night and feed it. Contraband from dinner would include tuna-fish sandwiches and hamburgers, along with the usual bread for the birds, which all the nurses overlooked.

When I gave my report the next morning, I thought the Director of Nursing was going to faint. She hated cats. It seemed the cat was on his way out, but the residents were up-in-arms, and there was a vote taken regarding the cat's fate. The vote was 41–1 for the cat.

Nights can be very lonely for residents and nurses in a nursing home. One night while I was feeling sad, the cat jumped up on my med cart. It made itself at home next to the juice and tongue depressors and went on the medication rounds with me. From then on, he accompanied me on my rounds every night, going for a ride on the cart. I kept this secret from the cat-hating Director of Nurses. I made sure the cat had a clean pad each night and I cleaned the med cart each morning.

The cat was the sensation of the nursing home. Then, one night, the cat did something unusual. It jumped on a resident's bed. The resident had been very sick, and she died in her sleep with the cat keeping her warm. Somehow, it didn't make the death seem as sad.

I gave my report the next morning and added the news about the cat. A wave of peacefulness traveled through the nursing home.

As time went on, the cat repeated this behavior every time a resident was about to pass away. The nurses were able to notify the residents' family and friends in time. The cat even predicted deaths that we didn't expect. He had a 100 percent track record.

That cat made the older residents feel comfortable, especially as they grew nearer to death. He brought peace to everyone in the nursing home — except for the Director of Nursing.

— Anna Heaney —

Dancing with Destiny

Cats' eyes seem a bridge beyond the one we know.
~Lynn Hollyn

Destiny was a small black cat with a tuft of white fur on her chest. Her name was perfect, as it turned out. How did she live up to her name? She knew the man I would marry, when I was pregnant, and how to give love when it was needed most.

I'd moved into a small apartment and wanted a furry friend as a roommate. I met Destiny at a small farm. A young girl greeted me and then scurried to the barn to grab the runt of the litter. I held the little black ball of love. Immediately, Destiny began to give me nudges with her small, furry head. Her purring was mesmerizing. She would not leave me alone. I had a new roommate. She had a new home.

Destiny could sense if I was sad or concerned. She would chase her tail, jump on my lap, and give me kitten kisses to cheer me up. I could not resist her unconditional love as I healed from fibromyalgia and chronic fatigue.

I began to date. Michael won my heart with his love for cats. He even taught Destiny how to fetch. They had a blast together and became fast friends. During the week, he left my apartment by 9:00 P.M. At 8:45 P.M., like clockwork, Destiny would crawl up on his chest and sit there. She would look intently into his eyes as if to say, "One day, you will stay!"

She was right. Michael proposed, we married, and Destiny moved from his chest to his lap.

Two years later, I became pregnant. Destiny sat on my stomach and did a little dance. She purred and pranced as her paws poked my belly. She stopped after about a month. She knew the bad news that was coming: I'd miscarried my child. Destiny was there to give me love and comfort. A year later, it happened again. We suffered two miscarriages in our marriage. I was heartbroken and afraid to get pregnant again. Her purring, cuddles, and whisker kisses comforted my husband and me.

"I think I'm pregnant," I said to my husband a year after the second loss. I went to the gynecologist to get a pregnancy test. I did both the blood and the urine tests.

The clinician doing the tests was new. "Your urine test came back negative. We will have to wait for the bloodwork to come back in two days to be sure." I left brokenhearted. I felt pregnant but did not dare entertain the thought.

I returned home. I cried, and my husband held me. Destiny rubbed up against our legs as we stood in the kitchen holding each other. I lay down on the couch, sad and depressed. My furry friend, Destiny, came up to comfort me.

"Honey, come look!" I called to my husband. "The test was wrong!"

We both cried happy tears as we watched Destiny do the pregnancy dance on my belly! The next day confirmed what Destiny knew: The bloodwork came back positive. I was pregnant.

On January 27, 2002, Michael Bisbano, Jr., was born, happy and healthy.

Destiny is no longer with us. Her kitten kisses will be missed. She was a feline future-teller, and she lived up to her name.

— Cherrilynn Bisbano —

Bossy and Frankie

Miracles are not contrary to nature but only
contrary to what we know about nature.
~Saint Augustine

Marie sat with her face in her hands, silently weeping. Her family had departed a few moments earlier, leaving Marie to her new life in a facility for patients with Alzheimer's disease.

As much as family members felt the loss of their loved ones to the ravages of Alzheimer's, it couldn't compare to the loss felt by the loved ones themselves. They lost the self they once knew, the person in the mirror.

Most staff responded to the grief expressed by new residents of the facility by telling them that they had a new home now. Personally, I advocated for validating the resident's feelings, even if they could not articulate them well. It was easy enough to recognize the fear and sense of abandonment they felt.

As the facility's activity director, I acknowledged their right to these feelings. The staff in the facility couldn't replace their families, but we could address the residents with respect and the compassion they deserved. Every morning, I made a point of greeting each resident, telling them how happy I was to see them and how I looked forward to spending time with them.

And I meant this sincerely. These precious individuals were a joy to share my days with, to share laughter and build friendships with.

They taught me valuable lessons about dignity in the face of supreme crisis and made it plain that there are some things even a disease like Alzheimer's can never touch—the capacity of the human heart for love and even hope in the darkest of times.

But Marie was new, and she was inconsolable. According to her family and medical paperwork, she was mostly uncommunicative. But there was no mistaking the devastation she felt, as evidenced by the daily tears. Usually, our residents adjusted over time and made friends, but Marie remained withdrawn.

Her family, doubtlessly struggling with their own emotions, very rarely visited, and then only briefly. "She's given up," said the charge nurse on duty one day. "She won't last long."

I didn't want to think of things that way. I always approached the residents from the perspective of their lives being in a different phase—certainly not the easiest one—but nonetheless having potential. I didn't want to watch them just bide their time until the end. But I'd tried everything and gotten nowhere with Marie, and daily I whispered a prayer in my heart that something would help where I had failed.

And as so often happens when we admit complete failure and see no way ahead, our prayers are answered in the most unexpected ways.

Marie was sitting in the afternoon sun in the facility's park area, in tears as always. The other residents were scattered about, helping me as I raked up leaves and removed dead petals from rosebushes. This was "gardening time," as I called it. The facility had a crew who took care of the grounds, but I found that many of the residents enjoyed this afternoon routine.

I was working with my rake, joining in the scattered conversation and laughter, when something caught my attention. Glancing over, I saw Marie bent over, petting one of the two stray cats that we had seen around the grounds for the past week. The other cat sat beside it, as if waiting for its turn.

I was surprised. These cats had always kept their distance. But Marie had apparently melted their reserve, and soon both cats were purring contentedly as they weaved in and out of her legs as she sat. I approached warily, but the cats didn't leave as I walked up.

"Marie," I said. "It looks like you have made some friends!"

Unimaginatively, I had referred to the previously aloof cats as "the orange cat" and "the gray cat." Taking my cue, the other staff and the residents referred to them the same way, usually when remarking about how the cats kept their distance despite friendly overtures. Marie, however, showed me that my prayers had been answered when, looking up with a smile instead of tears, she said the first words I had ever heard her speak.

"This one is named Bossy," she said with a nod to the orange cat at her feet. Reaching to pet the gray cat sitting beside it, she said, "And this one is named Frankie."

Marie rarely spoke after that, but the tears ended. Now there was something to look forward to every day: time spent with Bossy and Frankie. The two cats grew friendlier with the rest of the staff and other residents, but they made no bones about loving Marie first and foremost. The administrator, a down-to-earth and compassionate woman, allowed a small budget for their feeding, a daily task that brought Marie pure joy. They formed a trio — Marie, Bossy and Frankie — inseparable and bonded in heart.

Bossy and Frankie never missed a day with Marie and were with her until the day her heart quietly gave out. After that, they were seen no more, and all my calls to them during their regular feeding times failed to bring them back. It was as if they understood they were no longer needed, and so they went on their way.

But for the time they were needed, they never failed in their commitment, answered prayers of orange and gray, softly appearing on padded feet to bring comfort and dignity to a deserving soul. How Marie came up with their names, I do not know. Her family remembered no pets with those names and said that Marie had never even had a cat.

Perhaps the answer is simpler: They recognized each other with a vision that comes from the heart. All I can say is that some things have no human explanation, and we are fortunate that such mysteries grace our lives. When we have failed in everything and can find no answer, one comes unexpectedly, seeking out the individual who needs it and staying until the full miracle is finished.

Thank you, Bossy and Frankie, for being that miracle.

— Jack Byron —

27

Guard Cat

You are my cat, and I am your human.
~Hilaire Belloc

My sister Karen was five and I was two. We loved playing outdoors, taking full advantage of the warm Oregon summers, and exploring the wide-open spaces of our yard and the nearby tree-filled lots.

Enter one scraggly, longhaired black cat. Smokey showed up one day without a collar and in dire need of a meal. My dad tolerated this critter only because he would never allow the alternative — a dog — to set a paw on the premises. My dad also knew that once we fed a cat, it was ours forever. This was fine with Karen and me.

With adequate food and care, Smokey doubled in size in a few weeks. He would lie beside me on the bed, becoming my pillow when I buried my face in his fur. Soft, cuddly, and what a purr! It made me laugh but also became a soothing rhythm at naptime.

We met Smokey's demands like he was royalty: cuddle time before bed, out for an evening romp, breakfast in the morning followed by a vigorous brushing and hug from two little girls who adored him.

One sunny afternoon, my dear mother, frantic because she couldn't see her precious daughters through the kitchen window, dashed outside. My sister was contentedly making mudpies in the corner of our garden, but I had wandered to the end of the driveway, to the sidewalk that would take me onto the street.

Mom ran screaming toward me, but she needn't have worried.

Standing just beyond, at the edge of the sidewalk and no man's land, was our trusty sentinel, Smokey. He had taken up his post.

"Donna, I've told you about staying in the yard where I can see you." Mom spun me around to face her. "The street is dangerous, and I want to keep you safe."

I placed my hand on hers and showed her why she shouldn't worry. As I turned to face the street, Smokey pushed his head against my leg and shoved me back to safety. As I walked back and forth on the sidewalk, Smokey kept pace, blocking me from stepping out into the street.

Mom's furrowed brow disappeared, and a smile crept across her face. She bent down and gave Smokey a sweet chin rub. But he wasn't satisfied with that small token of appreciation. He flopped on his back, stretched his legs, and exposed his full belly. When rubbing time ended, Mom looked at me, shook her finger twice and reminded me that Smokey might not always be there to stop me. I needed to learn that skill on my own.

"I will, Mom. I promise."

But deep inside, my heart ached at the thought that one day I might walk to the sidewalk and not see Smokey, not feel his soft cat fur, not hear his calm purring, and not feel the nudge that pushed me back to safety.

God blessed us with an amazing, loving, protective cat named Smokey. And I was right. I did miss him when he was gone.

— Donna Hues —

28

Saved by the Cat

You learn something every day if you pay attention.
~Ray LeBlond

"**Y**ou're lucky," the doctor said. "A lot of times these conditions go unrecognized." I'd just completed a follow-up visit after spending the night at a sleep-study clinic. I was still grappling with the fact I'd been diagnosed with severe sleep apnea, a condition with too many side effects to count, including high blood pressure and exhaustion from waking up every two or three hours.

"So, how did you find out about it?" he asked.

"Not sure," I replied. I didn't think he'd believe that my cat's head-butting during the night had alerted me. At any rate, I went home with a CPAP machine, a full-face mask, and a hose designed to pump air into my nostrils and prevent those lapses of breathing.

Just to back-pedal a bit here: My cat Isis was prone to head-butting. In fact, it was the feature that attracted me to her. I had no intentions of adopting a cat the day I met her, but my friend Tammy had called and said, "They've got some black cats at Mississauga Animal Services. There's one you should check out." So, in I went, and there she was.

Many of the other cats cowered in the cage. Some made eye contact with soulful looks. Others turned their tails up and ignored me. But this one bumped her head against the door and gave a mournful meow whenever I left to look at another potential adoptee. According to the sign on her cage, she was a "drop-off" who'd been left outside the door of the shelter and was approximately six months old.

I already had another black cat named Syris, adopted from the Toronto Humane Society six years earlier. Although he wasn't exactly social, I figured another companion might help. At least, that was my rationale for getting this little feline. Besides, her topaz eyes had me the minute they fixed on mine, along with the head-butt she gave me when first removed from the cage.

Isis turned out to be the queen of head-butts. Whether I was on the couch, in front of the computer, watching TV or trying to make my bed, she was there with her head in my face.

According to the Internet, this is a sign of affection or marking territory. That's how I took it until the past couple of years when she would wake me up during the night. Every two or three hours, I'd get a head-butt on my forehead. I swore it was her waking me up, but now I realize she was just reacting to the fact that I was gasping for air and needed to be prompted to breathe.

As a registered nurse, I knew about sleep apnea, characterized by symptoms like loud snoring and periods of not breathing. I just never figured I had it, and it took some time to register. The doctor at the sleep clinic had just confirmed it.

So, in retrospect, I'm not sure who rescued whom. Yes, I may have adopted her from the shelter, but she had totally outdone herself. Thanks to Isis and her warning instincts, I was able to be diagnosed and now sleep a lot better.

Mind you, she loves the CPAP mask and plays with the tubing connected to the machine. So far, she's only managed one claw puncture in the hose, and that was easily remedied with a little patch of duct tape.

Now when she wakes me with a head-butt, it's usually early morning. I respond with a pat, maybe even a head-butt of my own. By the third one, I know it's more indicative of something along the lines of "Get up, will ya? There's an empty spot in the bottom of the food bowl!"

Isis is now twelve, and Syris is eighteen years old. I never sleep alone. God bless my furry friends.

— Connie Cook —

29

Storm Tracker

*Cats are mysterious kind of folk — there is more
passing in their minds than we are aware of.*
~Sir Walter Scott

It was the Sunday before Labor Day, and I was exhausted after spending the day at a picnic at a relative's house. I looked out the window before climbing into bed. Stars filled the night sky, and crickets gently serenaded me from the darkness. All seemed right with the world.

My big, old black-and-white cat, Oreo, stretched out on the foot of my bed where he slept every night, keeping my feet warm. I climbed into bed and promptly fell into a deep sleep.

I felt like I had just fallen asleep when Oreo woke me up by walking over my chest. I peeked at the bedside clock: 3:10 A.M. I had no idea why Oreo was bothering me. He'd never done that before unless I overslept in the morning, but that usually happened at 8:00 A.M., not in the middle of the night.

I pushed Oreo off me, rolled over and pulled the blankets over my head. But Oreo didn't stop. He stepped on my head and began meowing loudly.

"Oreo," I grumbled. "Knock it off. Go back to sleep."

But Oreo wouldn't stop. He kept walking on my chest, stomach, and legs, continuing to meow.

Suddenly, there was a crash of thunder, and I sat up in bed and looked out the window. Slashes of lightning filled the sky. A violent gust of wind blew through the window, whipping the bedroom curtains. A terrible storm had rolled in.

I hopped out of bed, pulled on my robe, and scooped up Oreo in my arms. We headed for the basement.

Once there, I sat on the stairs with Oreo on my lap as the wind howled and thunder boomed. Then there was an enormous crash that shook the house. I had no idea what happened.

The storm roared a few minutes more and then passed as quickly as it had arrived. Oreo and I headed back upstairs and discovered that the huge maple tree in the side yard had split in half and crashed onto the house, knocking a gigantic hole in the roof right above my bed. If I had been in that bed, I could have been killed.

I learned later on the news that the storm had been something called a microburst, and it had done damage all over the area.

Thank goodness that Oreo had sensed the coming storm and woke me up. That old cat probably saved my life!

— David Hull —

30

Local Hero

A meow massages the heart.
~Stuart McMillan

Tripod's story started one spring morning as I was finishing morning surgery at the veterinary clinic I owned. I was writing up medical records of the surgery patients when my receptionist stuck her head into my office.

"Dr. Godfrey, sorry to interrupt, but there's a lady on the phone who says she just found a cat in her back yard with a badly injured leg."

"I'll take the call," I said, picking up the phone on my desk.

"This is Dr. Godfrey. How can I help you?"

"Doctor, I apologize for calling, but I don't know what to do!" The women's voice quivered.

"There's a big tomcat lying outside my back door with a mangled front leg. The poor thing looks terrible, but I'm not really a cat person, and I'm afraid to pick him up."

"Do you have any idea who might own him?" I asked. "Do you see any collar or tag on him?"

"I didn't get close enough to check for sure, but I don't see any obvious collar." The woman was close to tears. "I really think he must be a stray. He's not been neutered, and he has some old scars on his head. The poor thing…"

I assured the lady I was more than willing to help and I took down her address. It was only about ten minutes away.

"I have two pre-vet students in the clinic today. I'll send them right out to pick up the cat."

I went up front and explained the situation to the students.

"If the cat's wild, you may not be able to get close to him. But from what the woman said, he sounds pretty sick, so he may not be able to get away." They eagerly accepted the challenge and ran to the clinic truck.

I went back to my recordkeeping, but it wasn't long before I heard the students returning with my newest patient.

"Boy, Dr. G, we had to drive with the windows down because the smell from that leg is so bad. This guy's in pretty bad shape."

We gently removed the large gray tabby from the carrier and placed him on a warm towel on the exam table. He lay very still, his breathing rapid and shallow. His right front leg was mutilated from just below the shoulder. The students hadn't exaggerated; the odor coming from what remained of the leg was overpowering.

"Looks like he was caught in a trap. See those ragged wound edges?" I felt the ice-cold toes and footpads, recognizing there was little, if any, chance of saving the leg.

"I wish we knew if he had an owner," I murmured, gently inserting a catheter into the vein on his good leg. "The only way I can save him is to amputate that leg, but he'd have to be an inside cat afterward with someone able to give him lots of care. And even with surgery, his chances are pretty slim."

I ran warmed fluids into his vein to counteract shock and dehydration and administered a large dose of antibiotics as well as pain medication. The students watched in somber silence as I carefully cleaned the wound. I knew from years of experience this guy didn't have an owner. My suspicion was confirmed when my receptionist stuck her head into the exam room.

"The lady called back. She's spoken to her neighbors. Several said they'd seen the cat roaming in the area over the last few months, but he doesn't appear to have an owner. At least not one who cares about him."

"Well, then," I sighed, "it's either remove the leg and see if we can find a home for him or put him to sleep."

Just then, one of the students began stroking the cat's head. Somewhere deep in the tom's throat, a faint purr began. As the student continued to pet the tabby, I noticed the cat's breathing became less labored.

"You're a fighter, aren't you, boy?" I whispered. "You deserve a chance."

After stabilizing the cat's vital signs, I performed the amputation in hopes of saving his life.

Over the next few weeks, Tripod, who the students had named, went through many ups and downs, but I was cautiously optimistic about his recovery. Word had gotten out about the three-legged "miracle cat," and a number of clients stopped by on a regular basis to check on his progress.

The day finally came when I decided Tripod had truly survived his ordeal. The surgical site had healed nicely, and new fur covered the scar left by the amputation. He had gained almost five pounds and was getting around well on his three legs. There was really no need to find a home for him. Everyone in the clinic had grown to love the big gray tabby, and he quickly became a fixture in the reception area.

"You know, Dr. G," my office manager said one day as we were going over the day's schedule, "we have clients come in without a pet. They just want to sit down, put Tripod in their laps, and talk to him while they pet him. They say he's better than a psychiatrist at treating their stress and anxiety… and a lot less expensive!"

Just then, one of my favorite clients, an elderly retired Army officer, came in the door. He had been undergoing treatment for a number of medical issues but had been one of the regulars keeping track of Tripod's progress.

"Good morning, Jeanna," he said as he sat down on one of the reception chairs. "Is Tripod around?"

As if on cue, the gray tabby came loping around the corner, headed straight toward the old gentleman, and jumped onto his lap with ease.

"My doctor told me yesterday my blood pressure hasn't been this good in years, even with medication. I somewhat jokingly told him it was because I was spending time with a special cat. Turns out, according to him, there is medical evidence to support it!"

"Well," I laughed, "maybe I should hang a shingle for him next to mine out front: Tripod, the best therapist you ever petted!"

—Jeanna C. Godfrey—

Why I Hate Cats

*Dogs kind of default to making friends unless
provoked. Cats seem to default to making
enemies unless convinced otherwise.*
~Perry Elisabeth Kirkpatrick,
The 12 Cats of Christmas

My name is Oreo, and I'm a ten-year-old, black-and-white Portuguese Water Dog. If you ask around the neighborhood, I think you'll find that I'm generally regarded as a lovable canine. I'm well-mannered, polite, and friendly. Heck, I don't even bark when someone comes to the door.

But there is one thing that does set me off: cats. Frankly, I can't stand them. With their messy hair, beady little eyes, and pointy teeth, they just set my curly coat on end.

If you asked me when I started hating cats, I couldn't really tell you. In fact, I can't remember any specific feline slight aimed my way that might have caused my tabby antagonism. I just know that from the moment I could draw breath, I've disliked them all. As far as I'm concerned, they're nothing more than overgrown squirrels.

I'm particularly not fond of the cats in my neighborhood. The gray-colored creature across the street is number one on my hate list. If she would just stay in her house or even her yard, it wouldn't be so bad. But, unlike me, she gets to go wherever she wants. No collar, no leash, and no boundaries from what I can see.

Like any responsible pet, I generally stay within the confines of my owners' enclosed back yard. And when I do venture out, it's on a leash held by a human and attached to a collar bearing various identification tags.

Ms. Gray Puss, on the other hand, wanders collarless across the street any old time she likes. She even does her business anywhere and anytime she prefers, including on my owners' lawn. I've never seen either of her owners following behind to pick up her mess in a poop bag.

I tell you, it just drives me wild to see this cat flaunt the rules so brazenly. I'm stuck behind a fence and a gate while she prances around like she's the cock of the walk or at least the cat of the block.

Ask anyone: I'm pretty laid-back. I have a very pleasant and calm demeanor. It takes a lot to ruffle my fur.

I try to be accommodating. My philosophy is basically smell and let smell. So, when the gray one comes waltzing across the street acting all high and mighty, I try to take the high road and let her be.

If she would just stay off my property, I'd be okay with her superior airs and standoffish attitude. I could almost ignore her.

But that's not how she rolls. Sometimes, she comes over and defiles my owners' front garden, knowing full well that I'm only a few yards away on the other side of the fence and powerless to stop her.

The worst, though, is when Ms. Crazy Claws flaunts her freedom right in my face. There's a small gap at the bottom of the front gate, just enough for me to stick my nose out but not enough to manage a full escape.

Well, what do you think that overgrown fur ball does from time to time? That's right: She comes over and plunks herself down on the sidewalk just in front of the gate so I can almost stick my paw out and swat that stuck-up puss of hers.

She lies there for what seems like hours, lounging in the sun and rolling back and forth as if I don't exist. But she knows I exist and obviously delights in torturing me.

Sometimes, when one of my owners takes me for a walk, I'll spot that poor excuse for an animal and take a run at her. Unfortunately, I always forget that I'm on a leash. Before I know it, I'm being yanked backwards.

What's particularly galling is that the gray one doesn't even budge. I guess she knows I can't get at her, and that's why she doesn't even deign to get up on all fours and at least hiss at me.

Mark my words: Someday, one of my owners will forget to lock the front gate, one of the fence boards will fall off, or my male owner Dave will forget to fully secure the leash. And when that day comes, someone's going to suffer. I'm not sure why, but Dave keeps saying he thinks it will be me.

— David Martin —

Whatever Works

There are no ordinary cats.
~Colette

One cold March morning, I discovered two adorable kittens snuggling together for warmth in a drain near our house. Covered in shiny, jet-black fur, they were small enough to fit in a teacup. When none of our neighbors claimed the animals or seemed to want them, I brought them home, and both kittens quickly became favored family pets.

We named them Boo and Scout after fictional characters in *To Kill a Mockingbird*. When they were older, I tried to teach them a skill for more successful cohabitation with our family. The truth, however, is that Boo and Scout ended up teaching me.

Both Boo and Scout were exceptionally sweet and cuddly, but it soon became apparent that they were very different representatives of their species. Scout ate anything we placed in front of him and enjoyed spending his days lounging on the couch in the family room. Boo had far more discriminating tastes and was very selective in what he would and would not eat. He was also more active and adventurous. From the moment he woke up, Boo wanted to be outside stalking the grounds. He loved exploring in the woods and often came home covered in mud and bugs. Scout, on the other hand, hardly ever wanted to venture outside. He disliked getting dirty.

Scout's idea of adventure was to maneuver off the couch three or four times a day in search of his food bowl. Because of these differences in their activity levels and eating habits, Scout weighed twice as much as Boo within a couple of months.

Boo was also more observant and inquisitive than Scout, and he seemed to learn routines and skills very quickly. We came to regard him as a very smart cat. Scout, on the other hand, did not seem very interested in skills or routines. He just wanted to do what he wanted to do, and he'd watch with amusement as I tried to explain that he could not sit on the drapes or drink out of our cups. He always adopted an affable look that seemed to say, "You're nice, but it's not going to happen the way you want!"

Both cats were loving and loved, but because of their differences, we came to regard Boo as a feline superstar, while Scout seemed more like a sloth wannabe!

Despite their different personalities, Boo and Scout got along well. They shared food, toys, and a bed. Even though Boo had his daily outdoor adventures, he always returned home at night to sleep in the basement with Scout. Our basement is separated from the rest of the house by a heavy door, and this door created a problem. In the morning, I found it difficult to know when Boo was awake and ready to venture outside or when Scout was ready to test the softness of the couch.

Both cats would sit quietly behind the door until I happened to remember them or opened the door for some other reason. Similarly, Boo would wait at the back door of our house to be let outside until I remembered his desire or went to the back door to leave. I frequently felt bad when it looked like one or both cats had been waiting for some time.

Early on, Boo carefully watched us turn the doorknobs on these two doors, and he quickly figured out that it was necessary to turn the knobs to get the doors to open. We watched in amazement as he would stretch out his body and reach up with his paw repeatedly, trying to turn the doorknob. Unfortunately, he lacked the strength to move the knobs, but we were astounded that he figured out what needed to happen.

One day, while I was describing this "door problem" to our oldest son, he told me about a "cat bell" that trainers use to train cats. Cats, my son informed me, had been taught to ring these bells when they were hungry or wanted to go outside. I'd never heard of such a device, but the following week, my son sent me two cat bells. They were the size of half an orange and had a button on their rounded tops. When pressed, this button made a ringing sound. The idea seemed simple enough, and since we had a problem with the doors, I tried to solve it by teaching Boo and Scout to ring the bells when they wanted out. I assumed Boo would grasp the concept quickly, but I wasn't sure if Scout would understand. I even joked that as soon as Scout realized the bell was not edible, he'd probably lose all interest!

For a couple of weeks, I worked with each cat. When I found one sitting in front of a closed door, I would gently press their paw on the bell and say, "So, you want to come out of the basement?" or "You want to go outside?" Then, I'd open the door and let them pass.

Much to my chagrin, Scout got the concept quickly. Within a week, he'd come up the basement stairs and ring the bell by the door to signal he was ready to be let out. When I heard the bell, I'd open the door, and Scout would scamper off to the couch.

Much to my surprise, Boo did not grasp the bell concept. He just didn't get it. I think he regarded the bell as an unnatural, foreign object, and despite my best efforts, he wanted nothing to do with the device. Boo would go to the back door, sit beside the bell, and wait for the door to be opened. Although the bell was right beside him, he never pushed the button.

Fortunately, the two cats solved the door dilemma on their own.

Somehow, Boo communicated his need to Scout, or Scout simply understood what Boo needed. Boo began to rub noses with Scout when he was ready to go outside. Scout would then get up off the couch, go to the back door, and ring the bell for Boo. When I heard the ring, I learned to go to the back door and open it. Boo would then go outside, and Scout would return to the couch!

I had planned to teach the cats, but they ended up teaching me.

Scout showed me that appearances can be deceiving, and one's preconceived notions about another's interests and abilities are often not accurate. Boo taught me that even if you're smart, talented, and successful, there are still times when you need help from family and friends, and you should not be too proud to take it.

— Billie Holladay Skelley —

33

Radar Ears

My relationship with cats has saved me from a deadly,
pervasive ignorance.
~William S. Burroughs

She roams the house and occasionally sneaks through the dog door. But Bella stays in the yard, content to listen to the birds and quarrelsome squirrels. Our Chihuahuas give her plenty of space — no rollicking or chasing back and forth as they sometimes do with our other cats.

Then Bella comes back inside and hops onto a bar stool, and without banging her head manages to climb onto the countertop. There's no telling her "No!" because she's earned her place up high, away from the other animals. The fact that she learned to jump, climb, counter surf, and make a nuisance of herself is a complete victory in my book. A complete victory over her blindness.

Apparently Bella was afflicted as a three-week-old kitten and ended up at a shelter, and then with a foster family who bottle fed her, and then with me and her forever family. She has no memory of being sighted and simply enjoys life to the fullest, a purring kitty, a happy kitty.

In fact, Bella is the most well-adjusted furry adoptee in our household. And the largest! I think she knows it, for she's very much the queen of the castle. I encourage this pecking order simply because a disabled animal can become frightened and unsure. I could not stand the thought of Bella hiding in fear or not living up to her full potential.

And so, we celebrate every conquest — she once caught a fly midair based on her keen sense of hearing. That was an applause-worthy feat.

We call her "Radar Ears." Whatever she misses due to her vision impairment, she makes up for with her other senses — especially her ears. I've never seen such rotation and twitching and head-turning! It's as if those fuzzy triangles are part of her toolkit. She may even have the gift of echolocation, for she responds more quickly than even the dogs to whatever noises excite her. Of course, I hear none of this with my limited human ears. But Bella's radar ears are a superpower times two!

Bella has other victories as well, pretty thrilling for a cat in general and especially for one who can't see. For instance, the top-loading litter box. I can't have a regular litter box due to the Chihuahua's keen interest in the contents, and so I bought the top-loading kind. Then I watched as Bella explored this new contraption, concerned that she'd fall through the hole in the lid.

But I shouldn't have worried, for she felt around the surface like an old pro, using her paw to detect the hole. Then, like an ordinary cat, she slid into the hidden chamber of litter, scratched like she was after buried treasure, and did her business. I was so proud!

Blind Bella is also gifted in getting my attention. As I walk by the couch or countertop or washing machine (you never know where her stake-out will be), she'll reach out and snag your sleeve. Gently. Never in a way to hurt or harm, but to signal that she wants something. That may be a can of food or a nice petting.

She's also very dog-like. Sometimes she yowls for attention, and I snap my fingers to let her know where I am. In she trots, responding to the snaps and putting her nose up to my fingers. Then she rubs like the sweet cat she is, and purrs and drools a bit too. The drooling is a leftover trait she developed as a bottle-fed baby, and my shirt can get quite wet at times. But how wonderful that this big, bold cat is so affectionate.

Friends sometimes ask if it's harder to care for a pet with a disability, and my answer is no. It's not really harder at all, for every animal is an individual with individual needs. Bella and her radar ears make it pretty easy for me to provide the time and attention she requires, with plenty of love left over for her "siblings" of whatever species.

So don't over-process the notion of adopting a blind cat. Several blind cat groups exist on Facebook, all really helpful as you navigate how to be a good blind cat parent. It's quite amazing the large quantities of people who have room in their hearts and homes for cats who face unusual challenges. Thank heaven for these animal advocates.

I'll never know the person who rescued Bella and her litter mates from the woods one spring day and brought them to the rescue. But I thank this person from the bottom of my heart for enabling me to have a radar-eared cat who brings so much joy and fascination into our household. Bella is very loved and very appreciated for exactly who she is, counter surfing habits and all!

— Melanie Saxton —

34

One of a Kind

Cats choose us. We don't own them.
~Kristen Cast

Years ago, when I was in college, my roommate Barbara and I shared an off-campus apartment. It was the lower half of an ancient garage apartment—yeah, we were living in the made-over garage. It had a large bedroom, a bathroom with an old doorknob, a living/study/dining room with gaps in the walls, and a yellow kitchen. Whoever lived there before us painted everything—and I do mean everything in the kitchen (cabinets, refrigerator, stove, ceiling, and floor) with water-soluble yellow paint. The more we tried to clean it, the more it bled yellow.

It had its drawbacks, but it met our two basic needs: it was cheap, and it was within walking distance of the campus. The landlady only wanted two things from Barbara and me—pay our rent on time and absolutely no pets. That worked for us.

One day as I walked to class, I noticed a lady giving away a litter of kittens to passersby. I declined and went on my way. Walking back home, I noticed the lady was still trying to find a home for her last kitten. It was without a doubt the most peculiar-looking kitten I had ever seen. From its head to its shoulders, it was short haired and gray, and from its shoulders to its tail, it had long, jet black fur. She offered me the kitten, and I was declining it when a dog ran up and started snapping at the kitten. The lady didn't seem to care, so I grabbed the kitten from her.

I didn't know how I would explain the kitten to Barbara and the landlady. When I walked in and told Barbara the sad tale, she was thrilled. She was a cat person and knew just what to do for this little fellow.

To my surprise, I liked having the little guy around even though I had always been a dog person. He really wasn't any trouble, even going outside to do his business like a dog. Most of the time, when we were home, he was with either Barbara or me.

He did have one disconcerting habit though. Every time one of us went into the bathroom, he would follow. Then he would sit on the floor in front of us and watch intently what we were doing.

Barney got big, weighing about twenty pounds. He ended up looking like a full Persian cat. He continued to try to go into the bathroom with us, even learning how to open the doorknob with his two paws. Eventually, he went into the bathroom alone, and we'd see him sitting on the rim of the toilet. One day, I found him meowing in there, and noticed he had made some cat poop in the toilet. I flushed the toilet for him and he stopped crying and jumped down.

The next few days, Barney and I went through the same process. Then I got it. He was using the commode instead of a litter box and knew it needed to be flushed; he just couldn't figure out how to do it.

A few weeks later, that changed too. I happened to be passing by the open bathroom door and saw Barney flushing the commode by himself. There was no more meowing on the commode or to go out — and no mistakes in the house.

I think that little kitten that no one wanted thought he was human. Never met another cat like him.

— Janice R. Edwards —

Chapter 4

Miracles Happen

35

Meant to Be

A beating heart and an angel's soul, covered in fur.
~Lexie Saige

For nearly a year, I searched animal shelters and pet-store adoption centers for a new cat. Although I'd seen dozens of cute cats, I didn't bond with them in the way you should. As I left yet another pet store empty-handed, I told the rescue volunteer how hopeless I felt. She suggested I visit their website, which included information about all the cats they had in adoption centers and foster homes.

When I got home, I scrolled through pages of cat profiles until suddenly the most beautiful, engaging green eyes popped out at me. "Brodie" was an eighteen-month-old, gray-and-white-striped tabby who was available for adoption. I immediately sent an email and left a voicemail for the rescue asking to meet Brodie.

I was at my office when they called back and said I could meet him that afternoon. When I got the address, I was shocked to discover it was the cross street I was looking at from my office window. Brodie had been living in the rescue owner's home-turned-cattery two blocks from my office!

When I arrived at the house, Nancy seated me in her living room. All floor coverings were stripped to the bare concrete slab, and the bedrooms had been converted to catteries. As Nancy walked down the hallway, I heard her say in a sing-song voice, "Brodie, you have a visitor." He raced into the living room, leaped onto my lap, and rolled and rubbed around me like a purring hurricane. All the while, he gazed at me with those hypnotic green eyes that bonded us immediately.

"I'll take him!" I exclaimed.

Nancy's prayers had been answered! Brodie was the longest resident at her rescue. They originally found him in a feral-cat colony in a South San Diego field near the Mexican border when he was about six months old. He was already neutered, so they assumed he once had a home and was dumped there.

However, when they took him in, he fought with the other cats. He also had a chronic eye infection, which prevented him from going to the adoption centers. Eventually, they put him in a room with all kittens, where he showed strong parenting instincts: affectionately grooming and playing with them. And that's where he'd been for nearly a year and would probably live the rest of his life. They had given up hope that he would be adopted, and despite being a no-kill shelter had considered euthanizing him… until they received my call.

If anything was meant to be, this was it. I signed their adoption papers, received his medical records, loaded him in a carrier, renamed him "Grey Boy," and drove him to my home two miles away.

Two years later, I had bilateral knee-replacement surgery. After a month-long stay in a skilled nursing facility and weeks of in-home physical therapy, I was finally able to leave the house and drive a car to my first outpatient physical-therapy appointment.

When I rolled to the front door with my walker on the way out, I nearly tripped over Grey Boy. He was panicked about something: incessantly meowing to a near howl, anxiously rubbing and jumping around my ankles and calves. His green eyes turned spooky as he glared up at me and tried to knock me down. When I opened the door, he attempted to escape. He was not allowed outside when I wasn't home, but my limited mobility prevented me from bending down to pick him up.

I was concerned and puzzled. He'd never acted like this before. He had settled into a routine that was as reliable as sunrise. Each morning, he'd wait by the sliding glass door leading to the back yard, where he had a poolside cabana. There, I'd serve him breakfast and fresh water on his table under an umbrella.

After his meal, he'd take numerous walks around the pool and tropical landscape to investigate "his" property. Once assured that everything was intact, he'd walk through the open gate my neighbors installed in the fence between our yards.

Grey Boy loved the couple who lived next door, especially the husband, "Rags." Although allergic to cats, Rags befriended Grey Boy, and they had quite the bromance going. Grey Boy would stretch out on the concrete outside the couple's kitchen door and meow until they opened it. When Rags appeared, along with a bag of treats, the rolling purr fest began. Rags would get on the ground, petting, scratching, brushing, and loving on Grey until his allergic reaction sent him running for Benadryl and some soothing hand and face washing.

After a leisurely saunter back to his cabana, Grey would then find the brightest streak of sunbeam under which to groom his glistening gray coat and take a mid-morning nap. By noon, he'd bang on the screen door demanding his return to indoor life. Other than his daily visits with Rags, Grey Boy was not a gallivanter. And I don't recall ever seeing him in the front yard or using the front door.

So, it was strange that this mellow, predictable feline would act so bizarrely, especially after making his morning rounds. But this went on for nearly two minutes.

Suddenly, as though the spirit or whatever had possessed him disappeared, he calmed down, walked away, curled up on the couch and went to sleep.

I wheeled myself out to the car and, for the first time in months, started driving to my appointment.

A mile from my house, I was the second in a line of cars stopped at a red light, waiting to turn right. As the car in front of me turned onto the northbound lane, an old panel van sped recklessly down the hill in the southbound lanes. It jumped the concrete divider, beelined toward the car in front of me and crashed into the driver's side door.

I immediately called 911. Nearby drivers leaped out of their cars and rushed to aid the victims, but I wasn't mobile enough to help.

The police and ambulance arrived almost instantly and pulled the driver, a young woman, and her backseat passenger, a baby, from the wreckage and loaded them into the ambulance. The tow truck and news crews arrived as the suspect was being handcuffed and taken into custody.

After giving my witness statement to the police, I cautiously drove to physical therapy.

Later that evening, I saw on the local news that, thankfully, the woman and her baby were going to survive.

Had Grey Boy not interrupted my departure by ninety seconds, that could have been me and my car. And, in my fragile condition, I might not have fared as well.

I may have emancipated this sweet boy from a caged existence, but he was destined to save my life.

— Melanie Maxwell —

36

The Angel Who Rang the Doorbell

When we believe that life is a gift,
life rewards us with miracles.
~Milan Ljubincic

The Christmas holidays were fast approaching, and we had ordered many gifts online. So, when the doorbell rang, I was sure some of the packages had arrived. I ran to the door and swung it open, but no one was there. I sensed something and looked down, only to find a beautiful calico kitten sitting there, looking up at me with big, intelligent eyes. There was no way that she could have rung the doorbell by herself, was there? Were my new neighbors playing tricks on me?

We had just relocated to Germany and had moved into a big, old country house that we enjoyed exploring while we began decorating for the holidays. It was a huge place with spooky service tunnels under the house and yard that led to the furnace room, workshops, unused pantries, and old wine cellars. Because some of the areas were dilapidated, my husband warned me not to go exploring without him or another companion.

In the meantime, we had begun slowly unleashing our large brood of rescue cats and dogs into the woods that ran behind our house. We wanted them to start getting used to the area so they could venture out on their own. It wasn't long before we began meeting some of the neighbors along the walking paths in the forest, and we gained a reputation for having lots of rescue animals with us.

That's how we thought the calico ended up on our doorstep. We figured that someone had found the kitten somewhere and left her there, and then rang the doorbell and ran away. They accurately guessed we would welcome an additional family member and take care of her.

My husband called her our little angel, so we named her accordingly. She had a calm aura about her as she walked straight into our home and hearts, fitting in perfectly. It seemed as if she was always meant to be in this big house with us. She was an old soul and turned out to be the perfect companion. Always by my side, she was more like a puppy than a kitten. Wise beyond her years, she enjoyed spelunking through the tunnels and mysterious rooms as much as I did, but with much less trepidation. Angelica the calico was courageous.

So, I took a page from her book and decided to be brave, too. There was an underground stone vault I had been eager to explore. The only way in was through a hatch that was partially hidden by the sod and grass that covered it, then down a rickety ladder to its murky depths. I surmised it was an old root cellar, probably twelve feet deep.

I had promised my husband that I wouldn't explore dangerous areas unless he or someone else was around. But he was away on a business trip for a week, and I didn't want to wait until he came back before doing more investigating. Though I knew I was stretching it, I figured that Angelica would count as my companion. I was ready to explore this cellar, and so was she.

I equipped myself with a good flashlight and warm clothes, and carefully started down the rickety ladder.

I don't remember what happened but I woke up with a splitting headache and pieces of the rotting, broken ladder lying around me on the stone cellar floor. My flashlight was shattered, as were my eyeglasses. My arm was throbbing. The only light I could see was a square of daylight that outlined the hatch above. Squinting, I could also make out a fuzzy, round object that began squeaking at me. It turned out to be Angelica, who was looking down at me from above.

Thank goodness, she hadn't fallen into the cellar, too.

I was in a pickle. There was no way I could pull myself out of this deep cellar, especially with a possible broken arm. With the ladder in pieces, I could never get high enough to make it through the hatch.

I suddenly remembered that I had brought my cell phone with me. Woo-hoo! Salvation. Excitedly reaching into my pocket, I pulled out a shattered phone. Sigh. I turned it on anyway and marveled that it actually lit up! Sadly, however, I wasn't getting any signal down in this pit.

That left my companion, Angelica, as my last hope. Perhaps she could somehow summon help.

Angelica could sense my dilemma. She seemed to understand that I needed help, but she didn't want to leave my side. She was smart and always responded when I talked to her. I really didn't know if I could survive down there in a cold cellar for a whole week before my husband returned. So, Angelica and I would have to think of something.

A last-ditch idea finally came to me. If I could get the still-functioning cell phone up through the hatch while it still had battery power, it might connect to the Internet so I could shout at Siri from down below to summon help. I had one shot, so I couldn't blow it.

Angelica kept her eye on me as I mumbled out my plan. I turned up the phone volume to the max. With a deep breath and a silent prayer, I heaved the phone upward. Angelica whacked at it with her paws as it shot through the hatch.

Miraculously, Angelica managed to bat the phone down right by the hatch entrance, close enough for me to yell at Siri. Once the phone picked up reception, I was able to instruct Siri to call emergency services. With them on the line, I screamed out my situation. I told them to look for a calico kitten. I prayed this would rescue me from my ridiculous and dangerous predicament.

In a serious tone, I instructed Angelica to lead my rescuers to me. She looked back at me knowingly and walked away. The next thing I knew, I heard her bold squawks accompanied by heavy footfalls. My rescue team was following Angelica to my side.

It turned out to be a wonderful Christmas in our new home.

My head was badly bruised. My arm, while also badly bruised, was not broken. My husband marveled at how our little angel had helped knock the phone into a position to let me call for help. Angelica, the courageous calico, along with a prayer, had saved my life.

I no longer wonder if it was Angelica herself who rang the doorbell that fateful day.

—Donna L. Roberts—

37

The Cats of Katrina

What is a miracle if not the manifestation of light
where darkness is expected?
~Leigh Ann Henion, *Phenomena*

'm ready to go home to my kitties," Poppy said matter-of-factly. "Y'all can drive me back to New Orleans. I feel much better today."

I stood there speechless. Poppy was reclining in our wingback chair with his leg propped up. Three days post-op, he was still wearing the padded Ace wrap on his knee along with a serene expression on his face. At that moment, I realized he was unaware of the chaos occurring in the city. Yes, Hurricane Katrina had blown over, but she'd left quite a wake! Water was rising at unimaginable speed. People were scrambling to escape with only the clothes on their backs.

"Umm," I stuttered, choosing my words with caution. "The city is a mess. It's safer here in Hammond," I said, trying to sound calm.

"Oh, I'm sure it's not all that bad," he said, waving his arm in the air. "Sniggle Puss and Thomas are waiting for me."

I wrinkled my nose. "It's quite awful," I said. "You haven't been watching this?" I pointed to the small, battery-operated television on the dresser.

Poppy shrugged his shoulders. "That pain medication had me so sleepy."

I wiggled the V-shaped antenna to clear the fuzzy broadcast that had been our only news access since the storm blew out the power.

Slowly, his peaceful expression changed to one of disbelief as he stared at the image of people being airlifted from their rooftops.

My husband walked in and broke his trance. "How are you feeling today, Dad?" he asked.

Poppy looked up with red eyes. "I didn't realize things were this bad, but I…," he said, struggling to speak, "…I have to go back."

My husband sat down next to him. "Nobody had any idea the water would breach the levee walls," he said sympathetically. "New Orleans may never be the same. I don't know if you will ever get to go back."

"Son, I have to go home," Poppy said. "The cats. Sniggle Puss and Thomas. They're locked in the house. I was only supposed to be gone a few days. The food and water I left won't last too much longer. And then," he said, his voice quivering, "it will be hopeless."

As each day passed in the aftermath of Katrina, the possibility that Poppy would return to his beloved cats became less likely. Most homes were either flooded or damaged by high winds. And the few that had been spared were being looted or vandalized. With widespread power outages, phone circuits were down, blocking communication to the city. So, Poppy had no way of knowing if his house, friends, co-workers, or cats had survived.

A week after the storm, we got back our electricity in Hammond, fifty-eight miles from New Orleans. Only then, by satellite image, did we learn that Poppy's house was still standing. In a desperate attempt to save Sniggle Puss and Thomas, my husband emailed out-of-state relatives for help. My sister-in-law, a cat lover herself, was able to contact the Louisiana SPCA, who added Poppy's address to their rescue list. At that point, all any of us could do was wait.

Finally, we received a ray of hope. The local news station announced that animals had been rescued and were being cared for at the Lamar Dixon Expo Center in Gonzales, Louisiana.

"I have to search for my kitties," Poppy said.

"The chance of finding those cats is practically impossible," my husband said.

"But I have to try. If I don't find them, it's not because I didn't try,"

Poppy said with determination.

So, a little over two weeks after Katrina, my husband drove the still recovering Poppy on the impossible mission to reunite him with Sniggle Puss and Thomas.

When they arrived at the open-air, barn-type structure, the hunt seemed overwhelming. Animals of all types were sheltered in different sections of the vast expo center. Poppy staggered on crutches atop the dirt- and hay-covered floor in the stagnant heat past sheds with horses and cows, and countless rows of metal cages containing dogs. With no walls, the different pitched barks and yelps echoed freely, bouncing off the metal roof. Workers, volunteers, and other displaced pet owners were flowing in and out of the crowded area.

Poppy and my husband roamed aimlessly, looking for any cats, until a friendly staff member approached.

"The cats are all grouped according to color," the lady explained, leading my husband and Poppy to the adjacent area.

"Sniggle Puss is older with black-and-white hair," Poppy said, following her. "That cat is quite special to me. He was born under my house in New Orleans and has even traveled back and forth with me to New York." Poppy struggled to contain his emotions.

A cameraman from the BBC network walked up. "I couldn't help overhearing your story. Can you tell me about the other cat?" he asked, adjusting his microphone.

Poppy nodded. "I adopted Thomas when he was six years old. I saw his furry gray face and just knew he needed me to take him home."

"Here we are," the staff lady said, pointing him and my husband to an entire section referred to as the cat barn. Then, she proceeded to relay his information to a young girl with a clipboard while Poppy and my husband began searching the many aisles of kennels and cages.

Suddenly, they heard a girl shout from the next row. "I think we have your cat!" she exclaimed.

As quickly as he could on crutches, Poppy walked over to her.

Right there in front of him was Sniggle Puss! There was no doubt about it. He was in his own kennel tagged with Poppy's address.

If that wasn't proof enough, dangling from the top of the kennel was Poppy's extra house key on a chain with his distinctive Saint Benedict medal!

An outburst of screams and cries from Poppy, the volunteers, and the BBC reporter filled the open-air barn with the pure joy of this reunion.

And the sounds of elation were not short-lived.

Only seconds later, another blissful discovery was made: a note indicating this was one of two kennels!

Yep, Thomas was safe too, in the section of gray cats.

That afternoon, when Poppy and my husband drove up with not one but both cats, it was the first good news any of us had gotten in weeks. Finally, we received a sign that some version of normal life would return one day.

Hurricane Katrina had destroyed almost everything around us, but not the power of the human-animal bond. The love between Poppy and his cats had survived. The rescue of Sniggle Puss and Thomas from the floodwaters of Katrina had restored Poppy's hope. One day, he hoped to step back into the home he loved in New Orleans, together with his kitties. And, eventually, he did!

— Pamela Cali Bankston —

38

Olivia, the Fierce

When I look into the eyes of an animal, I do not see an animal. I see a living being. I see a friend. I feel a soul.

~A.D. Williams

Cat lovers, please do not shoot the storyteller. Not liking cats does not mean I have no tale to tell. The tale is about Olivia, who ruled the cul-de-sac. Everyone knew her and warned all guests to ignore her as she would bite and scratch. No one ignored that advice twice.

Her owner family did not interact with her except to keep her water bowl filled and to feed her. I asked why they kept such an unfriendly cat. The answer was simple. "You don't get rid of someone because he or she develops a negative personality. You just continue to love 'em."

A few months later, I suddenly became homeless. Olivia's family took me in late one Sunday night. The following weekend, they left for a planned vacation in Washington, D.C.

I was to keep the water bowl full and to give Olivia one scoop of food when she sat in front of the pantry door where it was stored.

That night, I witnessed a different side of Olivia. Miss I-Don't-Care-About-Anyone padded from bedroom to bedroom... from bed to bed... as she searched for the family. I dozed off and then sensed her sitting in my bedroom doorway.

"No way! You are not coming in this bedroom with me. Remember? I don't like you, and you don't like me," I said. She left.

The next morning, I woke up looking into Olivia's eyes. They met mine, and she leaped off my bed and ran.

Later, she crept in and dashed under the bed. Not wanting cat hair on the fabric that was stored there, I attempted to chase her out. But I was overstepping her boundaries. Olivia hissed, nipped, and scratched at me. When I didn't back off, her eyes locked on mine, and her mouth opened lion-style to roar. It began as a hiss, just like a snake. And then, out came the tiniest squeak.

"That's it? That's your ferocious roar?" I was rolling on the floor laughing until I couldn't catch my breath. She shot out from under the bed and disappeared for hours — until she was hungry.

After that, Olivia always slept next to me — arriving after I fell asleep and leaving only a warm indentation in the blanket when I woke up. Officially, she continued to ignore my existence. But as my depression deepened, she became more attentive, and I often knew she was watching me. Occasionally, she would appear and sit at my feet, doze a bit, and then dash off on another outside adventure. When I worked 11:00 P.M. to 7:00 A.M., she would appear as I opened my car door and walk me to the house. Olivia offered no affection, no tiny purr, nothing… She was just there for me.

I moved into an apartment after a few months and was grateful for the unconditional love that had surrounded me when I was so fragile.

A couple of years later, the family was transferred to another state. I stopped by as the moving vans were pulling out. As I stepped out of my car, Olivia was sitting on a low branch of a small tree. She walked me to the door, and I think she knew I was okay but could not say good-bye. I never saw her again.

Cats still do not like me any more than I like them. However, for a brief time, a mysterious, fierce, four-legged, bad-attitude cat understood my troubled heart and mind.

— Constance Gilbert —

39

Connections

Explaining a miracle doesn't make it
any less of a miracle.
~Athan Fletcher, The Swordsman and The Priestess

love my job as a volunteer at a cat-rescue centre. Today, I enter the shelter, and one cat reacts to my entrance by racing over, skidding to a stop and throwing up a large black paw as if to give me a high-five. In fact, Angus, a big, longhaired, semi-feral cat isn't saying hello so much as demanding a treat.

I look past him into the small room of the shelter. Heidi and Garth snooze head-to-head on top of a cat tree. The owner refers to them as "the married couple" even though they arrived at the shelter as strangers. Heidi has a chronic respiratory infection that makes her unadoptable. Since she and Garth are inseparable, they will remain here together forever.

Lucy is my favourite. She is a small, shy orange tabby with a white chest and white paws. She has been moved into the small room because some of the other cats bully her. She is perfectly happy in her new home.

The two young tabbies I call The Brats are playing together.

Peter is an old tabby-and-white cat that was abandoned in a cage behind PetSmart. The centre took him, and he is doing quite well.

There are approximately thirty-five cats in the shelter. Each has a name and a story. Most of them are not adoptable for various reasons but will remain here and be looked after for the rest of their lives. I am always warmed by their presence and amused by their personalities.

The owner told me a story about a kitten that was born of a mother who arrived at the shelter pregnant. He was the runt of the litter and so small he fit into a teacup. They nursed him and fed him from an eye dropper. He slowly gained strength. At about five weeks of age, he took a turn for the worse. He was barely breathing. They found a small shoebox to be his coffin.

It was March 13, 2013, notable for two impending events. It was the date a new Pope was to be selected by the Vatican, and it was the day they expected to bury the tiny kitten. They turned on the radio and distracted themselves: replenishing food, changing water and cleaning litter. They cuddled the cats who would allow them and distributed treats. A newscast started as they finally turned their attention to Nameless. They stroked his fur and then gently placed him in the shoebox. They murmured a prayer, soft and low, and told him he would soon be joining St. Francis of Assisi, the patron saint of animals. Just then, the tiny kitten rallied and stood up. They decided to name him Francis after the Pope.

Today, Francis lives in the house. He is strong but cannot jump as high as the other cats. Every evening, at around 9:15, as if remembering the announcement of Pope Francis's appointment, he goes to the side door and cries, even though he has never been outside. Only after he hears a chorus of "Baby Francis, Baby Francis" will he come back into the room and settle down.

Saint and animal—Pope Francis and Baby Francis—an illustration of the universal connection among all of us.

—Janet Hodges—

This Is What We Needed

*Are we really sure the purring is coming from the kitty
and not from our very own hearts?*
~Emme Woodhull-Bäche

Two summers left before she leaves for college
Separated by walls and thirty-one years
So much time alone in her room and me in the kitchen

We went to look at kittens and fell in love with them
One cat each for mother and daughter

Baby cats closing the gaps between us
Filling our lives with weak meows and fish breath
Delicate bells muffled by fur, slow blinks and cheek rubs
Dainty paws on wooden floors
So much purring

Our eyes met in common adoration as we came together to swoon
over the kittens
This is what we needed, she said

— Heidi Kling-Newnam —

Our Little Old Lady

The way of the miracle-worker is to see all human
behavior as one of two things: either love,
or a call for love.
~Marianne Williamson

A few years ago, our home was a powder keg of meltdowns, controlling behaviours, and sleep deprivation. Our elder son had been diagnosed with autism.

The only time our little whirlwind paused was around animals, whether it was horses, dogs, or squirrels in the park. He was gentle, calm and fascinated by them all. Knowing this, we agreed to foster a geriatric cat called Cleo. She was a beautiful, gentle, green-eyed streak of black fur who immediately installed herself under our sofa and in the centre of our son's world.

To start with, we used Cleo as encouragement for our son to wash his face: "Cleo washes her face every day." We used Cleo's health as a reason for our son to clear his plate away after dinner, so she wouldn't eat people food that was bad for her. We asked him to pick things up from the floor so Cleo wouldn't have to walk around them. We encouraged him to sit still so Cleo could sit in his lap, and he began to use words rather than actions so he wouldn't disturb the sleeping cat. Our son was learning how to keep Cleo happy and safe through better behaviour. He was besotted with her, and she with him.

Nowadays, his meltdowns are less frequent. With Cleo's help, he is able to recover faster. She is our calm, green-eyed companion who likes to follow us around the house and garden, finding sunny spots and warm laps.

Cleo always seems to sense when our son's emotions are building up and will appear nearby. There are days when she just follows him around our home, outside to the trampoline, up to his room, or anywhere she can go to be with him.

When the pandemic hit and we went into lockdown, schools closed, and all usual activities paused. My elder son couldn't cope. He was on the sofa mid-meltdown, crying and lashing out. I couldn't get near him without being hurt, and words weren't helping. I felt utterly helpless.

Cleo appeared from the garden. As always, she didn't seem concerned by the behaviour; she just saw his distress and padded over to help. "Cleo's there. Keep your legs calm," I prompted. And with what must have felt like an insurmountable effort for him, he kept his legs still. Cleo leapt up onto him, turned around twice and settled on his lap.

His fists were clenched and his body rigid, but after a few minutes he was able to stroke Cleo's soft black fur with his knuckles. The stress ebbed out of his hands so he could stroke her properly, and from there the tension slowly released from his body. Cleo rested her chin on her paw, and I could hear the low rumble of her purr as her eyes gently closed, feeling safe on his lap and doing what I couldn't: making his world feel more manageable.

Cleo may be a cat, but in our home she is a superhero. She is able to see through our son's behaviours, offer him what he needs, and always trusts the kindness inside him. When he's had a difficult day and I'm exhausted, I think of how Cleo sees only the best in him and how far he's come, all because of our amazing geriatric cat.

— Naomi True —

42

The Scruffy Cat

How we behave toward cats here below
determines our status in heaven.
~Robert A. Heinlein

Our two cats had joined me on the screened back porch as I scooped out their favorite hard food from a bag. I had just gotten home from my job and was waiting for my husband, Tim.

"Eww! What's that smell?" I glanced down at our two cats. They looked up at me as if to say, "Nope, it's not us. Not this time."

What a smell! It was like very old kitty litter. Of course, that smell wasn't coming from our two cats, Squirrelly and Stamper. They didn't use kitty litter since they were mostly outdoor cats on our acre of land.

That's when I noticed what was causing the odor. There was a cat right outside the porch rubbing on the screen. Her fur was matted with big, mud-colored clumps around her belly and bottom. There were probably fleas in there, too. I couldn't even guess her fur's true color. Her tail was more like a possum's, with bits of hair sticking out. She opened her mouth and I could see she was missing her bottom teeth.

Despite all that, she had two amazing qualities. She had beautiful green eyes, and her purring was the loudest I had ever heard.

She lingered in our back yard and when Tim came home, we talked about how she might have ended up at our house. We lived on a road with lots of traffic and other houses close by. We certainly would have remembered if we had seen this cat in our neighborhood.

We decided the cat had probably been dropped off by somebody.

We'd taken in stray cats before. That's how we had ended up with Squirrelly and Stamper three years earlier.

We were surprised how our two cats casually accepted her. But we certainly did not need another cat, even one with that amazing purring. Without telling Tim, I included the stray in my prayers that evening. *God, please find her a loving home.*

The next day, Tim told me he had an interesting conversation with our veterinarian. The vet said he had been in our neighborhood a couple of days ago. One of our neighbors, an elderly woman, had been placed in assisted living. The sheriff had called the vet and our county's humane society because of the unsanitary living conditions in our neighbor's house.

Tim said, "The vet told me that they had to remove lots of cats and kittens and take them to the animal shelter." We couldn't be certain if the stray had escaped from our neighbor's house, but our compassion went out to the neighbor and all those cats.

That evening, when I saw the stray, I looked at her in a different way. I couldn't ignore her scruffy smell, but I saw a survivor now.

I kept watching her in our yard. She strutted around like a show cat. I wanted to applaud and cry at the same time. That evening, I repeated the same prayer for the stray to find a loving home.

For two more days, Tim and I went about our busy schedules. We talked briefly about the stray. Tim seemed surprised when I told him she was missing her bottom teeth. He described her as loving and sweet, and he said he didn't mind her smell.

I kept repeating the same prayer for her.

By the end of the workweek, I was actually looking forward to seeing the stray. As I drove up the driveway, I saw that Tim had gotten home early. He was carrying a can of cat food toward the stray.

I said, "What's going on?"

"I got a can of food for her."

Had I just heard him correctly? "Have you been feeding her?"

"I started feeding her some of Squirrelly and Stamper's food a few days ago. But she needed soft food."

I just had to laugh. *We* were the answer to my prayer.

And Tim was saying more.

"I've got a name for her: Scruffy. I'm taking her to the vet tomorrow for a checkup."

Tim was still holding the open can of food. Scruffy gazed up at him and rubbed against his leg. He placed the whole can down in front of her. She ate and purred.

This time, I didn't mind her scruffy smell either.

—Glenda Ferguson—

My Co-Pilot in the Storm

I believe cats to be spirits come to earth. A cat, I am
sure, could walk on a cloud without coming through.
~Jules Verne

I like to think that I always make good decisions, but Hurricane Harvey showed me that's not the case. Instead of blowing through in a few hours as most hurricanes do, Hurricane Harvey sat over Houston for days and dropped not inches but feet of rain all across the city. After the second day of near continuous rain, our home lost power. With at least four more days of rain in the forecast, it was clear the power wasn't coming back anytime soon. I sent my wife and two daughters across town to my mother-in-law's house where the power was still working.

I would stay behind, prepare our house for the rising waters, and join them later. I kept Mogli, our one-year-old orange tabby, with me for company. The only boys in the family would stick together.

Mogli and I hit the ground running. The first order of business was to move furniture to higher ground. Mogli followed me every step of the way as I carried our chairs and tables upstairs. Without air conditioning, the temperature inside the house was well into the eighties, and I had to take frequent breaks. Whenever I sat to catch my breath, Mogli would sit next to me and put his paws on my knee.

I could almost feel him encouraging me to keep going. We would split a bottle of water and, after a few minutes, we would get back to it.

After I moved all the furniture that I could carry, we got to work in the closets. I must have moved hundreds of hangers filled with clothes and dozens of my wife's shoes into the upper bedrooms. Mogli was no slouch in this effort either. I would tuck a T-shirt or scarf into his collar, and he would carry it up the stairs as he followed me. We ate dinner together that night by flashlight — Mogli had his favorite canned chicken and gravy, and I had a peanut-butter sandwich.

There was a pause in the rain the next day, and the power even returned in the evening. I called my wife to tell her to return to our house, but the forecast was grim. The rain was going to return with a vengeance on our side of town the next day, and our proximity to the river meant our house would likely be under a mandatory evacuation order. We decided I would take Mogli and go to my wife instead. With the sun already down and many roads underwater, I thought it would be best to leave as soon as the sun came up in the morning.

I woke up at 5:00 A.M. the next day and packed the car with everything I could, including Mogli's food, bowls, and litter box. I placed Mogli's cat bed on the front passenger seat so he could assume the co-pilot's position. We left a few minutes before dawn.

Five minutes into the drive, I knew evacuating was the right decision. The heavy rain returned. If I had waited much longer the roads leaving our neighborhood would have been impassable. With all the major streets closed due to flooding, I used my cell phone to find back roads to my mother-in-law's house. The going was slow as we were averaging only twenty miles per hour, but we were making progress. From time to time, I snuck a peek at Mogli. He was sitting with his full attention at the windshield as all good co-pilots do.

After taking almost an hour to go just eighteen miles, we were almost there. The back roads worked great. All we had to do was cross the highway, and we would be with our family within ten minutes. We only had one more traffic light to pass before reaching the overpass. As I got closer, I saw there was water in the intersection, so I stopped ten feet short of the light to weigh my options.

The rain was coming down hard, and I could not tell how deep the water was. On one hand, I knew that water can be deeper than it appears, and it can be very dangerous to drive into high water. On the other, we had encountered some water-filled intersections on our way to this point and been able to cross them just fine. Plus, I didn't see any flooded cars abandoned in the intersection, so I figured that other cars had passed through earlier unscathed. Turning back to go home didn't seem like a good option either as my house was already in an optional evacuation zone, and it was just a matter of time before it was made mandatory.

I decided to go for it. I slowly accelerated into the water. After just a few seconds, water was sloshing around my car doors, and I heard something that I had never heard before.

It came from the passenger seat. Mogli let out a "mrrrrrr" sound. I hit the brake and turned to my co-pilot. I was amazed because Mogli, for whatever reason, had never made a sound in the year since we had adopted him. I'd never heard him "meow" or "hiss" much less cry out in a "mrrrrrr." Mogli turned his head toward me and stared straight into my eyes. I immediately pictured what would happen if our car got stuck. If we were lucky enough to get out of the car, I would have to walk through waist-deep water in the rain while trying to keep Mogli above the water. We were still three miles from our destination, and there is no telling how long we would be in the pouring rain. How could I do that to him? What was I thinking?

I put the car in reverse and started backing out of the water. I would find another way. After twenty more minutes of driving, Mogli and I found a new route and finally reunited with our family. As I think back on it, I'm 100-percent sure I would have kept going if Mogli hadn't spoken up—and I'm 100-percent sure the car would have flooded if I did. Everyone needs a good co-pilot when they are in a storm, and I'm so glad Mogli was mine.

—Nikesh Patel—

44

The Cat's Paw

Seashells are love letters in the sand.
~Author Unknown

My falling tears got Kendra's fur wet as I cradled her in my arms. She had always been a good listener, and I could tell by the way her hazel-green eyes were fixed on mine that she knew I had something important to tell her.

"Kendra, you've been an important member of our family for fifteen years, which some would call a long life for a cat. You've been loyal and loving all that time, and it breaks my heart we will be forced to let you go tomorrow."

She adjusted her position, which made me think she might be getting antsy and want to get down. However, she continued to gaze up at me as if to say, "Go on, I'm listening."

I continued to explain why she would be leaving us. "We went into Dr. Martin's office — you know, the nice veterinarian we take you to now and then? He examined you to see if he could tell us why you have not been eating lately and spending most of your time sleeping. Well, he came back with the results of the blood tests and gave us the bad news. He said, 'I know this is not something you want to hear, but Kendra has a form of cancer that cannot be treated or cured. The only humane thing to do is keep her comfortable and end her suffering as soon as possible.'"

I continued my explanation to my attentive cat: "I must admit I had to sit down to keep my knees from buckling, and I don't recall hearing anything else. It was like I flipped a switch to turn him off. I wanted to ignore his advice and let you stay forever, but I realized that would be selfish because it would only serve to comfort us. So, we made an appointment to go back to him tomorrow morning."

I tried to comfort myself and her by saying, "You'll be happy in your new forever home where it's peaceful, and there is no illness or suffering. You'll feel good again and play with other cats — maybe even chase a chipmunk or two."

Kendra shifted her weight again, and this time I got her message — she had heard enough and wanted to return to her quiet spot to rest. I gently placed her on the floor and watched her disappear into our bedroom.

My family had said goodbye to many pets over the years, but this was different. Kendra seemed human to me, and I would often talk to her as I would with a friend who stopped by for coffee. I could tell she was listening by the way she sat at attention with her tail curled around her body and stared intently at me.

Just as a mother would brag about a well-behaved daughter, I would brag about Kendra because she would obey me when I told her "No." I frequently sat on our den sofa to watch television while I ate a meal. She would jump up on the opposite end and slowly approach me like a lioness creeping up on her prey. As she got closer, she would raise her nose into the air, sniffing what smelled to her like a banquet. Knowing what she was up to, I would raise one hand like a school crossing guard holding back traffic. She would sit down and patiently wait, knowing I would save a few tidbits for her.

It was interesting to see her habits change once she got sick. Her behavior mimicked her ancestors in the wild. They would find a secluded spot in the woods to be safe from predators during their remaining time and Kendra did the same. She chose the back of our bedroom closet as her safe haven, and no matter how much I tried to coax her out, she would curl into a tighter ball and pretend not to notice.

I sat straight up in bed the morning after my chat with her and told my husband, "I think Kendra slept on my hip last night like she always has. I can't decide if it was a vision in a dream or if it really happened."

He gave me a comforting hug and assured me, "No matter which it was, it must have been her way of saying goodbye."

"This is the last thing I want to do today," I admitted, "but I'm going with you. I need to be there for Kendra."

As the doctor stroked Kendra's weak body, he spoke in a soft tone and put his arm around my shoulder. "I know how difficult this will be for you but take as much time as you need to be alone with her. When you are ready, let me know, and I'll come back in." I was grateful to have a little more time, even though it would not change the inevitable.

I had no words that would let her know how much I was going to miss her, so I offered comfort by rubbing her head and cheeks. I felt blessed when I heard a faint purr of appreciation.

We called the doctor back in to administer the injection. I tried to be brave as I placed my face next to hers, but my heart was breaking. I couldn't think of anything to say except, "I'm so sorry, Kendra. We love you." Once again, her gray-and-white fur became wet with my tears.

When she was gone, I couldn't leave the office fast enough to get outside where I could breathe again. My husband put his arm around me and asked, "Do you want to go home now?"

Without hesitation, I responded, "No, I want to go to the beach."

It was a short drive, and we found a bench near the water. We sat in silence, hearing only seagulls squawking in the distance. I soon felt I could face our empty apartment and said, "Let's go home."

The sand shifting with each step caused me to feel unsteady, so I kept looking down to maintain my balance as we walked toward our car. I stopped short when I spotted a small orange-and-white shell lying on the sand all by itself. I recognized it right away as a cat's paw, which perfectly describes its appearance. Feeling this might be a sign from Kendra, I picked it up and guarded it all the way home, hoping to somehow preserve it.

When we entered our apartment, I passed the table holding our small, decorated Christmas tree. My arm brushed against the ornaments, including a small bell that jingled. That very moment, I clearly heard the little girl's voice from the movie, *It's a Wonderful Life*. "Every time a bell rings, an angel gets its wings."

I encased a picture of Kendra along with the cat's paw and bell in a shadowbox frame. It comforts me to believe our pets go to the same heaven as we do, and this is a constant reminder she isn't gone forever. She simply went ahead of us to wait for the day we will be reunited.

— Carol McCollister —

45

Miracle Cat

When the world says, "Give up," Hope whispers,
"Try it one more time."
~Author Unknown

Our family-owned business was pretty laidback, especially when summertime rolled around. When my children were out of school, I had the ability to take them to work.

The kids kept themselves occupied while I did my meetings, phone calls, and paperwork. As a reward for their patience in this boring corporate environment, we went on afternoon excursions to the park, pool, and ice cream shop.

Then the July week that my four-year-old son dreaded arrived. His nine-year-old sister would be spending the week with Grandma, meaning he would be on his own at the office while I worked.

As a consolation, I agreed to bring our Silky Terrier to work with us. Surprisingly, all went well. Until Friday.

Friday mornings were a bit hectic. We always arrived early to get some paperwork completed before I took my son to a local day camp. This morning, something was wrong with the dog. He wouldn't play with my son, and he appeared preoccupied. He was scurrying back and forth between the two office windows, his high-pitched yips growing louder and more demanding. Our little watchdog was trying to tell us something.

"He must hear a bird outside," I explained, urging my son to get his backpack together.

As we hurried to the car, my son stopped dead in his tracks. "Mama, do you hear that?"

I was too busy to acknowledge anything, although I did hear a strange, raspy sound.

"We're late! Get in the car!" I said, and my son did so reluctantly.

I leaned into the car to help him with his seatbelt and felt a soft tickle on the top of my sandaled foot. I jumped!

There was a cocoa brown cat standing behind me. It was making that strange sound.

"What is it, Mama?" My son hoisted himself up to get a better look.

The cat approached me, pawing my foot again, its meows weak and hoarse but very persistent.

"Aww, hey there, little fella." I crouched down to give it a pet as the feeble meows turned to purrs. As the grateful cat nuzzled me, I was startled at what I saw next.

At first, it didn't seem possible, but as I looked closer, I realized the cat's back-right leg was partly severed. This poor cat was pleading for my help!

I told my son to stay in the car and quickly called my mom, panicking as I told her about the cat. She knew of a nearby animal clinic, so I placed the injured cat in our pet carrier and rushed to the vet.

The vet said that nothing could be done even though I said I would pay whatever it cost. I quickly loaded my son and the cat back into the car. I knew time was of the essence. The receptionist, who was crying harder than I was, ran out to my car.

"Take him to Angels of Assisi!" she called out with her cell phone up to her ear. "I'm calling them now to say you're coming!"

Upon arrival, the cat was immediately taken to surgery. I watched as its brilliant green eyes looked at me through the pet carrier, as it cried goodbye.

The vet came in as I filled out the paperwork. "He's in really bad shape. Chances are, he probably won't make it, but I wanted to thank you for bringing him in."

The vet explained that gangrene had set in, and the cat had been in this condition for several days.

I called my mom with the disheartening news.

"You did the right thing," she assured me.

I was updated later that night. The surgery was over. The cat was heavily medicated and in critical condition.

I received another call from the vet himself the next afternoon. My heart stopped as I braced myself for the worst.

"I don't know how to tell you this..."

The cat had passed. I knew it. I sobbed on the other side of the receiver trying to remind myself of my mom's reassuring words. Through tears, I thanked the doctor for all he'd done.

"I have this cat here," he continued, "and he's going to need a very loving home." The vet continued through chuckles. "I'm not sure how, but your little guy made it!"

After a few more days, we were invited to visit the clinic. The vet met us in the waiting room, informing us our new pet still needed to stay another week to recover completely before going to his new home.

"I will warn you," he told us, "upon seeing him, you might be a little surprised, shocked even."

We all nodded in agreement. My children already knew that our new kitty would have three legs, and that he would need all the love we could possibly give him.

We walked into the exam room to see our recovering kitten and I gasped while both kids broke out in joyful laughter.

The most gorgeous snow-white cat we had ever seen was on the exam table!

"Our kitty was brown. A dark chocolate color!"

"Your kitty was dirty," the vet said with a laugh. "Very, very dirty."

I recognized those brilliant green eyes. And now the meowing was loud and proud.

Our sweet and thankful cat was lightning fast despite missing one leg. He lived a long and happy life with us and was a reminder that we are only as limited as we allow ourselves to be.

— Valerie Archual —

Chapter
5

Life Lessons from the Cat

46

Lessons from a Frozen Meatball

When life brings you full circle, pay attention.
There's a lesson there.
~Mandy Hale

"I have to be home earlier than all my friends," my teenage son, Jordan, said. "I'm seventeen years old, and I still have a curfew. Legally, I'm practically an adult."

"You're not an adult," I said. "You're still in high school."

"None of my friends has a curfew. You don't trust me."

"It's not about trust," I said. "It's about wanting what's best for you. I love you, and I want to protect you."

"Protect me from what? Having fun?"

I sighed. "Honey, we've talked about this before. As long as you live at home, there will be certain rules to follow. But those rules exist because I love you, not because I'm trying to control you."

He rolled his eyes and walked away.

I felt tears prick my eyes. Parenting teenagers was so challenging. How could I make Jordan see that I only wanted the best for him?

I decided to go for a walk, hoping the brisk October air would clear my head. I opened the front door and nearly stepped on him: a small black cat with a white-tipped tail. "Hi, Meatball," I said, scooping him into my arms. "Are you ready to come back inside?"

A few weeks before, I'd found the cat sitting on our porch like he belonged there. He was too thin, and he wasn't wearing a collar. We'd lost our last cat the year before, so we didn't have any cat food in the house. But this cat was clearly hungry, so I fed him some meatballs left from the previous night's dinner.

When my youngest son, Nathan, got home, he was beyond thrilled to see the cat. When I told him that I'd fed the cat some meatballs, Nathan thought that would be the perfect name for his new pet. "He may already have a home, honey," I warned him. "Don't get too attached."

But the next morning, the cat was still on the porch. He rubbed his head against my legs and allowed me to pet him. When I sat down on our porch swing, he jumped into my lap and started purring. "You are a sweet, little thing," I said, mentally adding cat food to my grocery list.

A week went by, and Meatball stayed on our porch. "I think this is his new home," Nathan said. When I nodded in agreement, Nathan picked up Meatball and carried him into the house. "Let me show you around," he told the cat.

Meatball seemed happy enough to come in the house, but after an hour or two, he sat by the door, meowing to go back outside.

"Why won't he just stay in with us all the time?" Nathan asked.

"Because he's used to living outside," I said. "It's going to take some time for him to get used to living in our house."

But as the weeks went on, Meatball didn't adjust to the life of a full-time indoor cat. After a few hours in the house, he'd sit by the door and meow, begging for someone to let him back outside. After a few hours outside, he'd sit on the porch, ready to come back in the house. He seemed happy with this arrangement, so I obliged him.

But because our other cats had been indoor cats, Meatball's behavior puzzled Nathan. "Why isn't he happy in our house?" he asked.

"He is happy here," I explained, "but he just really likes being able to come and go as he pleases."

"That must be nice," Jordan muttered from the other room. "The cat can come and go, but I can't. I wonder what time Meatball's curfew is."

Jordan's curfew had become an ongoing discussion that rarely ended well for either of us. I decided to ignore his comment. Thankfully, he didn't say anything else.

One night in January, when we'd had Meatball for a few months, temperatures were unusually low. The wind chill was near zero, and there was nearly a foot of snow on the ground. Meatball stood at the door, meowing to go outside.

"It's too cold out there, Bud," I said. "You'll freeze."

He stared at me and meowed again.

"I know you want out, but you're not going. You'll have to stay inside until it warms up a bit." I patted his head. "I know you're not happy, but it's for your own good."

"Mom's not being mean to you," Nathan told the cat. "She's just trying to keep you from turning into a frozen Meatball."

We both laughed at his joke.

The next morning, I couldn't find Meatball. I asked the kids if anyone had seen him.

Jordan nodded. "I let him out last night."

My mouth dropped open. "He was outside all night? It was freezing!"

Jordan shrugged. "He was sitting by the door, meowing. I could tell he wanted to go out."

I grabbed my coat and rushed outside, praying the cat had survived the night. It took me several minutes to find him curled in a tiny ball beneath my husband's car. I picked him up, unsure if he was alive or dead. As I carried him into the house, I saw him open his eyes a bit.

"Thank you, God," I murmured.

The next few hours were scary. While I called the vet, Jordan warmed towels in the dryer and wrapped them around Meatball.

"I'm sorry, Buddy," I heard him say over and over again. "Mom was right. Even though you didn't want to, I should have made you stay inside where it was safe."

As I drove to the vet's office, Jordan sat in the back, holding Meatball inside his coat for warmth. I could hear him talking to the cat, apologizing in soft tones. He was clearly near tears.

After examining him, the vet determined that Meatball had a mild case of frostbite on his paws, ears, and tail, but no permanent damage.

"But this could have been bad," the vet cautioned. "Severe frostbite usually requires amputation. In this extreme weather, this little guy needs to stay inside overnight, whether he wants to or not."

On the drive home, Jordan stroked Meatball's head and apologized again. Then, surprisingly, he apologized to me. "I'm sorry for how I've acted about my curfew," he said. "I know you're doing it because you love me and want to keep me safe."

I felt a lump in my throat. "Thank you, Bud," I said. "I'm glad you understand."

He nodded as he rubbed Meatball's back. "It looks like you and I are going to be spending more time in the house," he told the cat.

I smiled through tears, so grateful that our frozen Meatball was going to be all right and for the important lesson he'd taught my son about loving others enough to protect them, whether they want us to or not.

— Diane Stark —

Guilty

Cats are independent, by which I mean smart.
~Dave Barry

"He left the cupboard door open again," I muttered under my breath as I scooped a mound of dry cat food off the kitchen floor and plopped it back in the bag. The bright orange sack was much emptier now than it should have been. It was the third time this week our three cats had enjoyed a nocturnal feast, thanks to my husband's carelessness. I firmly closed the door and the drawer above it that had also been left open.

"No breakfast for you... or dinner either, by the looks of things," I announced to the feline faces surveying me sleepily from the back of the sofa in the family room. As usual, they didn't really seem to care. I swear I heard the furniture groan under the weight of their bloated tummies.

When my husband came into the kitchen, I reminded him about making sure the cabinet door was closed all the way before going to bed at night. I pointed out that it was not good for them to overeat, how much a bag of cat food costs, and...

"I did close it. I'm sure," he insisted.

I was not convinced. "Then how did the food get on the floor?" I countered. With no explanation for this, the discussion ended in a stalemate.

Meanwhile, the cats lay in a furry lump, digesting the spoils of their midnight raid. Kitty Cat (KC for short) was the matriarch, a reformed barn cat who'd come to us screeching, claws out, and full of ticks and

Life Lessons from the Cat | 131

fleas. Now three years old, she imposed order on the household with an iron paw. Beside her was Lucky, our Persian/Himalayan princess, who deigned to let the others serve and groom her. She usually weighed in at a wispy five and a half pounds or so, but this morning I guessed she would have tipped the scale around seven pounds. Finally, there was Stanley, the newest addition to our little family. He was pure white except for a grey smudge between his ears, and had mismatched eyes — one blue and one gold. He was a laid-back guy, but we never knew when he was going to suddenly scale the curtains or launch a glass from the counter.

I left for work, but throughout the day I pondered the kibble raid and the cat dynamic in our home. Stanley could be a handful, and the open door in the kitchen seemed to have started at the same time as he joined our family.

That night, we followed our routine to a T, with my husband coming to bed after me as usual. But this time, I slipped out of the bedroom before the door closed and hid in the hall around the corner from the kitchen. I felt ridiculous as I waited, but within minutes the game was afoot.

KC and Lucky padded into the kitchen and took their places in front of the cupboard. Stanley, the obvious ringleader, swaggered in. In one smooth motion, he leapt to the counter. Four expectant eyes watched as he hooked one white paw into the handle of the silverware drawer right above the cat-food cupboard. He pulled until it was open about four inches or so. He stuck his head into the opening and contorted his body until it was flattened atop the knives, forks, and spoons. With barely a sound of metal tinkling, he inched his way to the back of the drawer. After a minute of rustling around, Stanley gave a mighty push, and the cat-food bag burst from the cabinet, spilling its contents into a messy buffet on the floor.

The next morning, all charges against my husband were dropped. I washed and sterilized all the silverware and then headed to the hardware store to buy a set of childproof locks.

— Brenda Jefferies —

Perfect Excuse

Pets bring vital energy to our homes and lives.
~Laura Staley

A few years ago, on his normally uneventful drive home from work, Kyle found a donut-sized kitten curled into a tiny black ball on the side of a busy road. I was out of town when he texted the unexpected news.

"I found a kitten today!"

"Does your dad know?" I asked, confident my ex-husband wouldn't approve.

"Yes. He said I could keep him!"

I feigned excitement as I Googled "How to fake a pet allergy" to make it impossible for my youngest to bring his new kitten into our formerly fur-free home.

The day after I returned from my trip, I was prepared to lecture my seventeen-year-old about the pitfalls of pet ownership. I was eager to explain how his timing could not have been worse, especially with his impending move to college in two months. I was determined to strengthen my leave-no-cat-behind campaign by creating a gorgeous PowerPoint presentation, detailing what I hate most about cats: They walk, climb, and jump on countertops.

"They scatter enough kitty litter to open a private beach," I planned to tell him. More importantly, they walk through the house with litter clinging to their paws and it drops everywhere.

I had already made up my mind. No kitten. No way. My son was not going to change my mind.

A few minutes later, Kyle strolled into the house and handed me a fluffy cloud named Natty. As I held his fur baby above my head, I swore I heard the theme from *The Lion King* playing in the background. Natty's green, silver-dollar-sized eyes mesmerized me.

"She can keep you company when I go away to school," my son said.

"Thanks, but I'll be fine."

"But you'll have so much fun together," he insisted.

Within minutes, I realized that Natty not only was the cutest kitten I had ever seen, with her pint-sized paws and a nose the size of a Tic Tac, but also the first kitten I had ever held. Being a cat virgin, I almost dropped her when I heard what sounded and felt like a tiny motorcycle humming inside her.

So much for my "You don't need a cat" lecture. Still, I wasn't convinced I was ready to host a pet, especially a kitten.

"What if Natty stays with your dad during the alternating weeks you stay with me?" I suggested.

"Where Natty goes, I go," Kyle said.

When the stakes changed, so did my mind.

Begrudgingly, I have to admit that Kyle was right: Natty does keep me company. She also keeps me alert. At bedtime, she's eager to play and often awakens me from a dead sleep with a ninja-like sneak attack. But Natty does even more: She gives me a reason to text and call my son without coming across as an overbearing, pushy, "Why-don't-you-answer-my-texts?" type of mom.

Every few days, I text Kyle pictures of Natty eating, sleeping, or resting under my home-office desk. Or I post photos and videos of her on an Instagram account I started. Soon after, my son calls or texts to ask about his pet or to find out more about the pictures I've posted.

I never imagined I'd own a cat. Even the thought of buying a large bag of cat food made me break out in hives. Yet, living with Natty has changed my opinion and my life.

Not only do I love this pet, but I have an excuse to stay in touch with my son. And if that excuse is an adorable cat who doesn't mind posing for pictures, that's even better.

—Lisa Kanarek—

49

Class Clown

*Who among us hasn't envied a cat's ability to ignore
the cares of daily life and to relax completely?*
~Karen Brademeyer

"Quit playing around and get your schoolwork done!" I
called from my study where I was completing a work
assignment. I could hear my young son bumping
around and giggling, doing who-knows-what but cer-
tainly not his schoolwork! There was absolute quiet for all of thirty
seconds, and then the noise started back up, faintly at first and then
louder.

"What in the world are you doing in there?" I cried in exasperation. "You know you can't have your break until that work is done!"
As a single mom working from home and homeschooling my son, we
rarely had time for distractions, and I wanted him to be able to take
his break soon.

"Rosie stole my pencil, Mommy! I can't do my schoolwork!" came
the response in a voice that sounded as though it decidedly did *not*
mind having a pencil stolen. With a sigh, I dragged myself away from
the assignment that was due that day to go address the issue.

Entering the other room, I saw our black-and-white cat, Rosie,
sitting on the kitchen table with my son's pencil firmly in both paws.
She sat there tossing it back and forth and biting it playfully. To further
emphasize her utter disdain for my rules, she was also plopped down
right on top of my son's schoolbooks. Amusing as it was, I was forced

to remove her from the table.

This became the norm. Rosie would take my son's pencil and sit right on top of his schoolwork. They were the best of friends, and she was always in the middle of whatever he wanted to do, be it a board game, LEGOs, or soldiers. Once in a while, even he would get frustrated with her.

He never minded her interfering with his schoolwork, though. I finally offered my son a deal after what seemed to be the millionth time of trying to remove the cat from the table that week. "If you still do your work and don't let her distract you, she can stay on the table." I then moved Rosie firmly off his books and onto the side of the table, making her lie down. "Stay there!" I ordered, before returning to my office.

Of course, the giggles came not much later, and I peeked my head out to catch them in the act. Rosie was grabbing my son's pencil every time he tried to write, snatching it into her mouth and trying to bite it. She finally succeeded in stealing it completely away from him. Then she pushed it off the table and went back to rolling around on her back on his books and trying to lure him into rubbing her tummy.

I had to move fast to rescue the much-chewed pencil from the floor before it rolled under the refrigerator.

Though it was frustrating, I was grateful that my son had a cat who loved him so much. He was an only child without a father in the house, and she provided him with the companionship that he so yearned for.

Instead of constantly fighting a losing battle, I accepted that some-times you have to "take a little time to smell the roses." The schoolwork eventually got done and I always got my assignments in on time.

When we moved from that place several years later, we found quite a few lost pencils underneath the refrigerator, covered in teeth marks.

— H.M. Forrest —

50

Fox Poldark

A kitten is the delight of a household. All day long,
a comedy is played out by an incomparable actor.
~Jules Champfleury

We run an old-age home for cats. Some cats had elderly owners who had passed away, and they were going to be euthanized because the family didn't want them. Sometimes, we would get word of a cat that had been in a shelter for years and wasn't going to be adopted.

We have quite a few cats, but our home is roomy and comfortable, so we don't mind. We also built an enclosed sun deck on the windowsill so they're able to enjoy the fresh air and sunshine without going outside where they might encounter danger.

Even though we have tons of cat toys and cat trees, our elderly friends prefer to sleep most of the time. Some suffer from depression because they have been separated from their longtime owners or were abandoned. They all have different stories and personalities.

One day on social media, I saw a post from a man who had found a small kitten under his sun deck. His dogs had seen it and were going nuts barking. He thought it was a small rat, but upon closer observation, he realized it was a kitten and pulled it out from under the deck. He wrote that he was going on a business trip and could not keep the kitten because of his dogs. He was so sincerely worried and desperate about this kitten.

The man lived five minutes from my house, and I could see from the picture he posted that the kitten was only about three weeks old and sickly. I talked it over with my companion, and he said, "Go get him. We'll nurse him back to health and then find him a home."

I drove to the man's house and knocked on his door. The very big dogs were barking and barking. Thank goodness they hadn't reached the kitten first. I'm sure he would have been injured or killed. The man handed me the tiniest kitten I had ever seen. He had a closed, infected eye and was weak as could be. Apparently, he was the runt of the litter and had been abandoned.

We dropper-fed him for about a week and put medication in his eye. We then took him to the vet for his shots, but the vet said he was way too young for them to take. He was only about four weeks old. So, he would become a part of our household until he was old enough to get his shots in another month or so, and then we would look for a home.

This kitten was mostly gray and reminded me of a fox. Fox started to reign in the house, even though he was quite the pipsqueak. His curiosity and bravery reminded me of a gallant and dashing character in a British miniseries named *Poldark*. So, lo and behold, we added Poldark to his name. He was now Fox Poldark.

We had some mighty big cats, and he found it no problem to jump on their heads and backs, run up to them, and roll with them on the ground or whatever he felt like doing. At first, they were irritated, hissing at him or swatting him away. But he soon had their interest, and they started playing with him.

One night, it sounded like a tornado was swirling through the house. Downstairs, they were all running around with Fox, playing with their toys, and rolling all over the floor with him. The senior cats were no longer listless; they had found new life due to their little friend. I thought, *Oh, no, we are all falling in love with him.*

After he got his shots and I brought him home, I was torn as to what to do. I couldn't imagine anyone else having him. I looked at him sleeping on the sofa, surrounded by senior cats. They loved the little squirt. Well, darn it! He was Fox Poldark, and he was already home.

— Sonia A. Moore —

51

Nessie and Me

When you walk in purpose, you collide with destiny.
~Ralph Buchanan

When my husband retired, we moved from our suburban home in the West to his hometown in the upper Midwest, a small town fronting a huge fishing lake. There was a three-block Main Street with one stop light, and instead of a shopping center, antique shops shared space with two locally owned diners. Home-cooked hot beef sandwiches were a staple as well as fresh rhubarb pie.

It was another world to me, and even though the sub-zero winters froze the ice on the lakes so thick they supported fishing huts, I grew to love my charming new community.

But my thirty-year marriage was disintegrating. Ever since we'd lost our stocks and savings when a major commodities company collapsed a few years before, my husband had grown distant. Cold. I understood the devastation he felt and tried to be supportive.

I'd hoped the change of scenery would help us make a new start. Instead, one day I was served divorce papers. I pleaded for counseling, but I knew my husband. Once he made a decision, it was firm. Unshakable. I was going to have to start a new life on my own. But how? Where?

I didn't think I could survive alone in that beautiful, but at times terrifying, part of the country. Not only did we have snow that often lasted from October until May, but one winter the ice storms were so severe that trees in the surrounding forests froze and burst. The power could go out without a moment's notice. Living alone, how could I cope? What if I needed groceries, or if my electricity went out for days?

I'd made some casual friends, but my world had revolved around my husband. He was the one I'd counted on.

My son and his family lived on the West Coast, and I longed to be near them. I desperately needed someone to love and to love me, so I searched the Internet and found a gated senior apartment complex where I'd feel safe. I made the cross-country move.

But once I settled into my small apartment, I felt lost, in a city where I knew no one. I tried to be part of life by leaving my home for groceries or to walk to the shopping mall a few blocks away, but those outings made me feel more alone, as if I were living behind a glass wall that separated me from the rest of the world. My heart felt as frozen as the icy lakes I'd just left.

After a few weeks of isolation, I knew to survive I had to make changes, so I applied for part-time work at the mall, but as each day passed, instead of feeling better, I found it more and more difficult to smile. Finally, management strongly suggested I stay home. My son tried to help, but he lived a couple of hours away, and as each day passed, I retreated more behind my barrier walls. I lost interest in trying to make friends, in going outside, even in keeping up my appearance. Instead, I stared at the TV.

One day my son called. He and his wife had rescued a ginger kitten about four months old from their neighbor's barking dogs. They brought her inside with the intention of adopting her as a companion for their older cat, also a rescue. But the older one bullied the youngster, and the little one scampered under the bed and stayed hidden. No amount of treats could coax her out, so they named her Nessie, after the Loch Ness monster that also hid from the world.

"Mom," he said, "can you take Nessie? She doesn't have much of a life here, and if I take her to the shelter, I don't know what will happen to her."

I hesitated. All my life I'd had pets, and I especially adored cats. But at that time in my life, I could barely take care of myself, so how could I care for a kitten? I didn't even have plants. But I couldn't stand the thought of that little kitten sitting alone at a shelter.

"Bring her over," I told him.

He arrived in record time with his carrier, and while I caught a flash of orange movement within, I couldn't see the kitten. He also brought dry and wet food, a bag of litter, a bed, and assorted toys — everything I could possibly need.

When he opened the carrier, the little orange fluff of fur hesitantly crawled out. She was beautiful with green eyes, a white muzzle, and a pink nose. I instantly fell in love.

"Hello, little girl," I cooed, just as if she were a human baby. She darted behind my sofa, and no amount of coaxing from my son and me lured her into the open. Finally, I left food and water near her and went to bed.

When I woke up the next morning, instead of wanting to roll over and sleep the day away, I thought of Nessie, wondering if she'd ventured out. Eagerly, I crept to the living room to check. She still hadn't, but some of the food had been eaten. I knew it would take time for her to feel safe in my home, but I was willing to make the effort. That little soul needed me as much as I needed her, and she gave me a reason to face each day.

When she finally ventured out, I felt as if I'd conquered the world. And when she curled up in my lap and fell asleep, happy tears filled my eyes. As I stroked her silky fur, I thought about my online business, something I'd abandoned after my divorce. I dug out my computer and slowly went back to work. She became my constant companion, even jumping onto my desk and stretching out beside my laptop.

One day I stood at my patio doors with Nessie in my arms, and for the first time, I appreciated the beauty of the red setting sun dropping behind the distant rolling hills. Palm trees swayed in the gentle breeze. A sense of wellbeing came over me and I wondered what I'd discover if I ventured out to explore the area. I wanted to see the ocean, Disneyland, and more of the many wonders of Southern California. Suddenly, I was eager to check the maps my son had given me. Because of my love for a kitten and her trust in me, my frozen heart had melted, and I was ready to live again. Life was going to be a wondrous new adventure.

— Brenda Hill —

Learning to Be Sassy

*You know someone is very special to you when days
just don't seem right without them.*
~John Cena

I was greeted by Pumpkin, my neighbor's longhaired orange tabby cat, when I opened the door to get the newspaper. "How are you this morning?" I said, running my hand along his fluffy tail. "Sassy's sleeping in this morning." Pumpkin rubbed against my leg and then walked over to the long window. He stood on his hind legs and braced his front paws against the frame, peering into the living room.

"Hey, old boy, you can't wait to see her?" Smiling at him, I shook my head. "Maybe today is the day she'll be kind. Don't give up on love, Pumpkin."

Pumpkin lives across the street. He spends most days on my front porch, waiting to see Sassy, a shorthaired gray-and-white stray who purposefully walked through my front door one cold winter morning. At a mere six weeks old, she was dirty and sneezing from an upper-respiratory infection. Now, three years later, this healthy, little cat stays forever young-looking, having been the runt of a litter. She is the sweetest, gentlest, most friendly cat... except when it comes to Pumpkin. With him, she plays hard-to-get.

Sassy sits on the inside window ledge watching the world go by. Occasionally, she'll glance down at Pumpkin lying on his side in the middle of our front porch. He stares up at her adoringly. She acts completely uninterested. One afternoon, Pumpkin stretched his long body up to the window and pressed his nose onto the screen. I expected my cat to hiss and jump down. Instead, she simply turned her head away from him, glanced at me, and yawned.

"Sassy, give the guy a break. Give Pumpkin a kiss. He loves you so much." Sassy blinked twice, and then turned back to her suitor and snarled. That didn't faze her admirer one bit. He bumped his nose against the screen affectionately, and then took his place on the wooden floor and gazed up at her. Of course, the little flirt stayed on her windowsill.

I felt sorry for Pumpkin, but my loyalties will always be with my Sassy Girl. I'm not like Sassy when it comes to the opposite sex. I am much more like Pumpkin. I wear my heart on my sleeve.

One day, a stray cat made its way onto my porch. He looked up at Sassy sitting in the window. Before I could open the door to chase him, a flash of orange darted across the street and headed straight for this brazen tomcat. Pumpkin chased him all the way down the street until I couldn't see them anymore.

"Wow, Sassy, he's not letting anyone near his girl." Sassy licked her fur, obviously not the least bit impressed. Needing some fresh air, I lifted Sassy from the windowsill and carried her with me to the rocking chair on the porch. She snuggled in my lap until Pumpkin slowly made his way up to us. Sassy jumped down. Pumpkin moved closer to her and rolled passively onto his side. Sassy moved a bit closer. Pumpkin sat up. Sassy moved even closer, and I was surprised to see their faces almost touching.

"Aw, he loves you, Sassy. Give Pumpkin a kiss." Sassy gives kisses to all her humans on command. I thought I'd help them along. Sassy Girl stretched her neck and touched her nose to Pumpkin's. "Oh, that's so nice!"

"Hiss!" Swat! Pumpkin ducked just in time to avoid a scratch.

"Now, that was not nice! I'm sorry, Pumpkin," I said. "Sassy, get in the house!"

Opening the door, he and I watched as my haughty cat slowly stepped inside, her dignity always intact. Did Pumpkin give up? No, he went back to his spot on the porch and stared up at the window, always the gentleman. Sassy took her spot on the inside of the screen. I'm convinced he knew she would. *What loyalty,* I thought. If it were a man and a woman, the man would certainly give up and go away.

A few months later, I woke to the sound of Sassy vomiting in the kitchen. Terrible sounds were coming from her throat, and it seemed as though she couldn't close her mouth. There were puddles of bile all over the floor. Terrified, I called the emergency veterinary service. As I carried her to the car, Pumpkin ran over. He blocked us, struggling to see into the carrier's mesh window.

"I'm sorry, Pumpkin. We have to hurry. Sassy is sick. Go home now. Go!" I hated to do it, but I pushed him aside and rushed to the vet. My heart was breaking for both Sassy and Pumpkin. I don't know what we'd do without our girl. The vet admitted her to the intensive-care unit. I was devastated. Hours later, I pulled up in front of the house alone. Pumpkin ran across the street to me. He tangled himself between my legs, pressing his body against the empty carrier.

"I'm sorry, boy. Sassy's not in there. She's very sick." I looked into his crossed eyes and wept. Dropping to the grass, I pulled him into my lap. We snuggled there until my tears dried. Pumpkin climbed out of my lap and slowly walked back to his house.

The vet was cautiously optimistic. Sassy spent two weeks in the veterinary hospital. Every day, Pumpkin came and sat at my feet while I rocked in my porch chair and worried. I took comfort in telling him of each little sign of recovery.

The day I brought Sassy home, Pumpkin stood on the sidewalk in front of his house but made no move to come over. When I reached into the back seat and pulled out the pet carrier, Pumpkin raced to her side. "Yes, Sassy's home, Pumpkin!" Our loyal companion rubbed his side up against the carrier and purred. Sassy mewed.

"We're going in now. Sassy needs rest. You go home and rest, too." Ignoring me, he followed us up onto the porch and took his place under the window.

Hearts and bodies healed, and soon they were back to their old routine of Sassy being haughty and Pumpkin filled with adoration.

For as long as I lived in that cottage by the sea, those two cats taught me lessons about friendship, love, and loyalty. I don't know that Pumpkin would agree, but Sassy also taught me that when it comes to the opposite sex, I should stop wearing my heart on my sleeve — because a little "sassy" goes a long way.

—Mary J. Staller—

53

Big Guy to the Rescue

The cat has too much spirit to have no heart.
~Ernest Menaul

"Big Guy" came into our life when we discovered him sheltering in the aluminum boat we used on the nearby lake. He managed to undo a corner of the canvas cover for easy access. The first time we saw him, we thought he was a bobcat because he was big and had similar markings. We referred to him as "Big Guy," and the name stuck.

It was obvious he had been on his own for a while and didn't trust humans. When one of us would walk too close to the boat, we'd hear him growling, so we'd put a dish of food and water on the ground behind the boat and pick up the dishes so predators wouldn't come around the boat and challenge him.

Months passed before he developed trust in us and ventured out of the boat. He started meandering around our property. He gradually accepted us as "friendlies" and started showing affection by brushing against our legs and letting us pet him. We prepared a heated bed for him in the garage, which he readily traded for sleeping in the boat.

Big Guy blended with our other rescued cats, and the pecking order was established. He was the designated protector of the group. If one of the others was threatened, they ran behind Big Guy or followed him to a safe place.

When one of the cats was nearing the end of her life, Big Guy cuddled with her until she passed. Then he mourned her passing by lying in her bed and whimpering for hours. She was one of the abandoned cats he had befriended and led to our house.

Big Guy repeated that rescue act several times. I watched from a window one day when I saw him emerge from the nearby wooded area. He stopped abruptly, looked over his shoulder and waited. A small cat crept out and stopped a few feet behind Big Guy. Then it wobbled and fell to the ground. Big Guy went to the cat, nudged it until it stood, and then pushed it gently ahead of him. And when the cat wobbled again, he held it upright by leaning his body against the side of the cat.

When they finally made it within a few yards of our house, Big Guy left the small cat and began pawing on the back door. When I opened the door, he led me to the cat and watched when I knelt down to talk to it. The cat was obviously injured, so I called our vet, who said I could bring it right in.

Big Guy watched as I carefully wrapped a towel around the small cat and put it in the carrier. I patted him on the head and assured him his rescue would be treated well. He looked me in the eye with his big blue eyes, and I knew he understood. He was waiting next to the garage when I returned from the vet with the cat. He sniffed its bandaged leg and then groomed it. Another foundling was added to our furry family.

As I had with the other cats, I posted "Found Cat" posters with a photo and description of the cat and where it was found. Once again, there was no response. A local cat-rescue group helped find homes for a few of Big Guy's finds over the years, and the new owners had to agree to call the group if for any reason they could no longer keep the cat. So, occasionally, one of the adopted cats would come back to us, and Big Guy would greet and groom them when they returned.

I believe Big Guy's mission was to return the kindness he had been shown when he was abandoned, and he accomplished that for many years after he came to us.

—L.A. Kennedy—

54

How I Learned to Speak Cat

*As anyone who has ever been around a cat for any
length of time knows, cats have enormous patience
with the limitations of the humankind.*
~Cleveland Amory

When I was growing up, we had a dog — and a rabbit, guinea pig, three white mice, and numerous short-lived goldfish — but no cats. Then, as an adult, my first husband's severe allergies meant we needed a feline-free home. My dogs at the time agreed, as they always barked at neighborhood cats or treed any trespassers who managed to venture on our property.

But a new husband, a blended family, and several dogs later, the time seemed right to add cats to our household. To prepare for our new additions, I bought enough books to start my own library and explored every corner of the Web to learn as much as I could about cats and their care. Soon, we welcomed into our family two domestic shorthair kittens from a local rescue organization: Athena, a gray tortie, and her sister Dawn, a similarly colored tortie/tabby combination.

My dogs Lilah and Jasper had been fostered with cats before they came to live with us, but it still took a few months for everyone to figure out how to get along. The pups discovered that the kittens came with sharp and pointy parts that were best avoided, and the kittens learned how to wield those when someone got too close.

Like a canine posse, Lilah and Jasper followed me everywhere. I loved their attention, their in-your-face enthusiasm and doggy eagerness to please. The cats, however, were more like ninjas, silently melting away when I entered a room they were occupying.

I fed them, played with them, and cleaned their litter boxes. But if I tried to pick up Dawn, she'd wiggle and squirm until I put her down. If I so much as touched Athena, her entire body would twitch with the horror of it. With jealous resignation, I watched as the cats regularly crawled into one of my daughters' laps, and I wondered what I was doing wrong. I could not figure out why these tiny, sweet beings wouldn't let me get close or allow me to love them.

Dogs, I understood. I could read their minds by the lift and swing of their tails. I could tell their moods by how they walked or by the expressions on their furry faces. But Athena and Dawn seemed inscrutable. I didn't understand them, and it was obvious they didn't understand me.

I had lived in the land of dogs for decades, learning the language, customs, and unwritten rules. With cats, I was in entirely new territory, a nervous immigrant without a map, guidebook, or translator.

I needed to know more than how to care for cats. I needed to learn how they think. I needed to learn their language. So I bought another truckload of titles and spent additional hours surfing the Web, looking for information on the differences between cats and dogs, and how they communicated.

I also studied the kittens as if I were a scientist in the field observing the interactions of chimpanzees or cheetahs or naked mole rats. Watching them carefully, I noted how they interacted with each other, focusing on subtle cues and clues that offered insight into the essence of catness.

Experienced cat lovers would laugh at me, but I had to start with the basics.

I learned that, like dogs, cats speak with their tails, their body posture, their eyes, and, of course, their voices. But what they're saying is completely different.

Take tail-wagging, for instance. With a dog, it usually indicates a variation of "I'm happy." Sometimes, a low, slow wag means "I'm nervous," but that's about it.

Watching Athena and Dawn, I noticed that a tail held straight up — what I called "bumper-car position" — usually meant a happy cat, most often one on a mission. A slow twitchy tail indicated a hunt in progress; a toy or a piece of errant lint was about to get pounced on. Depending on the circumstances, a puffed-up tail could mean someone got startled or was super happy. And lots of tail wagging meant a very excited — or possibly annoyed — kitty.

I discovered hidden meanings in the size of a cat's squint or the relative position of her ears. If Athena flattened her ears and narrowed her eyes, it meant she was extremely displeased; perhaps a dog was occupying her favorite sleeping spot. When Dawn perked her ears and whiskers forward, she was signaling interest and curiosity: a bird just outside the window or a bug crawling across the floor.

I learned that a scared or upset cat will hump up like a Halloween silhouette or bunch down into a squinched-up package of anger. An alert and happy cat will sport big, round Puss in Boots eyes or crouch low with a wiggly butt and a twitchy tail.

Athena and Dawn taught me their vocal vocabulary as well, expanding way beyond the textbook "meow" to various "mews," "owls," "meps," and "rowls" — all meaning different things depending on the cat, the tone, and the circumstances.

But even though I was beginning to understand what was going on inside those bewhiskered little heads, and I continued observing and studying cat language and behavior, my lap remained empty.

One day, Athena was watching birds from her favorite spot on our window bench when Lilah gently placed her snout down next to her. Athena looked at the dog, blinked slowly and turned her head away. Lilah inched nearer, gently reaching out her tongue to clean Athena's ear. The cat leaned into it for a few seconds and then moved away, but Lilah glanced back at me and wagged her tail. Translation: "I got to lick cat ear!"

That's when I remembered something from my research. I had read that if a cat looks at you, you shouldn't stare back—which could be interpreted as a threat—but instead slowly close your eyes and turn your head. A cat will see that as a friendly invitation to interact—just like Athena did with Lilah.

A few days later, Athena meandered into the living room and glanced at me. This was my chance. I slowly blinked at her and then turned my head to the side. From the corner of my eye, I could see her pause. Then she began walking toward me. Again, I looked at her briefly and blinked. She hopped up on the couch, sauntered over the cushions, settled into my lap, and started purring. Then she looked up at me, blinked slowly, and closed her eyes as I scratched her chin. It worked! I had learned my first words in Cat.

Soon I discovered I could call Athena from across any room just by closing my eyes. I slow-blinked at Dawn as well, and she began responding with a friendly squint and head bonks.

Today, my cats—I now have four, along with three dogs—continue to teach me their language. I can tell their moods and understand their thoughts by the position of their ears, the look in their eyes, or the way they hold or flick their tails. My home and heart are full—and, more often than not, so is my lap.

—Susan C. Willett—

55

Finding Hope

One cat just leads to another.
~Ernest Hemingway

Life is divided into two stages. There's the acquisition stage in which one accumulates spouses, cars, children, pets, mortgages, and slow cookers. And there's the downsizing stage in which all the above are placed on the curb with a sign: "Free to a Good Home."

When my last dependent, a geriatric Siamese cat, passed away last year, I said, "Never again!" I focused on the advantages of indulging no desires other than my own. Oh, the joys of eating a tuna sandwich without little paws trying to snatch it away. Sleeping late without being poked in the eye. Writing on my laptop without a furry beast pouncing on it.

Like a new widow, I was subject to constant offers from friends to fix me up with a handsome tabby, a roguish tom, or an exotic Persian. I was tempted but relieved when each match fell through. I was fine on my own. A pet would only encumber me. Then, one day, out of the blue, I made the call.

"Linda? I'm thinking about adopting a cat," I said.

"No problem," Linda said. "Just fill out our online application."

Linda was a member of a local cat-rescue organization that fostered homeless cats until they were placed in a forever home. For the twenty years I've known her, Linda has shared her home with an ever-changing assortment of temporary feline guests, leaving every piece of furniture covered in fur.

Before filling out the application, I looked at the online gallery of available cats, not expecting to make any rash decisions. But OMG! I might as well have been on Tinder. I swiped two beautiful female calicos, and they both swiped me back. One was as big and fluffy as Dolly Parton's hair. The other was a "Hemingway cat," with a genetic mutation that causes six or more toes on each paw, as if wearing snowshoes. According to lore, Ernest Hemingway had a polydactyl cat that was as promiscuous as its owner, resulting in the breed being associated with the pugnacious author.

Like a lovestruck teenager, I couldn't resist meeting these seductive felines in person. It would just be for coffee, right? I filled out the application and received a call a few hours later.

"We've set up a date for you," she said.

I was nervous. It was happening so fast. Was I ready to commit? How could I choose between two contenders for my affection? I posted images of both candidates on Facebook and asked friends to help make the decision. They said, "When in doubt, take both!" My heart said, "Yes!" My checkbook said, "Not so fast."

The first cat I met was Ruby, the stunning, longhaired calico with the normal number of toes. I was smitten, but Ruby was so shy she wouldn't budge from her cage. I envisioned being on all fours, dangling mouse toys, trying to coax Ruby to come out from under the sofa. To sustain such a relationship, one of us would have to be on meds.

Then, I met Hope, with her jumbo paws and lime-green eyes. She sat on my lap and responded happily to my attention, rubbing her head against my hand. I loved her extra-big paws (size does matter). Plus, being a professional writer, I couldn't resist the idea of having something — anything — in common with Ernest Hemingway.

"She's got a lot of personality," said her foster mom.

I found out what she meant when I took Hope home. Her favorite pastime was walking between my feet. Did she really want to see how quickly medics would respond to a broken tibia? When not actively trying to kill me, Hope was a comedian who took more pratfalls than Kramer on *Seinfeld*. She cracked me up every time she lay down on her back, paws spread in four directions, and gazed at me upside down. Her taste in television was instructive. She watched cooking shows intently, perhaps hoping for a treat. She turned her back on Jerry Springer. And whenever I watched a Congressional hearing, she licked her paws languidly.

Like all star-crossed lovers, there was one aspect of our relationship I pretended not to see. I am a senior citizen who, when reading the obits, can't help but notice that my expiration date could come at any time, in spite of kale smoothies and probiotics. Hope, on the other hand, was in just the first of her nine lives. While no one chastises men over sixty for their perky paramours, some viewed my adoption of Hope as "inappropriate."

"What will happen to her when you are gone?" they asked.

Given Hope's fondness for trying to trip me up, they had a point. This agile, young feline could indeed outlive me. Then again, it's been medically proven that having a pet is good for the heart and increases longevity. If nothing else, having Hope has kept me on my toes. All ten of them. And all twenty-four of hers.

—Stacia Friedman—

56

A Change in Perspective

Any glimpse into the life of an animal
quickens our own and makes it so much
the larger and better in every way.
~John Muir

"A coyote attacked Thumper," my husband Rex blurted over the phone. "He's in bad shape!" I grasped the receiver with a white-knuckle grip as adrenaline shot through my system.

"What! How?"

I'd assumed our cat would be safe outside during daylight in our rural suburb. My eyes burned with unshed tears as I listened to Rex's terse explanation. Around noon, he ran from his backyard shop when he heard Thumper screaming. At the sight of Rex, a coyote dropped Thumper on the grass and vanished. The cat looked dead, lying on the grass with his tongue out, but was still breathing. Rex rushed him to the vet.

"I'll be right there," I said, my heart racing.

When I arrived at the veterinary clinic, my shoulders slumped at the sight of Thumper's sprawled-out form. The vet said Thumper did not break his neck and back, but his recovery remained questionable. "Hi, Thumper, my sweetie," I crooned, stroking his warm fur. He lay unresponsive. After a few minutes, I stood up and walked away, my face twisted with the effort of holding back my sobs.

But the next day, Thumper's big paws kneaded the air, and I heard a faint purr when I whispered sweet nothings to him. My heart warmed. *He knows me.* Several days later, Rex and I drove him home to recover.

After Thumper healed, I dreaded introducing him to a restricting leash and 3x4-foot cage. On his first lock-up on our deck, the puzzled cat sniffed the perimeter of his metal prison. Then he sat, cocked his head, and stared at me through the bars. His look seemed to say, *What's going on?* Over the next week, an apathetic Thumper sat in his cage. I missed seeing him contentedly lying on the grass in the sun, climbing a tree, or eagerly scanning the next-door field for mice. Something needed to change.

Rex solved the problem. He attached a car-sized, enclosed pen behind his shop. Thumper could sit on its perimeter benches, climb the installed center tree limb, and sleep in the shade or sunshine. The pen faced the overgrown creek area; it teemed with wildlife, but he would be safe. No cat or wild animal paws could reach through the pen's small, sturdy wire, and he could look out and enjoy the sights.

"Don't give me that look," I told an unwilling Thumper as I pushed him through the shop's pet door into the outside pen. "This is the best I can do to keep you happy and safe."

So began Thumper's year of change. Instead of hunting, he played with me. If I ignored him, he sat up and begged. He had learned to beg for treats, and now he used the trick to ask for attention. Trips from the house to the shop's pen became small adventures. One morning, as I bent to carry Thumper to the shop, he squeaked in protest. He did not like being held. I stared at him for a moment before deciding. "Okay, you can try walking on your own this once." First, he stopped and sniffed our juniper hedge and then started nibbling grass. After a few minutes, I insisted, "Thumper, that's enough. We need to get moving." He turned and ran thirty feet to the shop where he waited at the door for me. I chuckled, "Well, you old smarty."

On a balmy evening a year after Thumper's attack, I opened the shop's door. "Come on out, Thumper. It's time to eat," I called. No response. I walked to the pet door and repeated, "Thumper, come on out." Still no response. I hurried around back to the outside of the pen. Thumper sat on the bench, focused on the night sounds and smells.

"So, you're not ready to come in, huh?" I asked. "Okay, I'll check on you later."

I walked back to the house with a sudden lightness in my steps and no further concerns about Thumper's contentment despite recent restrictions.

I thought of Thumper's successful adjustment as I dealt with my restrictions early in the COVID-19 pandemic. Like Thumper, I grieved my loss of freedom. I missed hugging and visiting family and friends, going to movies and restaurants, relaxed shopping, and other activities. But if my old cat could adapt, so could I. Like him, I started to learn contentment within my new restrictions.

Instead of driving to my favorite public gardens and parks, I worked and sat in our front yard and enjoyed the beauty of roses, lavender, and the variety of wild birds at our feeders. The pleasure I gained from these simple at-home activities surprised me because I assumed away-from-home adventures were more exciting.

When our church closed, I hosted two or three women in my back yard to replace the weekly women's group we had enjoyed. The relaxed setting and flexible time allowed us to bond closer in friendship than the previous one-hour time frame permitted at church.

I plunged into the unknowns of ordering online groceries and virtual meetings. Having someone else navigate a store's aisles and avoiding heavy traffic to appointments turned out to be a blessing.

Thumper had survived his injuries from the coyote attack and learned to flourish in his changed world. I found that I could do the same.

— Darlene Ellis —

Cat-astrophes

57

The Riot in Feline San Quentin

I have studied many philosophers and many cats.
The wisdom of cats is infinitely superior.
~Hippolyte Taine

We had recently welcomed a handsome but feisty British Shorthair into our home after our beloved senior cat had passed. Tiki was approaching his first birthday when we had a family trip scheduled and needed to board him.

Finding a kennel wasn't hard as there was a delightful one named The Rainbow Farm that we'd used in years past with our previous cat. But even though the owners took excellent care of their boarders, including housing them in large, floor-to-ceiling enclosures complete with towering cat trees and lots of room to play, I still felt a twinge of guilt about leaving our fur baby in what we'd dubbed "cat jail."

Like any nervous mother, I packed Tiki's favorite meals and snacks so he wouldn't have to eat "prison food" and brought along his special quilted blanket to afford him the comforting smell of home. All of this, of course, was in addition to a boatload of cat toys.

But being a younger guy, Tiki well remembered that each time he had been finagled into his carrier, it ended in one of two ways: shots or neutering. Understandably, he howled incessantly for the entire fifteen-minute drive to the kennel. In his mind, he was preparing for the worst.

I fussed over him as I entrusted our little angel into the kennel's good care, and we got him settled into his spot. Each enclosure had a pretty, framed whiteboard pinned to the door bearing the name of the occupant. I smiled as we walked past Peanut, Muffins, Skittles and Artemis before reaching Tiki's assigned room.

Tiki rocketed out of his carrier as soon as we unzipped it, climbed to the top of his cat tree, and glared at us as we set up his food and arranged his toys. Although I was excited about our vacation, I also couldn't wait to get back to our little dude.

The time flew, as it always does on vacation. Before I knew it, I was back at the kennel. Payment settled and receipt printing, I began normal small talk.

"So, how did he do? It was his first time," I reminded the owner. Not that he needed reminding—I'd only mentioned it a hundred times when I dropped off Tiki.

"Ahh…," he said, running a hand over his hair as if not quite sure where to begin. "Has Tiki seen another cat before?"

I didn't state the obvious, that once upon a time he'd actually had littermates, not to mention being brought into this earthly realm via a four-legged feline mother.

"Might he have been the runt?" the owner continued as we walked into the boarding area where Tiki was being held captive in the feline block of San Quentin. I kept mum. Actually, he had been the runt, but I wondered what on earth had happened over the previous few days to make him ask.

Apparently, somewhere along the way, Tiki had learned or inherently knew that if one goes to prison, the Golden Rule, the only rule, is to establish dominance immediately. A fight is ideal, but if you can't physically reach your opponents, jumping and clinging onto your jail bars and puffing up like a wind sail at any and everything that moves is also acceptable.

I cringed as I got a play-by-play of Tiki's behavior toward his neighbors. The special food I'd brought for him had gone untouched as he entered a self-induced, one-cat competition to see how fast he could eat his prison chow. Then he climbed the mesh fencing of his cell and hissed and howled like Hannibal Lecter at his cellmates — to the point where they had to move several of his neighbors. The owner decided that trying to move Tiki might only ratchet up his quest for territorial dominance and reasoned it was probably best to leave him where he was.

The list of displaced cellmates was long. Tiki had originally been bunked beside a set of littermates, two cute little tabbies named Samson and Oliver. But after Tiki low-growled at them all afternoon from his cat tree, the poor pair kept knocking over their food and water dishes in an attempt to drag everything into the farthest corner away from Tiki.

Tiki's other neighboring cellmates, Figaro and Brewster, fared no better and became so frightened of Tiki's antics that they started using their beds as a litter box. Petunia took their place but started licking a hot spot on her chest from nervousness and was immediately moved.

With a full cell block, someone had to share walls with Tiki. After much re-arranging, the winning combination ended up being an equally grouchy Maine Coon named Medusa on one side and Pablo the Persian on the other. Both cats were unimpressed with Tiki and simply ignored his antics.

Relieved that he was okay, and embarrassed that he'd acted like an ingrate, I shuttled Tiki into his carrier, took him home and thought life would go back to normal.

Nope.

Boarding made quite an impression on Tiki. He created his own physical-training regimen and drills multiple times a day now.

He practices his foot-and-pivot maneuvers by dancing along the top of the quarter-inch-wide shower glass. He toughens up his paws by skittering across still-hot stovetop burners. He jumps onto the wire mesh of our floor fans to do his pull-ups and has started pouncing on the scale every day to see how his "gains" are.

And like a wanted man, Tiki no longer sleeps in the same spot two nights in a row. He sleeps behind the living-room television, under the couches, and on top of the fridge. He's also learned how to open doors, so on any given night, he may be sleeping in a closet, the pantry, or in the kitchen cabinets tucked away behind the pots and pans.

I could only imagine the look on the poor Rainbow Farm owner's face when I called to make another boarding appointment a few months later. I heard the clack of a keyboard and then a laugh as he answered, "Oh, yes! The little black Shorthair! We can put him on the end this time so he has just one neighbor."

— Kristi Adams —

58

Dial M for Kitten

Most of us rather like our cats to have a streak of
wickedness. I should not feel quite easy in the
company of any cat that walked about
the house with a saintly expression.
~Beverley Nichols

October 1

The shelter doesn't adopt out black cats during October. They wait until after Halloween because some people are messed up. So, I'm fostering this black kitten until November when she can find her forever home.

October 2

She's plotting my murder. I can see it in her eyes.

October 5

I'm cleaning her litter box, so she pees under the coffee table.

I'm crouched on all fours, dabbing pee. With my head at her level, she comes over to rub against my ears, purr, and act generally lovely. I'm distracted by her affection and bang my head on the coffee table.

Her purr sounds like laughter.

I crawl out from under the table and go to the freezer to pull out frozen vegetables.

I plop a bag of frozen peas on my head and myself on the couch as I contemplate the pee soaking into the carpet. The black kitten purrs in my lap.

October 8

I bring the kitten fresh water, and she trips me. I'm not sure if this is the murder attempt or part of a larger plan. I see contentment in her eyes, which worries me.

October 10

She meows a lot, but I don't know what she means. I name her Mrs. Meow.

October 11

I check out a book from the library to learn more about cats and try to understand what Mrs. Meow's different meows mean. There's a long hair in the book that probably belongs to a crazy cat lady. Mrs. Meow nibbles the corner of the book, and I realize that the lady isn't crazy—her cat is. I had always thought "crazy cat lady" meant a crazy lady with a cat (or many cats), but now I realize it's more likely a lady with a crazy cat (or many crazy cats). It's the cat who's crazy, not the lady.

October 12

Mrs. Meow is a mouthful, so I call her Mrs. M.

October 13

Mrs. M is a mouthful, so I call her M.

October 15

M walks all over me—literally, not figuratively. Maybe a little figuratively. My ears fascinate her, and she likes to help me tie my shoelaces.

October 18

An eerie dream jolts me awake. In my dream, a black rotary phone shook with a sinister ring. Vintage spiral telephone cords extended from the phone, and a black cat was tying my shoes with the cords. I picked up the phone. It was Alfred Hitchcock.

Hitchcock directed the murderous thriller *Dial M for Murder*, and I realize I've made a horrible mistake by naming the kitten M.

October 22

Today, I realize M gave me ringworm, a fungal infection that cats can pass to humans. M had been treated for ringworm before she arrived and has been asymptomatic, but the rashes on my arms tell me she needs more treatment.

When talking about the transmission of ringworm from cats to humans, the vet says, "Nobody dies from ringworm." That's little solace when a cat is laughing at your rashes.

October 23

I Google: "can ringworm get into the bloodstream," "complications of ringworm," and "how to get pee stain out of carpet."

October 24

I notice rashes on my lower back and more rashes on my arms. Apparently, you shouldn't let a cat with ringworm walk all over you, literally or figuratively.

October 25

M sits in my lap and purrs and sleeps. She's hoping I'll let down my guard.

October 26

I hear scratching, and my ear is full of pain and redness. I panic, thinking I have ringworm in my ear. This is disappointing because my research on complications of ringworm unearthed nothing about aural concerns. I'm optimistic the infection hasn't damaged my hearing because I can still hear M's meowing pleas for reconsideration when I put down Grilled Chicken Entrée instead of Meaty Morsels Chicken Entrée.

M continues to grill me for offering her the grilled chicken. But the Grilled Chicken Entrée and Meaty Morsels Chicken Entrée have the same ingredients and in the same order, including Thanksgiving favorites like sweet potatoes, cranberries, and pyridoxine hydrochloride.

October 27

Even though I still have seven cans of Grilled Chicken Entrée, I go to the pet store to buy Meaty Morsels Chicken Entrée, along with three new toys for M.

At home, I offer the morsels to M. I don't hear any meows, hopefully because she's satisfied and not because the ringworm has spread to my eardrum.

November 1

Today is the day to bring M to the shelter so she can start her journey to find her forever home. I give her extra treats in the morning and warn her about Flaked Chicken Entrée, just in case her new guardian makes that mistake.

I open the crate, and, thanks to M's natural curiosity, she walks right in to explore.

I put the crate on the front passenger seat so M and I can see each other on the drive to the shelter.

As I drive, M makes a meow I've never heard from her before — more of a scream than a meow. The book about cats I read said that type of sound indicates rage or fear. I reach for the crate and stick my finger through the grate, hoping to offer some comfort. She ignores my finger and reaches her paw out toward the clutch. Must be rage.

M bats at the clutch, trying to shift my existence into a fiery car crash.

I pull up to the no-kill shelter. A true no-kill shelter like this doesn't mean M can't continue to plot and attempt murder. It means she's one of the lucky ones who will have her entire life to try.

— Beth McMurray —

59

Cat Burglar

*A cat is more intelligent than people believe
and can be taught any crime.*
~Mark Twain

My university freshman year was almost over, but I could barely keep my pants from falling down. Like many other university students, I had experienced the Freshman Fifteen. But instead of gaining weight from eating too many snacks, I lost over fifteen pounds from cutting back on all the extras that my tight budget wouldn't allow.

I'd managed to get through the school year thanks to student grants and loans, scholarships, and personal savings. I'd budgeted as best as I could and even learned to cook my own meals to save money. But my bank account was depleted now, and my part-time job wasn't going to earn enough to pay all my bills. It was going to be a few weeks before my full-time summer job started, and I'd already hit up my equally poor student friends for a few bucks here and there.

As I contemplated my situation, I cleaned up my room. When I opened the window to let in some fresh air, a black cat jumped up on the sill. As bare as my cupboard was, I would find something for this furry friend to eat because I could never turn down anyone in need. I found a couple of slices of bologna in the fridge, which the cat scarfed down in seconds before licking his chops and scampering off again.

As I was bringing out the garbage, I met my fellow student Suzie, who lived in the same university complex. We exchanged pleasantries and talked about getting through the last days of school and our year-end exams. Like me, she had a minimum-wage diner job that she worked part-time. When I mentioned my new cat companion, she said that she had also adopted a cat during the school year, who had just showed up at her window one day. She named him Scamp because he was quite a scoundrel, often sneaking off with little trinkets.

When I asked where she'd be working full-time for the summer, she replied that she would just be increasing her hours in the job she had because it was too good to leave. What I hadn't realized was that she worked in an elite restaurant where the wages were low, but the tips were generous. She mentioned that her serving apron was stuffed with so many dollar bills at the end of a work shift that she didn't even bother to count them until the next morning. "That must be nice," I mumbled jealously before skulking back to my place. No wonder she was always cheerful.

In the meantime, my newfound cat friend kept visiting, often bringing me little gifts like pinecones and leaves, as if to pay for the humble bits of food I would offer him. I thought of it as the kitty currency he could come up with to let me know he appreciated the goodies. He made me feel better and forget my financial problems for a while. I began thinking of a name for the little fellow.

Then one day, my friendly kitty showed up holding something large in his teeth. My eyes popped open when I realized it was a banknote. And not just any banknote, but a fifty-dollar bill. I was stunned and couldn't believe it was real. However, I thanked him profusely and hoped for the best. When the cashier checked it with her marker later on that day, she declared that it wasn't counterfeit. Woo-hoo! The first things that went into my shopping cart that day were premium cat food and kitty treats. What a miraculous windfall! It came just in time, too.

Perhaps buoyed by my sudden lavish praise and upgrade in cat meals and snacks, the smart cat continued to bring in banknotes of all denominations. Sometimes, it was a one- or five-dollar bill. Other times, a ten or a twenty would arrive. It was a dream come true. I decided to name him Johnny after Johnny Cash.

However, there was a mystery to be solved here. Where was

Johnny getting the money?

I decided to try and follow him when he departed after his next visit. I didn't have to go far. When Johnny exited from my open window, he ran up the fire escape to another floor, jumping into an open window up there. Sigh. I was pretty sure I knew whose place it was that he had just entered. It seemed that my Johnny and Suzie's Scamp were one and the same cat.

Suzie's birthday was coming up, so now that my full-time job had started, I made sure to put a gift card inside a birthday card that matched the total of all the funds that our communal cat had borrowed from her to lend to me, plus an additional 20 percent to give a heartfelt thanks. Johnny-Scamp led the way as I marched up the fire escape with chocolates and card in hand. He looked up innocently at us, while Suzie stared wide-eyed as I revealed the whole unbelievable story to her.

— Sergio Del Bianco —

60

Expert Advice

*A sense of curiosity is nature's original
school of education.*
~Smiley Blanton

"To treat bee or wasp stings on your cat's pad," the article said, "put some elbow-tepid water in a glass jar and gently lower the cat's paw into it. "Then…" it said glibly, "hold it there until the discomfort passes.

"It will probably," it continued laughably, "take two of you to do this."

Yes! One human to scream and the other to mop up the blood. I wouldn't ask the Delta Force to put my cat's paw in a jar of water, not even wearing flak jackets!

Water has much the same effect on my cat as it did on Gizmo the Gremlin. Put a jar of water near my cat, and in an instant a cuddly, affectionate companion is turned into a whirling ball of claws that makes you think a depth charge has gone off in your face.

And where was the advice on what to do when this cataclysm had actually taken place, after you had gradually pieced together the strips of flesh that had once been half an arm and found your nose again? Hah! Nowhere in evidence, that's where. It was obvious they'd never tried it themselves.

These animal writers are all the same. They think everyone has the same sort of rapport with animals that they have. Silly, I call it. And anyway, my cat's too intelligent to go playing with bees and wasps.

Unlike me, who decides that 10:30 P.M. is a good time to dig out a wasp's nest at the top of the garden by torchlight, wearing shorts and a T-shirt because I figure by then they're probably all asleep. That's what it said on the instructions for the wasp-nest killer.

In a pig's eye, they are! I wonder if you can sue. True, the somewhat drastic measures weren't exactly specified nor, come to think of it, was the wearing of shorts and T-shirt... but it was summertime, and you can run much quicker when lightly clad. How was I to know that they posted lookouts? The instructions never said anything about that either! And it would have taken more than a jar of elbow-tepid water to remedy the damage, I can tell you.

Still, look on the bright side. By removing the source, at the cost of a few trifling little stings, I've got rid of the temptation for the cat to go swatting wasps. I've saved myself not only the trouble of heating up all those jars of elbow-tepid water but also the trauma of persuading pussy to dip its poor, swollen feet in. Who says there's no method in madness?

The trouble with these animal experts is that they don't think of all the ramifications before they come up with their silly advice. And I doubt they actually have a cat.

— Malcolm Twigg —

61

Tough Love

Where there is no imagination, there is no horror.
~Arthur Conan Doyle, Sr.

Rusty loved intrigue. A mild-mannered cat by day, at night he turned into the Midnight Marauder. Often, Bill and I would lie in bed squabbling over whether we should let the dang cat out to roam the dark Montana prairie or put up with another sleepless night. I resisted turning him out and always won, though, since a coyote had taken a previous cat. Neither of us wanted that to happen again.

So, instead, we lay in the dark each night and wondered if Rusty would wreak havoc. Some nights were quiet. Some definitely were not. And always in the morning, if I had forgotten to put the butter in the cupboard, there were marks from a rough, little tongue and once even a paw print.

Something had to give.

"I just read an article on how to keep cats off countertops," I said to Bill as I scraped the butter into the trash and gave him a piece of dry toast. "It involves cookie sheets and sinks full of water."

Bill took a bite of toast and a quick gulp of coffee to wash it down. "Do it."

"It doesn't sound completely nice, though. Maybe a little rough-shod? I don't know if I should do it."

"Do it."

My reservations were such, however, that it took me several weeks and the loss of nearly a pound of butter to decide we didn't have much choice.

Rusty was sleeping on the afghan I had over my lap when Bill suggested we turn in. I hated to wake Rusty, but I had some chores to do before bed — including put away the butter. I roused him by petting his orange head and then kissing him awake.

I smiled at Bill. "You go on to bed, honey. I have a couple of things to attend to, and I'll be in."

Bill nodded and yawned. "Let me know if you need help."

But I didn't really want help. I figured that if this was the absolute wrong thing to do, only one of us should have to deal with the shame.

I deposited Rusty on his cat bed and patted him a little guiltily on the head. Then I went into the kitchen. After I'd washed our coffee cups — and put the butter in the cupboard — I began filling the kitchen sink with about two inches of water. Rusty loved jumping into a damp sink and then tracking water all over the cupboards and across the kitchen floor. According to the article I'd read, cats used to jumping into your sink won't do it again if they jump in and find a couple of inches of water.

I turned off the faucet and secured the plug. Check.

Next, I cleared the cupboards of all extraneous clutter. Then I got out all my metal cookie sheets and a fork to go with each. According to the article, you should prop up a cookie sheet with a fork. When your cat jumps on the counter, he will knock down the precariously balanced cookie sheets, and the resulting racket will dissuade him from doing it a second time.

I balanced the cookie sheets on forks. Check.

On my way through the living room, I scratched my unsuspecting cat under his chin and headed for bed. He followed me in, but I knew he wouldn't stay. As soon as he figured we were asleep, he'd indulge in his normal indiscretions.

Bill and I snuggled under the covers and I told him what I had done. After about twenty minutes, Rusty jumped off the bed and headed stealthily into the kitchen. The anticipation was terrible.

We waited. But not for long.

Suddenly, there was a loud, metal racket. Despite our love for our naughty orange cat, we started to giggle. We heard a chain reaction of crashes next, and our giggling became louder. Finally, we heard a splash and the sound of paw treads too heavy to be a cat. Maybe a rampaging elephant, but not our little cat. As the sound of Rusty's footsteps came ever closer, we laughed harder.

He rounded the corner in the hall and leaped through our doorway onto the foot of our bed. On his belly, he shinnied under the covers all the way to the head of the bed and settled across the back of my neck.

His paws were wet.

As he lay there trying to gain safety and comfort from our presence, Bill and I were seized with guilt. But even with the knowledge that we'd scared our little friend half to death, we couldn't stop giggling.

And that was the night Rusty, the Midnight Marauder, retired. There were no more wet footprints on the counter. There were no more lick-marks in the butter, although I often forgot to put it away. Rusty was safe from coyotes, and the nights, well, they were suddenly peaceful.

— Leslie C. Schneider —

62

Bedtime Manners

*One reason we admire cats is for their proficiency in
one-upmanship. They always seem to come out on top,
no matter what they are doing, or pretend they do.*
~Barbara Webster

A few weeks ago, we went out of town for a quick getaway.
Mind you, we were only three miles from home, but being
by the beach allowed me to fantasize that we were in the
Caribbean, at least for twenty-four hours.

As any pet owner can attest, being away from the pets every now
and then is a real treat. Instead of three fur pillows crammed along
my various body parts, I was able to simply stretch out and enjoy the
space around me.

Cats and dogs seem to think it's their right to dominate the bed.
Every pet owner I know complains and then sighs at this behavior,
like it's some sort of bad weather they have to endure.

But in fact, we gladly move over, wedge ourselves into pretzel
positions, and let our limbs go to sleep as our cats dream about clean
litter and premium wet food. I know some owners shoo their pets from
the bed, but I'm too much of a wimp to let this happen. If I enforced
some sort of discipline, wouldn't my cat have a psychological complex
as it gets older?

Wouldn't it whisper to the other cats that I'm a bad mother, and
all three of them would revolt and ignore me for days? They already
ignore me enough as it is.

I couldn't take that. I spend hours alone as a freelance writer, and the last thing I want is for my "housemates" to give me the cold kitty shoulder.

So, when bedtime comes, I enjoy my space for about eleven minutes until, one by one, they assume their positions on the bed, and I plan my next visit to the chiropractor.

It's a small price to pay for the love of an animal.

— Mary McGrath —

63

Feline Frenzy

Curiosity killed the cat.
~Ben Johnson

Shortly after graduating from college, I moved from my childhood home into a small cottage on the other side of town.
While applying for jobs, I decorated my little house with tie-
dyed curtains and incense. My college roommate and I had
planned to get together since graduation, but I'd been on the road for
my summer job. Finally settled, I readied for her visit. There was only
one problem: Lynn's cat, Hortense, erroneously given a girl's name
based on his questionable genitalia at birth.

If Lynn came to South Carolina for a week, Hortense would, of
necessity, come as a houseguest as well. My landlord prohibited pets,
but Horty didn't belong to me. I figured we could sneak him in since
cats don't need a walk, so he wouldn't be seen. Who would be the
wiser, right? My three-room cottage might be cramped, but it certainly
trumped the space in our dorm room.

So, on the evening before my first day of real work after a fun
summer job, Lynn arrived with Horty in tow. He was a huge, gorgeous,
loving Siamese tomcat, obviously glad to reach the end of an eight-hour
car ride from Florida.

After dinner, we made up the sofa bed in the living room, laughing
and reminiscing until way too late, relishing each other's company like
girls at a pajama party. I enjoyed petting Horty for a while, stroking
his soft, downy coat. But he would not let me quit. He kept nuzzling

up under my hand. I didn't have to do anything much, just be there. He did most of the work, first pushing his head and then arching his back through the tunnel created by my cupped hand. He wanted more. I didn't. I wanted to relish Lynn's company, not massage the cat after his hard trip, which presented a dilemma. I didn't know how to stop petting him without offending Lynn or making her think that I didn't like Horty. I liked him fine. I simply didn't realize that he'd enlist me as his personal masseuse!

Lynn finally corralled Hortense by settling down on the sofa bed with him curled by her side. Unfettered from the demands of this beautiful kitty, I fled to my room, closing the door behind me.

"Jan?" Lynn called. "Remember that Horty needs access to the potty."

I swung open the door. "You mean you didn't bring a litter box?"

"Horty doesn't use a litter box. He's trained to the toilet."

"He's trained to your toilet, Lynnie. Not my toilet!" I shuddered, knowing full well this big guy would hold me captive again if he woke up and needed to wee-wee during the night. Tomorrow would be a big day for me. I required sleep.

"Oh, all right," I mumbled, and left the door cracked open enough for Horty to make his way to my bathroom.

New-job jitters consumed me, anticipating the worst with the all-male company. Sleep came slowly, but I had finally succumbed to the arms of Morpheus when a commotion scared the devil out of me. I awakened at the sudden sound of nails on a chalkboard. Then what felt like a huge, fuzzy sack of potatoes dropped onto my face. Not knowing what the heck happened, I flung that thing as hard as I could.

It catapulted into the wall adjacent to Lynn, and she bounced into the room before my eyes had even focused, crying, "Poor Horty! What have you done to him?"

Still shaking like a holly in a high wind, I struggled to my senses.

"What have *I* done to *him*?" I screamed. Lynn scooped up Horty, cradling him in his misery. "What about what *he* did to *me*?"

"Aw, he didn't hurt you."

"Well, he woke me out of a dead sleep and scared me into the middle of next week. That's something!"

Here's what we think happened: An oddly placed window near the ceiling above the head of my bed called Horty's name. Wanting to know what lurked outside that window, he leaped over me from the floor to get there. But he missed the windowsill. His claws screeched down the wall in an attempt to grab onto something, landing his full weight on my face!

I don't know who was more scared. One time, a huge palmetto bug crawled over my face in a no-tell motel. A mammoth mosquito, the size of a hummingbird, bit my cheek in the middle of the night while I camped out. But nothing ever dropped onto my face in my own bedroom, let alone a woolly, fifteen-pound bowling ball with claws!

The thing I remember most about that visit is the night curiosity nearly killed the cat, the cat's curiosity nearly killed me, and Lynn seemed to think I caused the whole fiasco. It concerned me for a long time, but then I recalled that cats are blessed with nine lives, and I only knocked off one of Horty's.

—Janet Sheppard Kelleher—

Cats That Go Bump in the Night

It is in the nature of cats to do a certain
amount of unescorted roaming.
~Adlai Stevenson II

The day I brought Gizmo home from the shelter, she was a sweet, cuddly kitten. Today, she's a sassy, feline teenager. She has a snarky attitude, has no interest in hanging out with me, and would rather be staring at a screen than interacting with her family.

Like any adolescent, she has an obsession with technology and staying up late. I first noticed the screen infatuation a couple of years ago when I caught her patting and swiping my iPad with her paws. She swished through images and apps, staring intently at the flickering display. Thank goodness I noticed she'd inadvertently opened the Amazon app. One more toe-tap and she would've ordered the toaster oven I had saved in my shopping cart.

No screen is safe in my house. If you set down your phone, Gizmo will help herself to your camera roll and social-media feed. And like any good teen, she expects everything to be scrollable. I once saw her pawing wildly at a magazine cover. I can imagine her frustration over the lack of animation on the paper device. She turned to me and meowed as if to say, "Hey, this thing is broken." I picked up her catnip-filled sock and tossed it for her. "Why don't you play with your own toys?" I asked.

She gave me a slow blink — the cat equivalent of a teenager rolling her eyes and muttering, "Whatever." Then she stomped off and spent the rest of the afternoon sleeping. That was when I decided it was time to limit her screen time. But little did I know, my house has more screens and blinking lights than I thought it did.

I was greeted by a variety of flashing error messages on my printer several mornings in a row. "Paper jam. Print job interrupted. Wi-Fi disconnected." It didn't take long for me to realize that Gizmo had discovered the machine's illuminated touch pad and had been doing some late-night swiping. After a call to tech support, I decided enough was enough. That evening, before going to bed, I closed my office door. If she couldn't get in, she couldn't make trouble, right?

Sometime around 2:00 A.M., I woke to the sound of my dog growling. I opened my eyes and listened. "Clunk-clunk-clunk." The dog growled again. The clunking continued, and my heart pounded. Oh, no! Was someone trying to break into my house? The noise sounded a lot like a door being rattled in its frame. When the dog cut loose with a full-on warning bark, I panicked.

Then the rattling paused, and I heard a soft "Meow."

I breathed an exasperated sigh of relief and got up. When I turned on the hall light, there was Gizmo, lying on her side with her front paw wedged under the office door, tugging repeatedly and making it rattle in its frame. "Stop that," I told her.

"Meow." I knew she wasn't going to give up, so I gave in and opened the door. The next morning, the copier was jammed, and a Barry Manilow video was playing on my iPhone.

Her paw-under-the-door trick has also helped her gain midnight access to my bedroom closet. She reaches under and gives the bifold door a few tugs, opening it just far enough to slip inside. Then she knocks down a few sweaters and curls up for a nap. Apparently, the little room where I hang my clothes is Gizmo's secret hideout.

A few weeks ago, I woke to a strange, whirring sound. Before I could process what it was, I dozed off. Several minutes later, I heard it again, louder this time. It was accompanied by a series of bumps and bonks. What in the world? When I finally sat up in bed, it wasn't the whirring that had my attention. It was the beeping. From somewhere in the house, I heard "deedle-dee-dee" over and over again. I got up and shuffled down the hall.

In the dining room, I discovered the robot floor sweeper beeping and blinking. The poor thing was practically choking to death on Gizmo's catnip sock. I tapped the flashing power button and pulled out the twisted fabric. My striped devil was sitting on the table, staring at me. I wondered how long she'd been up there watching the sweeper whir and bonk its way through the house. I gave the sock a toss and grumbled at her, "If you're going to clean the floors in the middle of the night, pick up your toys first."

My most recent sleep disruption came when I woke to a series of loud thunks and thuds. Something was falling and hitting the floor in the next room. As usual, the dog sat up and growled, and my heart went into overdrive, assuming there was a serial killer in my home. I sat up and listened, and then heard Gizmo meow. Of course.

When I checked to see what she was into, I found her on the top shelf of a bookcase. She was standing on her back legs, reaching up the wall with her front paws trying to catch a tiny moth. I took off my slipper to swat it, but it flew away before I could take aim. Gizmo backflipped off the shelf and galloped down the hall in pursuit of her new plaything. I stepped over the pile of books and stumbled back to bed. "At least it's not technology," I told myself.

The next day, I heard her meowing incessantly and went to the kitchen to investigate. She was sitting on the counter, hyper-focused on a black dot high on the wall. Her tail twitched, and her body was still as she waited for it to move. On the counter next to her was the clock I'd taken down earlier. I picked it up, changed the battery and set the time. Gizmo was still staring at the dot, waiting for her victim to take flight.

"That's a nail, you nitwit," I said to her, standing on tiptoe and covering it as I rehung the clock. She looked at me and gave a slow "whatever" blink.

At least once a week, this crazy, nocturnal cat finds something to explore — usually in the middle of the night. It happens so often that I'm afraid I'll get used to it. I hate to think what would happen if someone actually tried to break into my house. The dog would growl, I'd hear a thud, and then I'd just assume it was Gizmo trying to catch a bug or break into my office.

My only hope is that my would-be assailant will trip over the sock-clogged, robo-sweeper and break his leg, giving the cat time to dial 911 on my iPhone and allowing me time to hide in the closet. Apparently, it's pretty cozy in there.

— Ann Morrow —

65

Christmas Cat

Life constantly presents the greatest opportunity
brilliantly disguised as the biggest disaster.
~David Icke

We adopted a cat from a neighbor. She had a large litter of kittens, all of whom my kids would have happily adopted. Somewhat grudgingly, they were persuaded to settle for one beautiful, little tabby-colored creature. Being a new kitten, he came to us without a name. The search was on to find something suitable. We decided to wait a few days before deciding. There was no rush, and this would give us a chance to observe the kitten's nature and come up with something suitable.

After a week, there was still no name that struck us as appropriate. The kitten seemed to be a fairly calm creature with no obvious character flaws. There were lots of unsolicited suggestions, but none that seemed to be particularly obvious choices. The rest of the family decided to give our son the honor of naming the cat. It seemed to have taken a special liking to him. As it turned out, none of us was happy with his decision. Roosta didn't seem to be a suitable name for a cat, but we had agreed to let him choose. My son couldn't explain why he chose that particular name. Perhaps it came from his interest in reggae music. So, Roosta was to be the cat's name.

The kitten adoption had taken place in the weeks leading up to Christmas, a most exciting time for children and kittens alike. As in previous years, we had a freshly cut tree covered in sparkling, dangling decorations. Roosta spent many quiet hours learning how to decorate the tree. He watched closely as each decoration found its special place in the branches.

All was well until the day before Christmas.

Then, in the middle of the night, we were awakened by a loud crash. The whole family rushed into the living room. We arrived in time to see Roosta making a hasty exit. The tree, complete with water container, decorations and seemingly every last pine needle, was sprawled across the floor. That night of all nights, our new kitten had decided to see what it would be like to "roost" in the upper branches. He must have had quite a surprise when he discovered he was a lot heavier than a Christmas ornament.

We spent hours cleaning up the mess. The tree was a total wreck, way beyond salvation. Early the next morning, the debris was wrapped in plastic and taken down to the garbage room. We might be the first family in history who had to dump their tree on the day before Christmas.

In honor of his attempt to roost in the Christmas tree, we all agreed to change the cat's name. It went from Roosta to the much more appropriate Rooster.

—James A. Gemmell—

66

No Boxes, Please

Cats come and go without ever leaving.
~Martha Curtis

We lived in a trailer. Every day, we would see Buddy the cat perched on the railing of the next-door trailer's deck area. He rarely, if ever, seemed to move from that spot. We knew his owners had moved, and we thought that maybe Buddy had escaped from their new home. So, at first, we weren't concerned, sure that they would return for him.

Clearly, Buddy felt his owners would return too, and he was going to stay close to his home so they would see him when they came back. As the days passed, we saw him keeping his lonely vigil in all sorts of weather. We took food and water over for him and gave him some attention.

After many months had passed, we knew for a fact that Buddy's owners were not coming back for him. Winter was setting in, and in Prince George, B.C., our winters can be extremely cold with deep snowfalls. As the temperatures started to drop drastically, my mother or I would go and haul Buddy into our home every night.

Buddy seemed happy enough to be in where it was warm and to be given food and lots of attention by us. But every morning, he would practically beg to go outside and return to his vigil. Sometimes, we would keep him inside our trailer until things warmed up a bit, but all the time we would hear him crying to be let out. He had to get outside; it was important. He had to be there when his owners returned. He couldn't miss them!

For about a year, Buddy kept his watch, and for that year we were there for him, feeding, loving, and caring for him. Finally, he gave up and accepted us as his new people.

We knew that we had a very loyal cat on our hands and were happy to add him to our family and our other pets. Buddy had found his new home with us.

A while later, we planned on moving from our trailer to a house. Most of our animals had moved before and were not troubled by the many boxes being brought in to be packed up. Our other cats happily jumped in and out of empty boxes.

Buddy, though, was not happy. He seemed to be worried. He tried to destroy every box he saw by clawing it to bits. He would follow us around and pay close attention to us when we left. Clearly, he remembered what had happened last time when boxes came out. He had been left behind — forgotten!

We did our best to reassure him he was not going to be left behind. Yet Buddy was just learning to trust us when we had thrown these doubts and uncertainties at him. He didn't eat as much and started to lose weight.

Finally, the day arrived. We got some things moved over to the new home, and the rest would be moved over the following day. Mom decided she would stay in the trailer that night, and I would stay in the house so one of us would be in each place.

Mom brought the cats and dogs over to the house for the night and returned to the trailer. I didn't see much of Buddy that night. Not surprisingly, most of our cats were hiding in the house.

The next morning, Buddy was clearly visible, and it was a complete change from the panicky, stressed cat he had been for the past few weeks. As if a great weight had been lifted from his shoulders, Buddy was everywhere at once it seemed.

He walked behind the Dachshund, Jester, swiping a paw at the dog's wagging tail and butt, causing Jester to yip a bit when an errant claw caught him. He followed me, swiping at my ankles as I walked around the kitchen. He chased the other animals and tore around the house in cat-gone-crazy mode!

I just laughed at the gray-and-white streak. You would have thought that cat had found the mother lode of catnip, when in reality he had found something better. He got to go with the boxes! What a relief.

Buddy lived many years with us in our home. One thing never changed, though: Buddy's reaction to seeing boxes enter the house. Even if we brought in a box to fill with donations to the thrift store, Buddy would freak out. He would claw that box to bits. He was the only cat I have ever owned that didn't like to play with boxes.

—Loretta Olund—

67

Wreck the Halls

*Cats are a kindly master, just as long
as you remember your place.*
~Paul Gray

My wife and I unpacked several big boxes and contemplated the contents. The instructions seemed simple enough. Hopefully, this was going to be our salvation.

Christmas was coming and we were pulling out the decorations for the season. My wife Donna loves to decorate, and our place looks like something out of a designer magazine once she is finished. It makes the holidays even more enchanting. Or it did, until we adopted a litter of rescue kittens.

We've always had a large family of rescue animals call our place home, but we really bumped up our game once we moved to Italy. There were lots of stray cats that lived and bred in the balmy climate, making for more opportunities to bring some little furballs home.

More than any other beasts in our menagerie, our cats love it when Christmastime comes around. The bright lights, colorful decorations and twinkling tree are just some of the splendid attractions that make the season particularly fun for them. They grab at all the shiny, sparkly things with great enthusiasm.

Two years ago, Donna outdid herself and put up the best decorations ever. She had a big tree as a centerpiece, with smaller trees and decorations displayed throughout our living areas. It was as pretty as could be and she was proud of the results of her hard work.

A few months prior, a pregnant female found our rescue haven and soon bore five adorable kittens. By the time my wife started decorating for the holidays, the five scamps were just coming into their own. Even in balmy Italy, my wife would never dream of leaving new kittens outside in December. So they stayed indoors at night, admiring her decorating handiwork.

Kittens love to throw themselves into a tree and bat at the lights and decorations. Grown cats and dogs do not resist much either, so we made sure to close the doors to the decorated areas at night. We didn't want any damage to the Christmas décor, or to the animals who could injure themselves playing with it.

After finishing everything, the decorations looked fantastic. It was Donna's best result ever and the effect was stupendous. That evening, we enjoyed the twinkling lights while slurping eggnog and eating chestnuts in front of the blazing fireplace. Then we made sure to close the doors before heading to bed.

The door handles in Italy are built like a lever, so that a dog swatting it, or a cat hanging on it, can trip the latch and open the door. Because of this, we learned to lock the doors at night. But that fateful day, we must have forgotten one door. Intrigued by the Christmas decorations as they wandered around the house that night, one of the animals must have tried the door to the living room and managed to open it.

Needless to say, we found a disaster the next morning. All the decorations had been trashed, with our five new little kittens still playing in and around the large Christmas tree, which was now lying on the floor. The dogs all looked at us with guilty expressions on their faces. Happily, none of the animals had hurt themselves, but the beautiful decorating was destroyed. We didn't have the heart to begin all over again, so we salvaged what we could for the season and that was that.

Last year, we decided to do something unconventional. We ordered a variety of cat trees and adorned them with cat friendly decorations and treats. We figured that we could still have reasonably nice decorations throughout the living areas that would also serve as a kitty playground.

We assembled the biggest cat tree as the main attraction, with smaller ones situated here and there for effect. We tied strings and treats to them for the kitties to play with and chew on. We even strung some twinkling lights around the room for an overall holiday effect. After all was said and done, things didn't look too bad. Then we picked up all the wrapping paper and boxes that the kitty trees came in and put them in the storage room.

Congratulating ourselves on our ingenuity, we broke out the eggnog, preparing for a relaxing evening in front of the fireplace. We patiently waited for the kittens to discover their new kitty climbing trees. As we sat down, some of the cats and dogs wandered in to sniff at the cat trees and kitty safe decorations. But no one stayed to play, and there was no sign of the kittens.

After an enjoyable evening in front of a cozy fire, we finally headed to bed. Curiosity got the best of us though, so we decided to see what the new kittens were up to first.

We found them all in the storage room. They were happily playing hide and seek amid all the empty boxes and packing material that we had just put in there.

Best kitty Christmas presents ever.

— Sergio Del Bianco —

Chapter
7

We Are Family

68

Stupid Cat

When you're used to hearing purring and suddenly it's
gone, it's hard to silence the blaring sound of sadness.
~Missy Altijd

"What's your cat's name?" I asked. Amanda smiled and answered, "Snowball." I was puzzled because the cat was black. Before I could ask why she would name a black cat Snowball, Amanda shrugged her shoulders and said, "I always wanted a cat named Snowball."

Just a few minutes earlier, I arrived at Amanda's parents' house to pick her up for our first date. She was not ready, so I sat on the couch and waited. That was the moment when Snowball attacked. He appeared from out of nowhere and jumped on my head. When he landed, he dug all four claws into my scalp. Startled, and in agonizing pain, I screamed and vaulted across the room.

At that point in my life, I had been in the Army for a couple of years. Most of the soldiers in my unit used vulgarity. I was no stranger to filthy language. Still, I didn't appreciate swearing. I tried my best not to cuss. But when Snowball sunk his claws into my head, it wasn't "Praise the Lord" that came out of my mouth.

Amanda walked in as I apologized to her parents for my bad language. She laughed when she saw the cat still attached to my head. As I pried him off, I asked, "What's your cat's name?" That was when I was formally introduced to Snowball. I thought of several other names that I would like to call him. However, since I had already made a terrible first impression with my vulgar language, I looked at Snowball and said, "Stupid cat."

I loved Amanda from the moment I first saw her. Since I loved her, I started to love Snowball. Over time, Snowball also warmed up to me. When I came over, he rubbed up against my leg and purred. Sometimes, he hopped on my lap and let me pet him. One day, after I visited Amanda, the Sergeant Major called me into his office. As I stood at attention in front of his desk, he yelled, "Collins, what is that all over you?" I looked down and noticed my uniform covered with black cat hair. As the Sergeant Major wrote me a reprimand, I mumbled, "Stupid cat."

After dating for a couple of years, Amanda and I were married. We didn't have much money, so we lived in a modest apartment. Because of our busy schedules and small apartment, Snowball stayed with Amanda's parents. After a couple of months, I walked in one day to find Amanda sitting at the kitchen table. She didn't look happy.

"What's wrong?" I asked.

She looked up and answered, "I miss Snowball. I wish we had a bigger place so we could go get him."

"I wish that, too…," I started, but before I could finish my sentence, Amanda handed me a real-estate magazine with a circled listing.

She said, "I'm so happy that you agree."

The next thing I knew, I signed mortgage papers. As I wrote my name on the contract, I whispered, "Stupid cat."

Snowball ruled the roost at our new home. He came and went as he pleased. Sometimes, he wanted inside. Sometimes, he wanted out. He would roam the acres. Often, he would leave a dead rat on the front porch. Once, he greeted me with a dead snake. Fearing snakes, I jumped backward and started to run. If someone timed me, I would have qualified for the Olympics as a sprinter. I looked back over my shoulder and yelled, "Stupid cat!"

It was a bitter cold night when we lost Snowball. He didn't come home like normal. The weather was terrible, and Amanda worried about him being out in the sleet and freezing rain. I grabbed a flashlight and headed out to look for him. I searched the back pasture, the south woods, and over at the neighbor's place. Sadly, I didn't find him. Cold and frustrated, I went back to the house. Amanda was upset. So was I. Where was that stupid cat?

I found him in the barn the next day. He curled up in some hay to stay warm, but he didn't survive the night. I buried him in the back pasture under the live oak tree. Amanda cried. I did, too. Whoever heard of a big, tough soldier crying over the death of a stupid cat?

Over the years, I have come to understand that a little bit of our being created in God's image comes out when we love something for no reason. Snowball never gave me a reason to love him. Quite the opposite—he was often a nuisance. He scratched up our couch, hacked fur balls on the carpet, and left dead stuff on the welcome mat. Yet, Snowball was there with us during the first years of our marriage. He kept Amanda company when the Army sent me away. He sat in my lap as we watched TV. So, I loved him. I loved a little black cat named Snowball. I loved that stupid cat.

—James Collins—

69

Paw Prints
on Our Hearts

To a cat, "No" means "Not while I'm looking."
~Author Unknown

A hard smack hit my rear as I walked down the hall. My cheeks flushed hot and red. Indignant, I reeled around to see who would dare to be so rude.

My assailant? An adorable kitten with large, satellite-dish ears and long, spotted arms. His liquid-brown eyes met with mine, and he let out a protracted meow. I broke into laughter and immediately fell in love.

His name was Oscar, and he was born at the shelter I was visiting. The cats there roamed freely in a home-like setting. The volunteer let me know that the mother was an owner surrender. She and the rest of the litter had been adopted quickly, but Oscar remained, a bit too rambunctious for many potential adopters.

I could tell he was just what we needed. We were newlyweds full of love and hope, but we were also facing a few unexpected trials. Just weeks after our wedding, my husband was injured in an accident at work. The devastation had not only broken his body but his spirit. Grueling hours of physical therapy bled into sleepless nights. I hoped that this little bundle of joy would cheer up my husband.

When I brought Oscar home, I asked my husband to shut his

eyes and open his hands. I handed him the kitten, who reached up and rubbed their faces together. It had been months since I saw my husband smile like this, and Oscar himself couldn't stop purring.

Three in the morning was a different story, though. Gone was the genteel politeness of the new kitten. Instead, we had a hellion on our hands. Racing around the room in dizzying circles, climbing the drapes and exclaiming loud mewing war cries from the darkness, a small, fast shadow of a kitten overtook the room. We turned on the lights. Oscar froze. My husband laughed and called him to the bed. After giving a quizzical head turn, Oscar trotted to the bed like a puppy, jumped up and positioned himself on my husband's chest. With a loud purr, he snuggled in and found what would become his favorite sleeping spot.

Years passed, and our sweet Oscar continued to be quite the clown. He had an uncanny ability to know if someone was having an emotional moment; he would always try to help. One day, I received a phone call from my mother telling me that my father had cancer. I vowed to do everything I could to help him. Feeling upset and overwhelmed, I took a bath to try to regroup. Our little spotted bandit reached up, opened the closed door, and jumped directly into the bathtub with me. Hearing the loud splash, my husband ran into the bathroom to find a soaking wet, bubble-covered Oscar purring just inches from my face. That little guy was all heart.

My father beat cancer and recovered fully. Following his final treatment, he was given two weeks of rest at home. He asked if he and my mother could "babysit" Oscar for those weeks. We were more than happy to share.

On the final day of Oscar's visit, my father decided to bake cookies for me and my husband as an unofficial thank-you for "lending" him our cat. It was a sweet gesture. When we arrived at the house, the smell of warm chocolate-chip cookies hung heavily in the air. We went into the kitchen, grabbed plates, and dug in. It was only when I was on my third cookie that I noticed an adorable detail. There was a paw print on each of the cookies. I let my dad know that it was such a creative idea, to which he replied, "I didn't add those." We quickly put the cookies down and erupted into laughter. Oscar had added his own touch as usual.

Oscar made it to twenty. He fell asleep one warm spring night nestled softly on my husband's chest and didn't wake up. Oscar shared his love and joy with everyone and reminded us to always smile. Not only had he left paw prints on the cookies years ago, but he also left paw prints on our hearts.

—Robyn Milliken—

70

Saying Grace

*Looking at cats, like looking at clouds, stars or the ocean,
makes it difficult to believe there is nothing
miraculous in this world.*
~Leonard Michaels

My friend Terri asked me to feed her pets while she was out of town for a family emergency. "Of course. Just tell me what I need to do," I said.

I knew that she had pets — cats and dogs — but what I didn't know was how many!

When I opened her back door for the first time, I was met by an ocean of small, dark eyes and a lot of high-pitched barking. There were about fifteen Chihuahuas, plus a large number of cats. It was more than I had bargained for, but since I had told her I'd be the responsible party in her absence, I had to honor my word.

She never said that picking up poop and wet pads from the linoleum floor was part of the deal, but I was not about to leave "her children" to wallow in their own squalor.

After an hour of work, a stocky, firm-bodied tuxedo cat kept brushing my legs. Looking up at my face, he seemed to say, "Please, get me out of here."

By the fourth day, I had a routine. It didn't seem as bad as it had on the first day, but I'd still decided that Terri and I were going to have a discussion about "full disclosure."

Upon her return, she apologized for not telling me the whole truth — that there were twenty-one pets in the house, and there was more involved than "just feeding" them. She offered to pay me for my time and trouble.

"How about a trade?" I suggested.

"What kind of trade?" she asked.

I told her how the black-and-white cat had rubbed its body on my legs every day and seemed to be begging for a way out.

"You want to thin out your population a bit?" I asked.

"Yes, she does seem to be a bit overwhelmed."

We worked out a deal. I would take Samantha home with me for the three-day Labor Day weekend. If it felt like a good fit, Samantha would stay with me.

I also told Terri that I wanted to change her name.

"She's not a Samantha," I asserted. "I'm thinking BC."

"What does that stand for?" she asked.

"Black Chin," I said. "Or Beautiful Cat."

I took BC home and released her in the kitchen. I had already placed two clean litter pans in places where I thought she would most likely want to use them.

She didn't come out from behind the sofa for a long time. Finally, on Monday evening, she made an appearance, looked at me and meowed several times as if to say, "I would like a snack."

It wasn't long before she fully adjusted and found her favorite places to curl up for her many daytime naps. When I returned from school every workday, she greeted me with a lot of meowing, her black tail straight up in the air, telling me all about what she had seen and done while I was gone.

BC fetched just like a dog. It seemed rather odd to toss her favorite cloth mouse down the hallway for her to retrieve and drop at my feet. No matter how many times I tossed that mouse, BC would bring it back. It was good exercise for both of us.

BC had another "trick" that no one believed until they saw it for themselves. Whenever I gave her some food, she'd put her head over the bowl, close her eyes, and wait for about thirty seconds before starting to eat.

"That cat is praying," my friend's daughter pointed out. "Look, Mama, BC is blessing her food just like we do."

Several years later, I moved to another state about 500 miles away. My new roommate had two dogs. Since BC had spent much of her early life with dogs, I figured that she'd get along fine. After an initial adjustment period, it appeared that BC was going to accept her new home and canine "roommates" with the normal amount of caution. Everyone got along well.

As it turned out, I liked the work and stayed several years. As BC began to age, she started to have "accidents" on the beds and furniture. I took her to the vet, but an examination revealed nothing organically wrong.

I tried everything the vets suggested. Nothing worked. I was frustrated and embarrassed since it was not my house. Something radical had to be done.

One morning while talking to my cousin back home, he reminded me that his sister-in-law worked at a sanctuary for cats—the large jungle types and domestic ones. As a matter of fact, they had an entire two-story house for "retired" house cats. Some were blind; others had feline leukemia. Others were just older cats who needed some special attention.

He contacted his sister-in-law and asked if they had any vacancies.

"Yes, they have some spots. You can bring her this weekend for a trial run if you like. She might not be a good fit. The only way you can find out is to take her there and let them do an assessment."

Away we went for the long drive to the cat sanctuary. I had mixed feelings, mostly guilt. But I had to do something—and quickly.

I left BC in the assisted-living house for cats. As I drove away from the facility, my eyes filled with tears. I wanted to go back and pick her up, but I didn't.

I received a message three days later. BC was a perfect candidate for residence in the house. She was getting along with the other cats and had chosen a place on one of the beds for her daily naps. She liked spending time with a much younger cat who had trouble walking.

"It's the oddest thing," said Angie, "but BC seems to be praying before she drinks her water or eats her food. She's usually toward the front of the line at mealtime but refuses to eat before she bows her head."

I smiled and told Angie that BC had been "praying" since she was a kitten.

Even though we found BC another home in which to spend her senior years, a place full of love and care, I missed her beyond words. I have many blessings in my life, and one of them is having spent time with a cat who helped people understand the importance and art of gentle living.

—John Dorroh—

71

Pick Me

I love cats because I enjoy my home; and little by little,
they become its visible soul.
~Jean Cocteau

had seen *Hoarders* on TV, but I'd never actually been to a house like that. I didn't know what to expect… a basement filled with cardboard boxes? Bookshelves lined with hundreds of creepy porcelain dolls? I expected it to be cluttered, dusty, and maybe a bit unclean, but it was worse — so much worse than I had ever imagined.

I actually recoiled when I pushed open the front door of the large house. The stench was unbearable.

Tugging the neck of my sweater over my nose, I tried not to gag. This was the last place I wanted to be at 6:00 on a Saturday morning, but Natalie needed my help, and she was, after all, my friend. Everyone in town knew Natalie as an angel on Earth. She selflessly ran an unofficial cat rescue, so when an elderly woman was taken to the hospital with asthma complications, the family called Natalie to help with her cat-hoarding situation.

For years, the family had been trying to help the elderly woman with her compulsive hoarding issues, but she was reluctant to give up any of her "treasures" or her furry friends. With the medical complications ahead of her, the family took matters into their own hands and decided that she — and the cats — needed better care.

Natalie and I inched deeper into the house, slowing picking our way through stacks of old newspapers, broken chairs webbed with dust, stacks of empty cans, moldy couches, and endless mountains of debris. It was like wading through a Dumpster.

Every now and then, a cat leapt from beneath the wreckage, its hair matted and mangled. It was heartbreaking.

I quickly lost count of how many cats I saw... fifteen, twenty? And that was only on the main level. The sheer number of cats that would need to be fostered was staggering. It occurred to me that I could take one. We were, after all, in the middle of a pandemic. Rescuing a helpless animal in need would be a good thing to do, something positive I could contribute to the world. But as quickly as the thought came, it evaporated — mostly due to the pungent sting of ammonia and cat pee engulfing my nose, cementing my conviction to stay pet-free.

After all, I'd never really wanted a pet, despite the insistence of my twin daughters, age ten, who had been begging me for a kitten or puppy for ages. I liked my freedom. Pets meant arranging a sitter every time we took a family vacation. There's also poo to pick up, feedings, and vet bills. It just wasn't for me.

After luring ten or so cats into crates with salmon-smelling treats, with some more eager than others, Natalie and I decided we were done for the day and would return again soon.

As I turned anxiously to leave and give my lungs a much-needed reprieve, a sudden movement caught my eye. I spied a box tucked into a shadowy corner. Praying it wasn't a mouse, I bent low.

It was a litter of white-and-gray kittens, all pink-nosed and fuzzy. I looked around for the mother but didn't see her. Two kittens were asleep, one was bouncing up and down, and the fourth was staring up at me expectantly. When I reached for her, she literally jumped into my arms as if to say, "Pick me!"

I held the kitten close my chest, her soft fur grazing my arms. I stared into her ocean-blue eyes. She let out the tiniest meow, and I was done for. All my doubts and reservations melted into a puddle on the floor. She needed my family to love and care for her, and why not? We had a lot of love to give. Without another thought, I was sending my husband pictures, and he instantly agreed. Suddenly, we had a kitten.

When I arrived home, it was like Christmas morning. Somehow sensing they needed to be calm and not scare the tiny bundle in my arms, my twins traded their usual happy squeals and jumps for heartfelt tears and gentle snuggles. The kitten was a real live (fuzzy) baby doll that my daughters fussed and fawned over in the most joyful display I had ever witnessed.

The girls named her Marshmallow due to her mostly white fur with a few patches of gray. Marshmallow has fallen into complete step with our family's routine. My perfect little lady has never had an accident and is a litter-box champion. Believing she is one of the children, her favorite game is hide-and-seek. Each night at bedtime, as my husband and I finish saying goodnight to the girls, Marshmallow will promptly run under my bed. Right on cue, the twins will call, "Where's Marshmallow?" and pretend to look for her. After a few minutes of hiding, she will shoot out from under the bed, "find" the twins in their bedrooms, and choose one to hunker down with for the night, although she often hops from one bed to the next, giving each of the twins a chance to shower her with affection.

Life has changed. I have a litter box to scrub and cat food to buy. She needs daily meds due to a health condition, and my teal accent chair is her favorite scratching post.

It's different, but it's also wonderful. My daughters are responsible for feeding her dinner each night, keeping her water fresh, and playing with her each morning to use up some of her energy (which happens to be their favorite chore). They have stepped up to the plate and done a beautiful job of caring for her. I'm proud of the responsibility and maturity they have shown, and how loving and protective they are with her.

The pandemic was tough. My children missed their friends. They were confused as to why everything in their lives shifted so drastically and without warning. A kitten brought a light into our gloomy days of isolation, cut off from the world. I may have rescued her, but she rescued my family, too. Marshmallow brought fun, meaning, and purpose into my children's lives and mine, at the exact time we needed it the most.

In the hectic afternoon hours, I'm in my home office, frantically trying to put out the latest fire at work, when a soft tail curls around my legs. In no time, she's on my lap, purring loudly. My jaw unclenches, and my shoulders relax. All the troubles of the world fade away because I remember what really matters — we are all together, and, finally, we are all content.

Suddenly, I hear the rapping of little fingertips as my daughters push open my office door.

"Mommy, I think Marshmallow wants a friend. Can we get a puppy?"

Sigh.

—Annette M. Clayton—

The Tabby Who Taught Me to Love Myself

Cats are cats... the world over! These intelligent, peace-
loving, four-footed friends — who without prejudice,
without hate, without greed — may someday
teach us something.
~James Mackintosh Qwilleran

I waited for a cat to choose me at the shelter. An orange tabby kitten came up and rubbed my leg. Putting her in my lap, I melted when she curled up and fell asleep.

I had a secret. I was a chronic shelter visitor on a mission doomed for failure.

My husband had a rule that we were only allowed to have the "boxed variety" of pets, such as guinea pigs and a parakeet, which wouldn't be underfoot. They were sweet, but something was lacking. They didn't fill our hearts the way I knew a dog or cat would.

Our young son Paul wanted a dog so badly. Everyone he knew had a dog or cat — or both. Paul adored his friends' dogs and told me stories about them. He made the best of the situation, which killed me. Paul was basically an only child, as his half-brother was ten years older and didn't live at home. The child needed a buddy.

I tried to convince my husband to get a dog for years. Paul changed his plea from a dog to any pet that "walks around the house." I wondered

We Are Family | 209

about a cat. I'd always wanted one and heard they were easier to take care of than a dog. No, my husband said. A bunny? No. A ferret? No. One time, I saw a painted hermit crab and thought Paul might like that for fun. No.

When Paul was eighteen, my life went off a cliff. My husband had a new Mercedes-Benz convertible and fewer pounds. I later discovered he also had an old friend of mine. How much more clichéd could it get? My husband moved out, and Paul and I occupied the house together.

Then I went to the cat shelter and met that kitten. It was a dilemma. After nineteen years of marriage, we might try to work it out. But if I brought a cat home, I'd be undermining that possibility.

I thought about that little cat for days. It became an emotional tug-of-war—to love myself, to be true to myself, or to continue without her, putting my broken marriage ahead of my own desires.

A few days after my cat-shelter visit, Paul called me at about 11:00 P.M. "You'll never believe what I found! A kitten!"

He had been driving in a remote area surrounded by grassy fields. He saw a kitten in the middle of the road, as if it had fallen from the sky. Paul picked up the kitten and put it in his lap. It kissed him on the cheek. There it was: a bold answer to my prayers—a tiny orange tabby handpicked from the wilderness.

We named him Teddy, short for Theodore, which means "gift from God." Teddy was a prize that rained down on us. Like a message in a bottle, he came with a personal note addressed to me: "It's time for you to be you. Here's a start."

Teddy became the house toddler. We laughed at things we never knew a cat would do, like play fetch with a ball. He sat on a barstool at the kitchen counter and played cat games on the iPad. "Catch a fish!" we would say, as he batted at the fish swimming around on the screen. Paul would hold him on his lap and pretend Teddy was playing our piano. Like a kid about to jump into a pool, Paul would say, "Watch this, Mom!" and show me Teddy's latest trick.

Paul announced our new addition to everyone. He was proud to finally have a pet that didn't live in a box. Whether Teddy was awake or asleep, Paul petted him and silently confided in him. My son was mourning the unbroken family he no longer had, and Teddy was the pillow he could cry into.

But Teddy turned tears into laughter. He wasn't problematic. He was pure joy. I was right. My desires weren't selfish; they'd been buried. Maybe Paul wasn't the only one healed by a tiny kitten.

Months later, Teddy and I piled into the car to drive to my hometown. I had an apartment lined up and would wait for Paul to join me. I set up a cat fort in the back of the car with food, water, and a small litter box. After several days of driving, crying, and arranging, we settled into our new place.

The days that followed were filled with jarring echoes of my past. I had a lot to unlearn at age fifty-six. But I wasn't alone. I had my furry little boy.

Eventually, I met a new man. Early on, I texted him, "I have a nightlight for Teddy so he can see better. Is that silly? Do people do that?" He texted me a picture of his cat nightlight! I'd struck gold.

Teddy is now seven years old. I share him with my man, and we got him a pal, Tommy. We are family now. Teddy and Tommy are a big part of Paul's life, too.

This little cat has changed my life in ways I never imagined. He tells me it's never too late to start over. He shows me truth every day. And through his big, round eyes, he reminds me to love and respect myself.

—A.J. Hughes—

73

Bump and Leonard

Meow is like aloha — it can mean anything.
~Hank Ketchum

No one knew the cat who was found balanced on top of our only street sign. Cathy saw him first and called me. I'd never seen him, but the sign he was perched on said "Bump" so that became his name. Bump was missing two toes on his back left paw. He probably felt safe high above the ground all by himself where other animals couldn't reach him.

And no one ever understood why the county repaved our quarter-mile country road and added a speed bump. Two weeks after the bump appeared, they'd put up the sign, as if no one realized there was suddenly a bulge of blacktop on our otherwise flat street. Whatever the reason, Otter Creek gained its bump, its sign and its striped orange cat in the same month.

Everyone knew Bump, and he knew all of us. He kept track of whose windows let in the most sun and when everyone ate dinner. He went to Ed's house for table scraps, Carl's house to get combed, and our house for a bowl of cat chow. He attended everyone's social events and didn't leave until the last guests said their good-byes.

Bump routinely spent the morning with Hal, who always cooked a big breakfast. Hal would lay a placemat on the floor next to his chair and serve Bump a bowl of scrambled eggs topped with grated cheese and chopped bacon. He placed a human version of the same thing on the table, and the two of them ate together. As soon as Bump finished, he returned to his perch on the sign and Hal did the dishes.

Hal had another regular visitor. His name was Leonard. For years, the two men had been postal clerks together at the Bridge Town Post Office until they retired one year apart. Leonard was as quiet as Hal was talkative, which is probably why they had such a successful relationship.

Leonard was not memorable. In fact, people often couldn't come up with a better description than to say Leonard had enormous feet and an endless collection of plaid shirts that he tucked smoothly into his pants and belted high above his waist.

We got used to seeing Leonard's classic yellow 1950s Morris Minor Traveller parked in front of Hal's house. The two men often took it to cultural events together — the symphony, a museum exhibition, or a recital of some kind. No pair of friends looked less alike — Hal in his gray sweatpants and his long gray hair, and Leonard with his salt-and-pepper crewcut, heavy black glasses and plaid shirts.

In a way, Otter Creek tried to adopt Leonard like it adopted Bump. For years, villagers invited him to take a walk or visit their houses. Leonard always declined, leaving the inviter feeling as if he or she had said something wrong. Eventually, people stopped asking and left the job of entertaining Leonard to Hal.

A conversation with Leonard was never a positive experience. Even if he told a cheery story, it sounded like bad news. He had skied in the Alps and lived in New York City, but he had nothing positive to say about any of it. The accepted conclusion was that Hal was either hard of hearing, or he talked constantly and never listened to anything Leonard said.

The one Otter Creek resident who didn't seem to mind Leonard's vinegary disposition was Bump. It took more than a year for their relationship to take hold, starting with mutual gawking and hissing. That progressed to months of avoiding eye contact while sitting at opposite ends of Hal's couch. Then, fifteen months after Bump arrived, Leonard reached out a gnarly finger and poked Bump on the side of his neck so awkwardly you might think it was the first time he ever touched a cat.

One morning when Leonard arrived at Hal's, Bump met him at

the door. Leonard let himself in, and there was Hal, still in bed with the covers pulled up to his eyes. Hal had a bad cold and had not been up to make breakfast. Leonard stepped in, made Hal a cup of tea and scrambled some eggs for Bump. He made himself a cup of black coffee and drank it while Bump ate.

That night, a cold, harsh wind blew in from the ocean and brought a violent storm with it. The rain didn't let up for days and flooded a low section of Highway One, the only road from Otter Creek to town. Unfortunately, Leonard had stayed at Hal's house the first night of the storm, and his old car was not up to driving through the small lake that formed on the highway. He had no choice but to stay put.

The rain turned to sleet, and on the last morning of the storm, we woke up to see the village covered in a layer of frost. Frost on the coast is rare, so by 9:00 A.M. nearly everyone in town was outside covering plants or throwing snowballs. We decided to walk around to get a better look. As we headed down the street, we saw that someone had walked this way before us. We bent down to look at the footprints. One set was from an extra-large pair of men's shoes and alongside them was a set of paw prints. Three paws had four toes each, but one only had two toes. Bump and Leonard had already taken an early morning walk together. And from that point on, the unlikely friends were inseparable.

— Suzanne Cushman —

74

Sprouty's Story

No amount of time can erase the memory of a good cat,
and no amount of masking tape can ever totally
remove his fur from your couch.
~Leo Dworken

My time with Sprout was short but precious. The best friend I ever had left his indelible mark on my heart and soul, and the grief from his loss shook me to my very core. At the same time, I can't ignore the rich reward his time and love left me with. I am a disabled veteran of the U.S. Navy and have a lot of time on my hands. Sprout helped me more than I will probably ever know.

Our journey together began when my wife saw his picture in the newspaper. Sprout was a cat whose owner had passed away; the family surrendered him to the SPCA in Benbrook, Texas (a suburb of Fort Worth). He had been there for a relatively long time, as no one seemed to want him. His picture revealed messy fur and sad eyes.

At the time, we had two other kitties — Kat-Meer and Kit-Meer. We decided that we had room in our home and our hearts for "Sprouty" too. So, we made the ninety-mile trip to Benbrook and adopted him. The drive was filled with anticipation and excitement as we couldn't wait to start showering him with love in his new "forever home."

Sprouty and I bonded from the moment we met at the shelter. I felt a warmth in my heart I had never felt before. It was almost as if he were my long-lost brother, and we hung out together as much as we could. We played, and when late-night zoomies came over him, I called out, "Katy, bar the door!" The evening's entertainment was about to begin. Instead of meowing, he barked like a cheetah. His tail would twitch a couple of times and he'd be off. If you got in his way, he could knock you down. He weighed more than twenty pounds, and it was amazing how fast he moved with all that weight onboard.

His ability to understand, even mimic us, was uncanny. My wife Carolyn, my mom LaFon, and I went to Cooperstown for the baseball Hall of Fame inductions. We were to be on vacation for a week and needed to make sure the kitties would be taken care of. Diane, a close friend who lived with us for a time, volunteered to take care of our cats while we were gone.

The day after we got home, I was in our back room looking for something when I heard someone call out, "Hello!" Carolyn was upstairs, and it didn't sound like her, so I turned toward the door to the kitchen and saw Sprouty walking in. His mouth formed the word, and the vocalization was clear. I was stunned! When he saw me, he ran to me and stopped the vocalization. Apparently, he had heard someone say "hello" at the door and must have figured out that helped you find who you are looking for. I was able to make a video a few weeks later of his vocalization, and I play it back every now and again.

We had our "guy time," too. While Carolyn was at work, Sprouty and I would cue up my favorite movie, a western called *Mackenna's Gold,* and he would take his place in my lap. One time, I opened a bag of potato chips that were called "fiery hot" and started snacking on them. I was flabbergasted when Sprouty stuck his head in the bag and came out with a fiery hot potato chip in his mouth. He licked off all the spice and spit the naked potato scrap onto the floor. Then he got another chip and did the same. Again. And again. It seems that Sprouty didn't just like the spice; he loved it!

Sprouty had his way of showing me affection, too. He climbed into my lap at close to the same time every day and put his paws on my chest while looking into my eyes. He kneaded my chest while lowering his head onto the space between his paws and slowly raising his head. He'd close his eyes and then open them slowly with an almost dreamy look in his eyes. The kneading continued for sometimes thirty minutes. His purring had a deeply calming effect. Often, we both dozed off. This action seemed almost spiritual and gave me the sense that these "pets" we adopt have souls, and they love and demonstrate the same affection we give them.

When Sprouty passed away a little over a year ago, it was devastating. I'd lost my dad in 2013. Sprouty came into our home and hearts about a year and a half later, and I felt that he was there to fill the void left when my dad died. Even though I feel a sadness that has been tough to get over, I accept that pain because of the deep, spiritual connection I feel we had. He had almost a magical — or mystical — way about him, for which I will be forever grateful. But for now, I go forward convinced by Sprouty Kat that we will meet again in heaven, and we will have our "guy time" once again.

— Pete Commander —

75

Buckley

One must love a cat on its own terms.
~Paul Gray

The houses along the route to my cousin Bob's apartment slid by in a blur of bricks and shingles. Our trip seemed to take as long as my campaign to convince Mom to take Bob's cat. For two weeks, I tormented her with pleas and promises. "If we don't take the cat, she'll be put down. The superintendent told Bob to get rid of her, and Bob can't find anyone to take her. Please, can we take her? Bob will be so happy if we rescue his cat. I'll look after her. You'll love having a cat."

"We might not be able to keep her," Dad said. "Your mother can't help being afraid of cats. She's brave to try, but if she can't get used to Buckley, we'll have to find the cat another home."

I sighed. "I've waited all my life to have a cat."

Dad smiled. "All ten years?"

A half-hour drive, a ten-story elevator ride, and a thirty-second walk down a gray carpeted hallway brought us to Bob's door. He stood in the hall and shook Dad's hand. He closed the door, nudged a black-and-white kitten from his shoulder, and said, "Meet Buckley." Buckley squirmed and jumped down onto the parquet floor.

We followed Bob past a cardboard box poked with holes and another box filled with canned cat food, bowls, and a bag of cat litter. Bob sat in an armchair and motioned us toward the couch. Buckley jumped on the chair and perched on Bob's shoulder.

"My shoulder is her favourite place. She's pretty calm for a five-month-old, but she's playful. You're a lot of fun, aren't you, Buck? Come and say hello to Lynn." Bob placed Buckley in my lap. "She loves being scratched under her chin." Bob demonstrated, and Buckley lifted her head to reveal her white goatee. I took over the scratching. Buckley purred and rolled onto her back, exposing her white tummy. She wrapped her front paws around my hand. They were black with white toes that looked like furry little spats. Her back paws were white up to her knees. White whiskers brushed my arm.

We chatted about family and Bob's studies. Dad stood. "I guess we should get going."

Bob lifted Buckley from my lap. He nuzzled her and slid her into the perforated box. He whispered to her and slowly closed the flaps. "I'll help you carry her stuff to your car," he said.

All the way home, long, pitiful meows escaped the box. I tried to console Buckley, telling her about her new home with a big back yard to explore.

Mom stood at the front door as we pulled into the driveway. Dad and I carried Buckley and her luggage into the house and set everything down on the living-room floor. I had only two box flaps open when Buckley jumped out like a jack-in-the-box. Mom moved into the kitchen. Buckley sniffed the couch, end table, curtains, and bookcase, meowing loudly with each new discovery. Having explored the living room, she entered the kitchen. Mom circled through the dining room and hall, back into the living room.

"Why don't you set out some food and water for her?" Dad said.

"In the basement," Mom added.

Dad took the litter box downstairs. Buckley watched him from the top step.

Mom held Buckley's dish as I spooned food into it. The smell of fish filled the room. A black blur flew from the kitchen chair to Mom's shoulder, and she screamed. "Get it off me! Get it off me!" The dish clattered to the floor, and Buckley followed. "I can't stand a cat jumping on me." Mom's voice quivered. "This will never work if she jumps on me."

I knelt on the floor beside Buckley, who was now eating her tuna. She purred for the first time since leaving Bob's apartment. "Mom's afraid of you," I said. "You can't jump on her."

For the next week, the cat stayed in the basement when she and Mom were alone in the house. I rushed home from school to bring Buckley upstairs and play with her. She chased the crinkly foil balls I tossed across the floor. She chased the string I dragged in circles around me. Buckley chased everything. Mom enjoyed watching until Buckley decided to rub up against her legs. Mom cringed and hurried into the kitchen. The cat trotted alongside. I caught Buckley's attention by scratching the carpet. She pounced on my hand. "Don't get so close to Mom," I said. "She's still not used to you. You'll have to win her over slowly."

The next morning, entering the kitchen, I overheard Dad tell Mom, "No one can say you didn't try. I'll see if anyone at work would like a cat."

I gasped. "Are we giving Buckley away already?"

"It's not fair to your mother to be afraid in her own home," Dad said, "and it's no life for a cat to be stuck in a basement all day."

I ran home after school, afraid Buckley would be gone. My breath caught when I saw her sleeping on the stereo, curled in a patch of sunlight. I'd forgotten to put her in the basement when I left for school. I couldn't believe that Mom was sitting in the living room with the cat. "It's okay," Mom said. "She's been good. She hasn't moved from the stereo all afternoon."

Buckley stretched, jumped down from the stereo and crossed the living-room carpet to jump up on the opposite end of the couch from Mom. Buckley licked her paw and wiped her face. She watched Mom while Mom watched her. The cat moved six inches toward Mom and sat again. She licked her shoulders and moved two inches forward, meowing softly, never taking her eyes from Mom. The kitten moved onto the next cushion. Mom moved closer to the couch's edge. Buckley retreated to the first cushion, stretched out a hind leg and licked her toes. Mom sat back and crossed her legs. Her hand patted the arm of the couch. I expected her to ask me to take Buckley to my room.

Slowly, Buckley stood and approached Mom. Mom's hand stilled. Her legs uncrossed. She and Buckley eyed each other like two movie gunfighters at high noon. Buckley reached out a front paw to tap Mom's arm. Mom stiffened. Buckley reached out again and left her paw on Mom's leg. Mom didn't move. A minute later, Buckley's other front paw rested there. The kitten slowly lifted one hind leg and then the other to settle in Mom's lap, all the time keeping eye contact with her prospective new friend.

The phone rang. "That will be your dad," Mom said, "wanting to know if we still want fish and chips. Tell him to buy extra fish." She stroked Buckley's head lightly, tentatively. "I bet my pal here would like some halibut."

That night, Buckley enjoyed the first of many halibut filets.

— Lynn Tremblay —

76

For as Long as I've Known Him

Time spent with a cat is never wasted.
~Sigmund Freud

When I first met him seventeen years ago, he didn't growl. He certainly didn't purr, not that he wasn't pleased to be rescued. The sound he made when we met at the shelter reminded me of the engine brake on an eighteen-wheeler. It's called a Jake Brake. We shortened it to JB and hung the name on him. It stuck.

JB has stayed with us through two local moves, relocation across the Sierra Nevadas, and another two moves within our new hometown. Most cats would have given up on us and found another free meal. That might have required effort, however, and he hasn't been a great proponent of exertion, except when bare feet pass by him as he hides under the bed. Motivation is everything.

Like nearly every feline ever born, JB has never come when called and can't be shooed away when you wish he'd leave. When we go for a family walk, he tails us at enough distance that we won't mistakenly assume he has any affection for us. That would be so un-catlike. When we turn to see if he's still there, he quickly rolls in the nearest patch of dirt as though that had been his original goal.

More than once, I've been halfway to work when a furry tail has brushed the back of my neck. Fellow motorists have, for the most part, been patient with my sudden erratic driving. It has likely been educational for them to practice defensive driving while the man in the car next to them has a heart attack, followed by a mad scramble and flying fur. Upon returning home, JB leaps lightly from the vehicle, tail held high, and struts away as though peeved to have been rudely inconvenienced.

I suspect we should have sought permission from him before we brought home a puppy. To be hounded by such a bumbling, flop-eared interloper must have cost him dearly in the neighborhood pecking order. The coup de grâce came when Max, the now teenaged dog, chased JB up the side of the chimney in full view of his rival, the cat next door. It's probably a good thing we don't speak feline. The late-night screaming matches between JB and the neighbor's cat would have offended tender ears.

That cat wakes us at all hours of the night. At 3:15 A.M., he wants out, but he won't stay out. At 3:20 A.M., he wants in, but he won't stay in. He scratches at the side of the bed. The pillow I throw at him usually misses. He ducks and runs for cover only to return and scratch again. He brings nameless squishy things into the house and leaves them for us to discover. He sits nearby grinning, as though to say, "Look what I have bestowed upon you, ungrateful peasants." So it has been for all of his nine lives and much of ours.

Time flies when dealing in cat years. JB is already eighteen, quite the senior citizen. I guess he can be forgiven for expecting us to wait on him hand and foot. Of course, he's expected that since he condescended to accompany me home an eternity ago. He can't reach the toilet anymore for a drink of water, and his vanishing teeth can't handle dry food. He has shed more hair than I have. He can no longer reach all the places cats need to reach to stay clean and smug. It is good that Max, his aging nemesis, is too old to chase. JB's hyperdrive is worn out.

He doesn't like that I need to carefully lift him into the truck for the ride to the vet. To signify his distaste, he refuses to sit up front with me. He pouts on the back seat until we are nearly there.

It's easier this way, I think to myself.

We're almost there when a feeble, furry head pushes its way under my arm, and JB nestles onto my lap one last time. Lying there quietly, he endures my fingers methodically scratching the back of his neck and his deaf ears. His weary head rests between his paws. The engine brake revs up deep within him, the only thing that remains intact from the old days when we first met. My vision blurs.

Reaching our destination, I take a deep breath and carry him into an empty waiting room. He is silent now, the rumble stilled. I pay the required fee. When the vet comes to take JB away, my voice fails me, and I can only whisper, "Please, be kind."

"I will," she promises and takes him from my arms. Just like that, my old friend is gone.

On the long and lonely drive home, I wait in vain for a furry tail to brush my neck. I wish, but it doesn't happen. I hear a Jake Brake, but it is only a big rig slowing down for the hill ahead. It is difficult to breathe, and I swallow hard. I call to him, but as always, he doesn't come. He's been like that for as long as I've known him.

— Edwin F. Smith —

77

Audience of One

There are two means of refuge from the miseries
of life: music and cats.
~Albert Schweitzer

The Alabama sun was intense that lazy Saturday afternoon as we strolled about the shopping center. As we walked by a pet store, we noticed there was an adoption event underway. But with no intentions of adopting, we kept walking.

A minute, maybe two, had passed when my husband suddenly blurted out, "Want to get a cat?"

I looked at him to see if he was serious and, sensing that he was, I replied with an enthusiastic, "Yes!"

We quickly backtracked to the adoption event and greeted the rescue volunteer, who was surrounded by felines of all sizes and colors. We peered inside the stacked crates at the mewing mass of kittens inside. In one crate, a trio of gray-and-white kittens stared back at us — fluffy cuteness small enough to fit in the palms of our hands. But in the back of that crate, a lone orange-and-white kitten stood out.

He reminded me of the orange-and-white tabby from my childhood. A few minutes later, we were a party of three. We left the store with a cart full of food, toys, and all the necessary supplies needed to welcome our new family member.

Sneezer was the first pet we adopted as newlyweds, and from day one, he was contraband. To avoid a monthly pet fee, he went unreported to the landlord for the duration of the lease. Sneezer, though, soon lost his undocumented status when we relocated north and bought our first home. As we settled in our new house, I wanted to make it feel homey. Sneezer, snoozing in front of the fireplace, certainly added ambiance. A piano seemed like it would also add some hominess. As luck would have it, we found an upright at a nearby liquidation sale, and music came into our home.

There was just one problem: Years had passed since I had touched a piano. I had forgotten a lot, and it was necessary to start at the beginner's level and re-learn the basics. I was discouraged by this until one day when Sneezer hopped up on the piano bench beside me and began to purr. I took this as a sign of encouragement and pressed on.

From that point forward, Sneezer joined me whenever I played. Curled up on the bench, he listened intently and purred non-stop. Never a howl, nor a heckle. No pulled-back, flattened ears; just looks of pure contentment. Regardless of what or how I played, he was always there, cheering me on. My audience of one never missed one of these private concerts. I knew that my playing was not music to most ears, but to Sneezer it was.

Over the years, these impromptu concerts became one of my favorite ways to spend time with him. I played, and the applause was delivered in the form of purrs. Whether the music selections were familiar Christmas carols or pieces from the great maestros, it was fun to imagine that this small performance was held in the presence of a distinguished audience. Suddenly, the humble living room of our home was transformed into Carnegie Hall. And Sneezer was there in dress-circle seating for every single show.

As the years passed, other cats came into our home, but Sneezer was the only one who ever showed any interest in music.

— Jennifer Heilman —

78

Manny

Since each of us is blessed with only one life,
why not live it with a cat?
~Robert Stearns

Now I've gone and done it
I've become one of the stats
Those boring types of "senior"
Residing with their cats.

I said I wouldn't do this
But it's ever so uncanny
How my mind abruptly changed
When I met precious "Manny."

So I'm not apologizing
And it's plain for all to see
That this kitty who I rescued
In turn has rescued me.

When I'm lacking entertainment
His antics bring me laughter
And curled up beside me
He's the company I am after.

Now Manny isn't perfect
He's got his little glitches
But he's more than worth the trouble
When he's keeping me in stitches.

He's got no special talents
Nor any superpowers
But Manny with his presence
Has filled my lonely hours.

—Judy Schwab—

79

Perfect All Along

If you want to make God laugh, tell him your plans.
~Jewish Proverb

always knew I'd be a cat mom. My vision was a studio apartment — perhaps above a café overlooking a park — where I'd write award-winning novels with a loyal feline companion by my side. She'd be plump with white, rabbit-soft fur and a pink nose, maybe five or six years old. I'd have chosen her — the perfect cat — at the local animal rescue. Together we'd have a perfect life.

But the dream would have to wait. Like many twenty-somethings, I was working full-time, sharing a flat with two recent college graduates. My priorities included going to parties and jet-setting to exotic locations. I wasn't ready to be a pet owner.

In the summer of 2008, I was a case manager at a women's shelter. When a resident came home with a tiny black kitten, the whole house was abuzz. Maria begged the senior staff to let her keep it and they ultimately relented. She named him Chulo, Spanish for "cute." True to his moniker, he was all ears and paws.

Seeing an opportunity for kitten therapy, I offered to watch him while Maria was at work. The minute she'd leave, I'd sneak him into my air-conditioned office. He was a welcome distraction, climbing the shelves and sharpening his claws on the couch. Before long, he'd collapse in my lap for belly rubs.

Over the following month, his visits became more frequent. Maria picked up as many extra shifts as possible, determined to pull herself and her two young daughters out of poverty. We rarely saw her at support groups or house meetings. Later that fall, she appeared in my office and slumped onto the sofa.

"Well, I got my housing voucher," she announced rather indifferently. The waitlist for subsidized housing was long. Some of our residents had been on it for years.

"That's amazing news," I said. "Aren't you excited?"

"They don't allow animals."

I instantly understood. If Maria wanted to escape homelessness and give her girls stability, she'd have to surrender Chulo. She had no choice.

"I know how much you love him…" she went on, setting up her pitch. I knew what was coming.

Still, I was holding out for my dream. My cat was going to be of my choosing, not one thrust upon me. Anyway, I was too irresponsible to own a pet. Too busy. Too self-involved. I had recently returned from two weeks in South America and was planning a trip to Europe. I told Maria I'd look after Chulo, but only until I could find him the perfect home.

However, the universe had other plans.

From the moment he peeked his head out of the cat carrier in my foyer, he wouldn't let me out of his sight. Every morning, he stuck his paw under my bedroom door and demanded snuggles. When I was in the kitchen chopping vegetables, he was on the table. If I was reading on the balcony, he draped himself across my lap. My roommates teased me about my "little shadow."

As his attachment grew, so did my own. I'd come home on my lunch break just to see him. I melted every time he curled up on my chest. His antics made me laugh — he once entered a living room full of guests, my bra dangling from his teeth. Chulo brought me a sense of joy and fulfillment I didn't realize I was lacking.

None of his potential adopters met my standards. They were too old or too young. Too far. Too many kids. I was beginning to think no one out there could adequately care for him. Whenever an inquiry popped up in my inbox, my stomach clenched. Eventually, I stopped opening them altogether.

When Chulo was old enough for his neuter surgery, I set up an appointment at our neighborhood veterinary clinic. The receptionist chuckled as I strolled into the lobby, the pint-sized furball trotting beside me on a leash.

"Name?" she asked.

"Chulo."

"Not the cat's name. Your name."

I hesitated.

"You're the owner, right?"

I glanced down at Chulo, gold dinner plate eyes staring back at me.

"Yes," I answered, the hint of a smile forming at the corners of my mouth. "I'm the owner."

We became inseparable. The motifs of my life shifted rapidly in those days. Jobs came and went. Friends drifted in and out. Romances began and ended. My apartment saw a steady turnover in housemates, yet Chulo was always present, the one constant. He was an impeccable judge of character. Any man who wanted to date me had to pass the Chulo Test. Finally, when Chulo was two, one man did.

My husband and I are childless by choice; our pets are our children. Now thirteen, Chulo is as much our son as any human child. As I reflect on over a decade of memories with him, I think of how close I came to rejecting this priceless gift. My allegiance to a fantasy almost blinded me to the blessing that was purring away right under my nose. Chulo was the perfect cat all along.

— Laura Plummer —

Chapter
8

I Knead You

80

The Thing

*There is, incidentally, no way of talking about cats that
enables one to come off as a sane person.*
~Dan Greenberg

was jerked out of a sound sleep. I looked at the clock: 2:08 a.m.
It was very quiet in my moonlit bedroom. Then I heard it: a deep,
low growling that vibrated through the floor, ending in a battle
yowl. It was coming from the bathroom.

I sat up in bed clutching the blanket and called out in a croaky
voice, "Juna? Juna!"

Silence.

Without warning, a black shape exploded out of the bathroom,
catapulted across my bed and hurled itself against me, trying to burrow under my arms and squeaking at me as if there were a big, mean,
awful, horrible, demonic cat-eating monster in the bathroom!

I attempted to calm Juna as she tried to crawl inside my night-
gown. In the darkness, with her eyes glowing, I imagined the story she
would tell if she could. *She'd gone into the bathroom to get a drink and a
little smackerel of something when she was attacked. It jumped on her out
of nowhere, wrestled her to the ground and tried to gobble her up! But she
fought bravely, fighting tooth and claw, only managing to escape by losing
one of her nine lives and some of her fur.* She turned and growled in the
direction of the bathroom again, and then looked up at me hopefully.
I'd keep her safe, even at the risk of my own life, right?

With visions of snakes dropping from ceiling vents or rats coming up through the toilet, I slithered quietly out of bed with Juna meowing encouragement to me from her safe place under the covers. I stopped long enough to grab one of my fuzzy slippers and, brandishing it like a floppy club, I crept down the shadowy hallway to the bathroom. Juna had gathered up enough courage to follow me at a distance now. If I got attacked and eaten, she could still make a quick getaway. Brave and loyal kitty.

With my heart pounding against my ribs and a dry mouth, I reached a shaky hand around the doorframe, groping for the light switch. Finally, my fingers found it, and I snapped it on. I had to blink several times before I could see through the white glare. Would I be the monster's next victim in that moment of vulnerability? Then I saw it.

The Thing!

Words can't describe the horror of that most unassuming yet vicious night hunter: the predatory bath towel! Juna was right; it had been hanging above her water dish, patiently waiting for the precise moment when it could drop on her like a vampire bat in the darkness and suck out her furry, little soul. But she had escaped, and it had to satisfy itself with merely soaking up the water in her dish.

It sat there gloating at us, its heavy wet folds smiling evilly. It taunted us deliberately by doing absolutely nothing! This creature was clever and unrelenting; it would stop at nothing to get to the ground and continue its deadly hunting. Juna was lucky she escaped, losing only one life.

Finally, having plucked up her courage, Juna peeked around my ankle to give the towel one last growl. Then she looked up at me, mewing urgently, as if to say, "See! I told you there was a monster in here!"

—Deborah Kellogg—

81

The Cat Girl

It is impossible for a lover of cats to banish these alert,
gentle, and discriminating little friends, who give us
just enough of their regard and complaisance
to make us hunger for more.
~Agnes Repplier

was a horse girl. As a child, I rode rocking horses and uncles'
knees. I pretended I was atop my Palomino with its mane whipping in my face and its withers trembling beneath my jockey body.
I thrilled at the size, grace, and power of horses. I pictured myself
riding my horse in the Kentucky Derby, winning the Preakness, acing
the Triple Crown. But my parents explained horses wouldn't make
good house pets, and our toolshed couldn't house a Shetland pony.

So, I became a dog girl. I'd pet, play, and roughhouse with any I
could get my hands on at friends' or relatives' houses. I liked the ones
as big as ponies, with shaggy soft hair and beseeching brown eyes. I
wanted one badly.

I got a two-month-old Terrier from the pound when I was twelve
and was ecstatic. Banjo was full of energy and love and goofy as all
get-out. He could jump high and make me laugh as hard as anything.

But losing him made me cry harder than anything. He'd jumped
over our fence and leapt onto a child in play, teething on the boy's leg
like puppies do, and his parents called the warden. My parents didn't
plead for his freedom very hard. My mother was tired of him nipping
and shredding our socks. My father was tired of curbing him on the

frozen snowdrifts of the Connecticut winter.

I dreamed of living in my own house with a horse in a big back yard and a dog in the parlor. I fantasized about my dog sleeping before a roaring fire, warming me in the night, protecting me from intruders, and walking with me and my horse in the hills of Hollywood when I moved there.

Until I could own a house, cat-loving friends recommended I adopt a cat, but becoming a cat girl was furthest from my mind. I think one had snarled, scratched, and nipped me when I was little, so I bore a grudge against the entire species. Cats seemed stuck-up, untrustworthy, and never goofy enough to make me laugh, like dogs, or thrill at their size and power, like horses.

Many years later, I was living dogless, horseless, and friendless in a one-bedroom, upstairs corner apartment in California, homesick and lonesome. I enjoyed sunning myself on my balcony in a shaft of winter sunshine as it migrated for two hours across my quick-cooling porch. I'd inch myself and my Wandering Jew plant, the only living thing I had for company, to follow the sun. I liked sending photos of myself tan in January to friends shoveling snow back East.

One day, while freckling my shoulders and meditating, I felt I was being watched. A rustling sound interrupted my repose. I looked up to the wooden posts dividing my balcony from my next-door neighbor's, and there was his big, old orange tabby cat. His scary cat face stared me down.

I had overheard him being called Sugar Ray by my neighbor, and looking closely, this was fitting. He was bigger and more muscular than the usual cat. One of his ears was forked and scarred, probably from one of his fights, which I overheard often at night. His nose had been slashed, leaving a deep gash between his nostrils. Sugar Ray and I stared each other down, his twitching tail the only evidence he wasn't a statue. Neither of us moved or made a sound.

"Hi," I said nervously. I thought he might pounce at any moment if he saw me as a threat or saw my turf as his turf. So, I slowly scooched on my butt backward, flung my screen door open, and slid inside.

The next sunny day, tanning and meditating, I felt his presence again, but now Sugar Ray purred and gazed into my eyes for a full minute. I smiled up at him, and I guess he felt this was permission. He jumped down gently and made himself at home on my towel. After a few minutes of getting used to being so near another creature, and hearing no calls from my neighbor, his owner, I fell into an alpha state, comforted as Sugar Ray purred by my side.

In time, I grew far closer to him than to anyone else in my new world. My patio became his "catio." I'd occasionally see his owner at the mailboxes in the morning, and we'd nod at each other. Did he know? I said nothing about Sugar Ray's visits. Our relationship felt illicit.

One night, I came home brokenhearted. A work project of mine had been rejected on the same day a guy I liked rejected me. I was in personal and professional hurt, feeling all alone in the world, when I heard a thump against my patio screen door. I heard it again and then again. I looked out, and there was Sugar Ray, shoulder against it, looking up, beseeching me to let him in. He'd never been inside my house before.

It was a big step, but this was not a moment for negotiating boundaries. He strolled in gracefully and sniffed the air. He leapt uninvited onto my couch, circled twice, and then made himself at home. I tentatively perched by his side, offering my open hand. He snuffled it and then sinuously pressed his ear against it. As bidden, I stroked his scarred head. After a moment, he pulled his head back and met my teary gaze for a long, still minute. I felt some sort of understanding pass between us in the stillness that I'd never stayed still enough to feel from any creature before. I sat back on the couch, and Sugar Ray burrowed into my side, the engine of his empathic purr inviting me to burrow back.

We nestled on the couch together as I cried from deep in my gut. Sugar Ray pressed harder against me, moaning, inviting my grief, moving into my lap against my belly. He held me as well as any human might've if I'd been intimate with any. And when I fell asleep, he stayed near, occasionally standing atop me and massaging my belly with his paws. I was in the middle of a miracle, I felt, bridging whatever gap existed between cats and people. And the miracle superseded my hurt.

Sugar Ray continued to visit me in the months to come, comforting in his cat way. I was his rescue human. The next time I saw my neighbor at the mailboxes, I summoned up the courage to confess about my intimacy with his cat. But he spoke first.

"Hello," he said. "I just wanted to tell you I'll be moving out tomorrow morning, so it might be noisy for an hour or so."

"Oh. You're not taking the cat, are you?" I stammered.

"Well, yeah. Sugar Ray goes where I go, so he'll be moving, too, to a nice, big house in the hills."

"I'm glad for you—and him," I lied, my stomach roiling with sadness. It was time to let go of Sugar Ray.

And, soon, I became a cat girl....

—Melanie Chartoff—

Super Trooper

There is something about the presence of a cat…
that seems to take the bite out of being alone.
~Louis J. Camuti

When I began searching the shelters for a feline friend, I never suspected the companion I'd end up with would soon gain neighbourhood notoriety in the midst of a global pandemic. I'd already visited several shelters and petted dozens of cats. I was overwhelmed by how many needed homes. I decided I would wait for the cat who'd give me a special sign to show that he was choosing me, too.

Finally, in the last room at the last shelter, the volunteer had pointed to a giant black-and-white tuxedo cat resting atop a cat tree. "And that's Trooper. He's been here nearly half his life."

I walked over and thought, *This is it, cat. Choose me if you want me.* Trooper stood up so we could examine each other eye-to-eye. Then he climbed onto my shoulders, wrapped himself around my neck, and fell back to sleep. My heart nearly exploded.

I like to take my time to make decisions, so I drove home, mulling over the pricey adoption fee. The other shelters were cheaper, but the other cats hadn't chosen me. I couldn't get that giant, fluffy cat off my mind, and I called the shelter back later that day.

"You can't adopt Trooper. He's one of the cats we selected to go in a shipment to a pet-store adoption centre tomorrow."

I was confused. "But I want to adopt him, and the purpose of sending him away is to find him a home. Can't I come pick him up right now?" I hadn't realized how badly I wanted him until I was told I couldn't have him. He'd spent nearly a year in that shelter. What were the odds I'd find him the day before he got sent away?

"Well, we'd have to pick a different cat to go to the pet store, but I guess so. Goodness knows the other cats will be happy to see him go."

She wasn't exactly selling him, but… "I'll be right there," I promised. I knew I'd made the right decision when a different shelter worker who was sent to collect Trooper came back with tears in her eyes. "I'm going to miss you, buddy," she said. She waved as we left. Clearly, not everyone at the shelter was happy to see him go.

This cat turned out to be the living embodiment of the term "separation anxiety." He was immediately obsessed with me. Every morning when I woke up, he'd be tucked beside me under the covers with his front leg around me. He'd wrap himself around my neck like a warm winter scarf, and I'd usually prepare dinner and even bathe with a giant cat around my shoulders. He was petrified to be left behind again, and I wondered if I'd made a mistake. I valued my personal space, and clearly that was a thing of the past.

Trooper was so needy that I considered returning him to the shelter. But as the weeks went by, he relaxed a little and became slightly more secure in the fact I'd always come back for him. When I had to go on a short vacation, I dropped him off at a friend's cat-boarding kennel for a few days. It was devastating to see his heartbroken reaction. He thought I was abandoning him at another shelter.

When friends saw photos of him wrapped around my shoulders, they'd gush, "You're so lucky. My cat wants nothing to do with me." I began to come around to the fact that my tuxedoed gentleman was indeed a catch. When he wasn't wrapped around my shoulders, he was usually resting his paw on my leg, reassuring him of my presence and reminding me of our connection.

When the coronavirus pandemic hit in March 2020, I was forced to self-isolate at home alone after long hospital shifts. I went months without any physical human contact — no hugs from family or hand-shakes with colleagues. Friends were afraid to risk catching hospital germs and visited from a distance. But when I got home, Trooper would run to jump on my shoulders. He'd nuzzle into me and purr the day's stress away. Having him curled up on my lap and holding my hand with his paw kept me sane. When he began vomiting and looking pale two months later, I rushed him to the emergency vet. I had to stay in my car while the clinic staff rushed him inside. They did bloodwork, and the results were concerning.

The next few days, after Trooper had recovered enough to return home, I found myself doing all his favourite things. I willingly threw pinecones for him to chase at dusk rather than staying inside to watch Netflix. I relaxed on the front porch for hours with him, watching the world go by. Rather than feeling isolated indoors, we watched children hopscotch past, and neighbours stopped to greet Trooper and recounted how much they enjoyed his neighbourhood antics. I saw the world through his eyes. A week later, he got the all-clear from the vet. It's likely he had consumed a toxin, and his body had fought it off and recovered.

A trend had popped up in my neighbourhood called "wine ninjas" where (primarily) women would put together gift baskets and sneakily drop them on the doorsteps of unsuspecting strangers to make their days brighter. One evening in May, I was "ninjaed" when the doorbell rang, and I found Trooper investigating a beautifully wrapped basket full of goodies.

I discovered who did it when the ladies posted on a local Facebook page, laughing about how they nearly got caught after their boozy ding-dong ditch. After ringing my doorbell, they had noticed the cat and couldn't help but stop to pet him, delaying their quick escape.

I discovered the duo lived just around the corner from me. That night, we crept over to leave a gift of our own on their doorstep, complete with a card from the cat thanking them for giving his human mom such a lovely basket and inviting them to come pet him anytime. They later posted a selfie with their gift, captioned, "THANK YOU SO MUCH, TROOPER!" They laughed about how they got "wine ninjaed" by the neighbourhood cat.

I'm not sure what I'm more scared of: my looming vet bill or how much more obsessed Trooper's going to be with me now that I've saved him twice. Luckily, I have a basket full of wine to sip on the front porch as we greet neighbours passing by, re-connect to the world, and put our problems in perspective.

—Cassie Silva—

Angel in Waiting

Not all angels have wings.
Sometimes, they have whiskers.
~Author Unknown

've always loved cats. In my neighborhood, I'm known as the Cat Whisperer by some and the Crazy Cat Lady by others. It makes no difference to me. I love cats no matter how you label me.

I have a theory that cats pick us more than we pick them. I've only rescued a couple of cats from a shelter. The cats I have had over the years have mostly just shown up on my doorstep. I've literally had cats run onto my front enclosed porch as I opened the door. Cats instinctively know who they can trust.

As much as I love cats, I cannot keep all of them. I try to find the original owner — usually to no avail — or find them new homes. But I always give them a few days to figure out if they want to go home if they can.

Several years ago, a cat I named Katie showed up at my doorstep. I tried to gently encourage Katie to go back to her original home. Katie opted to stay with us. I took Katie to the veterinarian to get spayed and that's when we found out that Katie was a male! We quickly changed his name to KD and adopted him into our home.

KD had a sixth sense about him. He always knew when one of us needed extra loving. KD would sleep with whomever he felt needed him the most each night. He was quite the therapy cat.

In 1992, my mother suffered a debilitating stroke. She could no longer care for herself. At home, she needed a cane or walker. When she was outside the home, she had to be in a wheelchair. My father and I took care of her.

My mother became KD's mission on Earth. KD wouldn't leave her side. In the afternoons, KD would nap beside her. He would nestle up next to her, and we could hear his purring anywhere in the room.

The stroke took a toll on my mother. She could no longer articulate what she wanted to say, and her eyes looked sad and vacant; but she came alive around KD. She would scoop him up and pull him close to her chest. The only time we saw engagement from my mother was when she was cuddling KD.

My mother could only use one arm after the stroke. KD knew which side of her to lie on so she could stroke his fur. There were times I believed I heard my mother uttering a few words to KD, although she never said anything to the rest of the family.

After my mother was fast asleep, KD would come out and spend a few minutes with the rest of the family. He would go around making sure we were all okay, then eat and watch a little television with the family. Then he'd go back into the bedroom to spend the night with my mother.

During the last year of my mother's life, she spent many nights in the emergency room. Some nights, she came back home; some nights, she stayed in the hospital. KD would always be lying on the bed waiting for my mother's return.

That cat was persistent, dependable, and faithful to my mother. Thirteen long, arduous years after my mother had her stroke, she left this Earth. KD continued to wait for her return, lying in her spot on the bed. We cried and mourned my mother's death and KD's fierce loyalty to my mother.

A week or so after my mother's death, KD made his transition. He was almost sixteen years old. I'd like to believe my mother and KD are in heaven together. The two were inseparable on Earth for a little over thirteen years. I believe on some level that KD kept my mother alive by giving her a reason for living. He gave her a kind of love nobody else in the family could give her.

— Darlene Parnell —

Obsession

I think having an animal in your life
makes you a better human.
~Rachael Ray

Today, I should really
clean the house.
It's been a while —
but first I'll find the cat.

And my desktop
is piled high with mail
and undone filing —
but first I'll feed the cat.

I should go outdoors
to start the spring cleanup,
put the deck furniture out,
after I freshen his litter box.

He loves when I play piano,
so I'll play a few tunes
as he sits by me on the bench,
purring his own melody.

There's laundry to do
and dishes to put away,
but he's begging me to throw
the toy he loves to retrieve.

In between times, he needs
lots of stroking, along with
words of love over and over —
precious, darling, sweetie pie.

His favorite time of all?
Our daily rendezvous —
he curls up against my back
while we take our afternoon nap.

—Margaret M. Marty—

Chicken Soup
for the Soul

Uncommon Bond

*When you touch a cat with your spirit, in return
they touch your soul with their heart.*
~Author Unknown

rowing up in Damascus, Syria, I was accustomed to seeing street cats all over the city. My sister and I watched a neighborhood cat give birth to dozens of kittens right behind our house. I connected deeply with one of them. He was a yellow tabby cat with beautiful hazel eyes. He and I communicated with our eyes, and we knew what the other was conveying. We played our version of hide-and-seek around the yard. He would sneak up from behind a tree until he reached me, and I would act startled. He would then run away, and I would chase after him. Then he would turn around and start chasing me. He knew when it was his turn in the game to run away and when to chase me. I named him Skippy because he would skip across the ground while we played. Our bond traveled beyond the boundaries of our yard. When Skippy was old enough, he would walk with me to school every day.

My mother wanted Skippy to be an outdoor cat because she was afraid he would bring germs into the house. But I would sneak him into my bedroom through the window at night, and he would sleep by my feet until dawn. When the sun started rising, I'd let him out the window, and he would make the short trip around the house to greet me at the kitchen glass door. It was as if we hadn't seen each other since the previous evening. Skippy knew my mother's rules, and he knew how to get around them. This became our daily ritual.

After feeding Skippy every morning, I would head off to school, and Skippy would follow. An elderly neighbor who always sat by his front door asked me once, "How did you train the cat to follow you?"

I said, "I didn't train him. He just likes to be with me that much."

Of course, Skippy didn't come into the school building. But every afternoon when I got back home, he'd be there to greet me at our building entrance. He would hear my footsteps and know it was me regardless of which shoes I was wearing. He'd jump to the top of the pillar framing our home entrance and start meowing, letting me know in his own way how much he'd missed me. "I missed you, too," I'd tell him, certain that nothing would ever separate us.

One day, years later, after I had graduated high school and started college in Damascus, I made a life-altering decision. I'd always dreamed of traveling to the United States to finish my education, and I knew it was time for me to pursue that dream. It was the hardest decision I'd ever made up to that point in my life because I would be leaving my family and friends behind. I would also be leaving Skippy. How would I explain to him that I was leaving, and he would no longer find me every day when I came home from school? I wondered if he would ever forgive me.

While attending college in the United States, I called my mother back in Damascus. I asked her how Skippy was doing. She didn't have much to say about him. On the next phone call, she gave me an update on everyone in the family back in Syria. I asked about Skippy again, but she still didn't say much. Finally, a few months after I'd been in the United States, I called my mom and told her, "Look, Mom, there must be something you can tell me about Skippy."

I heard her sigh softly on the other end. "He kept coming to your bedroom window every morning to look for you. Finally, I told him Rihab was gone. She won't be coming back for a long time."

It was crushing to hear my mother's words. I wondered what had happened to him. My mother said, "I'm sorry, sweetheart, but he most likely died." There was silence on the phone, interrupted by the sound of my sobbing. I prayed for Skippy's soul. He had been my true companion for seven years, and I bid him farewell in my heart.

Over a year later, I went back to visit Damascus. During my flight home over the winter break, I reflected on all the family and friends I was going to see again. But there was sadness in my heart knowing I would not find Skippy.

My mom was driving the car from the airport, and when she reached the route Skippy and I had walked together to school, I could almost imagine him following me. When we arrived at the house, I saw the pillar where he would sit and wait for me to get home from school. I carried my luggage into the house and went to the kitchen for a glass of water. As I was standing at the sink, I saw movement out of the side of my vision. I turned to look down and had to do a double take. I couldn't believe what I saw: Skippy! He was waiting for me outside the kitchen glass door, as he always had. I opened the door and squatted down to pick him up. I hugged and kissed him profusely. I was in tears, and he was meowing in his usual affectionate way. This time, I didn't consider any of my mother's old house rules. I was thrilled my cat was back. I kept apologizing to Skippy.

An uncle who was visiting from overseas watched the emotional exchange between Skippy and me. As soon as it passed, he said, "I was in the kitchen yesterday, and I saw this cat at the door waiting. I asked your mother who this cat was. And when she came to the kitchen, she couldn't believe it. Her jaw fell open." My uncle proceeded to inform me how my mother had told him about Skippy's disappearance for over a year after I had left. My uncle said, "You must share something very special with your cat such that he sensed you returning. That's a very uncommon bond."

Over the next three days, Skippy and I relived our old rituals. This time, I told my mother I wanted him to stay with me overnight. I didn't want to hide him anymore. At the end of those three days, Skippy bid me farewell in his usual affectionate way, and that was the last time I ever saw him. Skippy lovingly shared beautiful moments with me that I carry in my heart to this day. Those precious bonds defy time and space, and they open our hearts such that we are never the same again.

— Rihab Sawah —

86

Yours, Ferally

*God made the cat in order that man might
have the pleasure of caressing the tiger.*
~François Joseph Méry

Betty's eyes meet mine through the steel bars of her prison. Her eyes are flaming, burning deep holes through me, testing my perseverance and mocking me. I take a step closer, willing myself to look away, spellbound. Staring. Despite all cost.

All the training I have courses through my mind, telling me to look away lest it incite aggressiveness. Still, I can't shift my eyes from the incandescent globes that are Betty's eyes.

I lift the latch and slowly swing open the metal door. Betty hisses at me, fangs bared. Her ears rear back stiffly, tension writ on her gorgeous tabby face. She has nowhere to run; her cage is just a few feet wide. At five weeks, Betty has already learned to deeply distrust the two-legged world.

I am firm; I won't back down. My mission is kitten love, and kitten love I shall get. Does anything else in the world come remotely close to this?

Making soothing noises and humming lullabies, I inch my right hand closer to Betty's forehead. I must remain steadfast.

Slowly, my hand reaches its destination. I start scratching her forehead, right at the center of the taut, tipped pink ears.

And I count down. Thirty, twenty-nine, twenty-eight, twenty-seven...

It always takes thirty seconds for a feral kitten to fall in love with me. A blessing bestowed by powers beyond me, its magic has never failed me yet.

My countdown comes to an end. Thirty seconds have passed.

Betty's eyes are still fixed on me. She's forgotten to hiss. She's purring now, a deep reverberation that trembles through her vocal cords, up her chin, through her baby whiskers, straight up her pink nose, right up to her forehead and to my fingers. Toiling as they do in Betty's service.

Her teeth are no longer bared.

At the one-minute mark lies the second test. I lift my hand back toward me by seven inches. Betty follows my hand, pawing up to rest her forehead against my fingers. "More scratching, please."

After a while, she allows me to take her out of the cage and wrap her in a towel, her face peering out. I take her to the window, pointing at cars and trees. Showing her the world. She conveys her understanding by looking at me, purring intermittently.

From a test of perseverance to a taste of pure, decadent love — this is the journey to loving a cat. And all it takes is thirty seconds.

— Paroma Sen —

87

The Demon Assistant

*My cat came out of nowhere and
became my everything.*
~Author Unknown

"Could you please take back your assistant?" I looked up from the keyboard to see my husband holding Tonks in his hands. Her black-and-white face was creased in a Cheshire Cat grin of feline pleasure. I smothered a laugh.

"She started an outreach program for her services and decided to work with you today," I remarked.

He dumped her into my lap. "She knocked everything off my desk, played with the cords under the desk, and bit a hole in three pages I printed."

Hiding a smile, I looked down at the eight-pound cause of exasperation. She promptly threw herself onto her side, the awful sound of a cement mixer rising from her chest.

"You're terrible. You know that?" Her green eyes slit just shy of closed. "That's what I thought."

Shaking my head, I turned back to my computer screen, her purr competing with the music pouring from my speakers. Names tend to become prophetic; naming her for the mischievous character from Harry Potter was no exception. The tiny demon got into more trouble than the other three animals in the house combined, with a complete lack of remorse — in true feline fashion.

"Just goes to show you can't trust those cute kittens," I said.

Taking my words for permission, Tonks jumped onto my desk and began batting my pen back and forth. I sighed. Unlike my husband, I tolerated her desktop shenanigans with grace and patience, accepting the necessity of restoring order to my knickknacks and sacrificing pens regularly. With all she did for me, even tolerating her knocking books off my shelves seemed a small price to pay.

She draped herself over my right arm as I tackled an article about aquarium maintenance. The soft rumble drifting from her little body resembled an actual purr this time. She remained oblivious to the movement of my hand and arm, content with her choice of sleeping arrangement. It wasn't the first time she fell asleep there while I worked, and I knew it wouldn't be the last.

As assistants went, she was horrendous: easily distracted, prone to stealing office supplies, disrespectful of supervisor space (she'd decided my office chair was her throne from the moment we put it together), and a shameless camera hog on Skype or Zoom. She also made up her mind regarding my schedule, chasing me down if I dared to step away from the desk for any reason. The little monster would reach up and claw at my leg, insisting in a loud voice that I get back to work.

Looking down at her, the warmth of her body transferring to my arm, I knew she was worth the headache. Where else would I find an assistant willing to help me choose my clothes every morning? Or help me brush my teeth? Or sit with me under a blanket when the bottom fell out of my world?

I saved the document on my screen, switching tabs to look at my calendar of writing assignments. It felt like years, although the dates confirmed that only a few months had passed since I'd embarked on my dream of freelance writing. "And just two months before that…," I murmured, scratching Tonks behind the ears.

The wound from losing my previous job still felt raw, and the depression and self-loathing that resulted were only beginning to relinquish their hold. I wanted to credit my friends and family for seeing me through that despair, but their constant barrage of positivity and encouragement made me feel like more of a failure. If I were everything they said, then none of that misery would have happened. Every day turned into a battle to reassure them — and myself — that things were fine.

Beneath the fragile exterior, though, was the conviction that I was worthless and doomed to failure. But while I slogged through the pit of depression, Tonks bounced into the room each morning to wait for me to decide what we were going to do. Stay in bed for three hours? Okay — she snuggled beside me the entire time. Wander to the couch and pretend to research job options on the laptop? She curled up on the blanket and watched the screen with me. Drag through the house like a zombie? She trailed behind me with her tail and whiskers up, convinced we were on a grand adventure. Sit under a blanket and cry? She poked her head beneath and licked my cheeks, content to wait until the tears ebbed.

Everyone else, as much as I loved them, tried so hard to pull me from the shadows and throw me back into the sunlight. She asked for nothing more than I was ready to give. They wanted me to be excellent, fantastic, and triumphant. She wanted me to be myself. In the end, that small, constant presence of acceptance helped more than anything else. I'd hit a bump in the road, but I was still me, and that's all she expected. That's all she wanted.

Opening her mouth in a yawn that displayed her sharp teeth, she chirped a happy sound at me. "You're probably the best demon assistant out there. But you knew that already, didn't you?"

Stretching across the entire keyboard, making sure to press as many keys in the process as possible, she jumped onto the bottom shelf and swatted my stuffed tiger. Watching it bounce to the desk and then the floor, her ears pricked forward in interest. She jumped back to the desk and whacked the pen.

Rolling my eyes, I returned both to their previous positions and picked her up, holding her at eye level. "You're a real pest, you know that?" I heard another rumble, vibrating the soft fur beneath my fingers. I pulled her close and whispered into her ear, "Now, go bother Daddy for a while."

I set her on the floor and she streaked in the direction of my husband's office.

—Andria Kennedy—

The Elements
of Argument

The cat does not offer services. The cat offers itself.
~William S. Burroughs, The Cat Inside

Dad was a country lawyer for more than fifty years, a sort of circuit-riding attorney in the small West Virginia towns where we lived. Often, his clients were financially strapped, so he accepted whatever they offered in trade for his services.

This resulted in a never-ending series of surprises at our home. We received bushels of produce, including some things unique to our area, such as pawpaws and chinquapins. During my childhood, I was given a pure-bred Beagle, a Cocker Spaniel, and a Basset Hound. There was a mama cat, a kitten, and two ducks. We also acquired an endless supply of wedding bands from divorces and a complete set of solid gold dentures, which puzzles me to this day.

One of the more astonishing contributions was a promised side of beef for the freezer, which turned out to be a live cow tethered to our back stoop. (We did not eat Bossy. We donated her to a friend, and she happily lived out her days as a farmer's pet.)

But most intriguing of all was a mysterious cardboard box that Dad brought home. He said it contained "The Elements of Argument." The box had perforated holes through which peered out six yellow eyes. Inside the box were three kittens as shiny and black as the West

Virginia coal fields into which they had been born. They were long, lean, sinuous, and shorthaired. They appeared fluid as they seeped out of the box in one viscous motion. Dad named the trio Ethos, Pathos, and Logos.

Dad explained to me that to win any case, one must carry all three elements to a judge or jury. He said no one should attempt to convince (which means "with force") anybody of anything. His motto was: "A person convinced against his will is one who is unpersuaded still." So, an argument should, to be persuasively successful, go like this:

Ethos: This means ethics. What is the moral or righteousness of a case?

Pathos: What is the emotional weight? Could the points of the argument pull at the heartstrings?

Logos: What is the law and/or logic of a situation?

My mother joked that the cats should be named Motive, Means, and Opportunity because Dad's client had seized all three to dispose of the cats while simultaneously dispensing with the bill.

Dad did not find the humor in that, so Ethos, Pathos, and Logos they remained.

The Elements moved as one in a long, straight line while following Dad everywhere they could. To me, they were indistinguishable from each other, but Dad knew, or at least swore he knew, which was which.

When my father was working on a speech, he would pace on the front porch, which went three-quarters of the way around the house. Dad was short and wide and had a walk that sounded like the gait of a sailor on a storm-tossed deck — left foot heavy, right foot soft — and all three cats followed in single file, a "danse macabre" (my mother's term). Sometimes, he and they paced for hours. Many nights, I drifted off to sleep to the synchronicity of his rolling gait and the syncopated whisper of twelve following paws.

In the winter, Dad would sit by the fireplace with a tuffet of black hair in front of him, for all the Elements slept in a pile. Should anyone in the room make the slightest disturbance, six glowing orange embers would appear suddenly in that black tuffet, and equally suddenly all six eyes would flame out. It was unnerving to the uninitiated.

The Elements operated as one. None ate, even a single bite, without the other two, and none drank a drop more or less than the others.

Winter or summer, when my father had completed a speech to his satisfaction, all retired to the back porch. The Elements would assemble on the railing and sit in silent judgment of his arguments. Occasionally, I would hear a blood-curdling screech and a thump, and then my father would mutter something. Out would come the pencil and legal pad for revisions. Then, the pacing by human and felines would recommence.

My father explained to me that if he could not hold the attention of a tomcat, he could never sway a judge or jury. He told me he could tell which of the Elements his plea was lacking. Ethos yowled — okay, what was wrong morally? Pathos? How could he alter his appeal to the audience's emotions? Logos? Back to the law books.

These three distinguished (or indistinguishable) gentlemen tolerated my family, but they were completely disinterested in anyone's speeches except Dad's. He and they were one another's mutual judge and jury.

Dad was quite successful in his courtroom appearances, and I, sometimes sitting in the gallery, wondered what the assemblage would think had they known the first audience had been three tomcats on a porch railing.

Whether through listening to years of his speeches or my appreciation of his enthusiastic entourage, this had a profound effect on me personally. I was a state debate champion in high school, majored in speech in college, and became a teacher and debate judge.

As Dad always said, "A good lawyer understands the elements of argument."

To this day, whenever I see a black cat, I smile and wonder whether it is Ethos, Pathos, or Logos in search of Dad.

— Anne Oliver —

89

Tortitude

Know in your heart that all things are possible.
We couldn't conceive of a miracle
if none had ever happened.
~Libbie Fudim

M y friend Pam and I happened to lose our senior cats within days of each other. We were adamant that we would need to wait a while before we got another cat. She felt she wasn't ready, and neither was I.

However, days after we had the "not yet" conversation, Pam called to tell me she couldn't wait. She'd just adopted two cats! She had also seen a compelling rescue cat online named Kelly, and I decided that I would adopt her if Pam couldn't.

It was a sunny fall day when Pam and I headed to the shelter. Entering the cat room, we looked for Kelly in vain. There were plenty of cute kittens and cats available for adoption, but no Kelly in sight.

I approached the young woman in scrubs with the shelter's name embroidered on it. "I'm looking for Kelly," I said. "My friend saw her on the website, and I'd like to see her. Has she been adopted already?"

"Oh, Kelly is in the unadoptables room. Her last owners had to surrender her," she said. "But you can still see her."

We followed her into the office — a separate room with a closed door. Inside were a number of cats roaming around the counters and desks, meowing for attention. Kelly was easy to spot. She was the only tortoiseshell in the room and was definitely the loudest. I approached the counter Kelly was sitting on, and she stalked toward me. Immediately, I realized where she got her name from. She had the most beautiful kelly-green eyes. She stopped before me and reached up, her front legs circling my neck as she lay her head against my chest.

The volunteer gasped. I looked over to her and said, "Well, I guess she's picked me, too!"

It took the volunteer a little while to gather her emotions. "I'll just get the fostering papers for you now."

I stopped her before she left the unadoptables room. "Oh, I'm not fostering Kelly," I said. "I'm taking her home for good." Kelly was still cradled in my arms purring. The volunteer looked between Pam and me in disbelief.

"Before you commit," she said, "I have to tell you that Kelly is not an easy cat. She has issues."

I let Kelly nuzzle my chin. "I have issues, too," I declared. "I think we'll get along just fine."

The volunteer ignored me and pressed on. "She hates to be picked up. She doesn't like people to touch her ears. And when she wags her tail, that's a sign she's going to bite. That's why she's considered unadoptable. She's been here for three years now. And Kelly can't go outside at all; she'll run away."

I didn't change my mind. The volunteer was still in a state of shock that the shelter's longest resident was being adopted. She had to phone the manager at home to tell her the good news. By the end of the phone call, she and the manager were both in tears.

The papers were completed and Kelly left the unadoptables room for a permanent residence with me.

The life lessons began right away, and I learned all about "tortitude."

Kelly was extremely affectionate — but on her own terms. She loved having her ears rubbed, at least by me. Her tail wagging wasn't a sign of her biting, although she did bite if I didn't pay attention to the growls. She wagged her tail like a dog. I tried to keep her inside, but she was an escape artist. She'd race out the door to sprawl in the sun, but she never once ran away. In fact, she'd often go on walks with the dog and me, greeting the other dogs and their walkers in the park behind my house.

She's gone now, my orange-and-brown bundle of tortitude, but the lessons I learned from her are for life. Don't judge a book by its cover or a cat by its tail. Second and even third chances are important. Stay true to yourself and live your life to the fullest. And always, always have lots of tortitude.

— Amanda Ellis —

90

Mortimer

Blessed are those who love cats,
for they shall never be lonely.
~Author Unknown

"How many were there this week?" The bubbly voice of my doctor drew me back from my thoughts, sounding as light-hearted as if she were making small talk rather than asking about my debilitating panic attacks.

"Three," I replied quietly, examining my cold and sterile surroundings. The door to the small, square room was comically tall, almost twice the height of my short, bustling doctor. Her fingers flew across the keyboard of her laptop as she feverishly took notes on my condition.

"Do you still live alone? Was there anyone there to help you?"

I shook my head, my fingers twitching as more anxiety crept up from the pit of my stomach. It was one of the bad weeks, which were occurring more often.

"Have you considered getting a roommate?" my doctor asked suddenly, looking up at me with wide brown eyes.

I shrugged awkwardly. "I have, but I don't really want to have these... attacks, in front of someone I don't know that well."

She nodded knowingly and continued tapping for a moment before looking up at me again.

"What about a pet?"

The thought of adopting a pet had crossed my mind many times before that day, but I never pursued the idea despite growing up with them. At twenty-one, I didn't want the responsibility of a dog, especially when I lived on my own in a small basement apartment.

"I think a dog would be too much for me right now, unfortunately." I sighed. My doctor shook her head.

"What about a cat?"

Growing up in a dogs-only household, getting a cat had never occurred to me. Despite my apprehension, when I got home I sat at my computer and searched cat rescue sites. As I scrolled through the many adoptable cats, I resolved to only inquire about one if it was the absolute perfect companion for my lifestyle.

After two days of searching, I found him. Mortimer was described as "the perfect companion for a single person or student, a quiet and extremely affectionate cat who just enjoys being in the same room as his person." With a write-up like that, I had to meet him.

When I got to the house where Mortimer lived with his foster mother, I walked in hesitantly. After a moment or two, he emerged from the basement confidently, leisurely padding across the linoleum floor to see what was happening. I crouched down to allow him to investigate me. Mortimer circled me slowly, sniffing me as he went, and stopped as he reached my front once again. Without warning, he sprang up and placed his two front paws on my shoulders. He sniffed my face and then began licking my nose, offering his apparent approval.

I hadn't expected to take him home that day so I wasn't prepared. But Mortimer's foster mother and I made it work. With a borrowed kennel and large freezer bags of food and litter, Mortimer accompanied me to my humble home.

After an hour of inspection, he settled into his new living arrangement, comfortably roaming the space and claiming my favourite green chair as his own. He was, as promised, a very friendly and quiet cat. We spent the first few days together, Mortimer purring beside me as I worked on university papers. Things were going well until the inevitable happened: another panic attack.

As I lay in bed, the familiar feeling started in my abdomen, causing my whole body to shake. Tears pooled in my eyes as I gasped for breath, feeling my throat constrict and watching the walls move in closer. I threw back the bedsheets, startling Mortimer in his peaceful slumber at the end of my bed, and collapsed onto the cool floor, desperate for something grounded and stable to hold me up. I rocked back and forth, trembling helplessly in the darkness.

Then I felt soft fur brush by my hand and felt two small paws on my legs. Mortimer climbed into my lap sleepily, curling into a circle and purring. I grabbed hold of him tightly — a lifeline. Despite his usual aversion to being held, Mortimer hung limply in my arms as the waves of fear and anxiety crashed over me. I was going to throw up.

I plopped Mortimer down on the floor and fumbled my way to the bathroom, barely making it to the toilet before I retched. I curled up on the bathroom floor and sobbed. Once again, soft fur filled my arms as Mortimer snuggled in with me. He calmly tucked himself into my stomach, patiently waiting for the attack to pass. When it was finally over, I scooped him up carefully and carried him back to bed.

Mortimer became used to these attacks, dutifully getting into his consoling position every time the panic arrived. As time went on, the attacks occurred less often, and they were easier to deal with because I was no longer alone. Mortimer was a natural caregiver, and I showered him with love and adoration in return for his loyalty and affection

My panic attacks never went away, but I faced each one with Mortimer by my side. Despite him being a rescue cat, it quickly became apparent to me who truly rescued whom.

— Rachel Esser —

My Very Good, Very Bad Cat

91

Delightfully Devious Dora

Some people say that cats are sneaky, evil, and cruel.
True, and they have many other fine qualities as well.
~Missy Dizick

Dora, our gray-striped tabby cat, grew up (we believe) as an alley cat, prowling the neighborhood, running her own life, and doing things her own way. When Dora decided to move in with us, we had no say in the matter. She had a mind of her own — although what cat doesn't?

My mom had a mind of her own as well, and a twisted sense of humor. She saw humor in all sorts of odd circumstances, and she loved to play practical jokes on people, keeping a straight face the whole time.

Put that cat and my mom together and, boy oh boy, it was an amazing combination.

Our house was two stories high but very small. If you came in the front door, you'd walk through a little foyer not even large enough for a coat hook. Then you'd choose whether to walk up the stairs in front of you or make a slight turn into the front room. As soon as you walked into the front room, you'd see a nice, comfortable sofa, which Mom kept clear of clutter.

That sofa was the focal point of the room. It was large and comfy, with a few throw pillows here and there. It was the kind of sofa you'd sink into and almost get stuck in its depths. It was irresistible.

My mom never met anyone she didn't like. She greeted strangers with her sweet smile and chatted with anyone anywhere. Therefore, she never turned away a door-to-door salesperson. She loved to chat, and strangers made for interesting and diverse topics. But Mom never mentioned Dora the cat. No warning.

So, door-to-door salesperson encounters went like this. Some innocent individual would knock on our door. Mom would rush to answer. The salesperson would step inside, chatting already, and then spot our deliciously welcoming sofa. The unsuspecting visitor would plop onto the sofa, slip out of her coat or jacket, and get herself nicely settled, chatting all the while with Mom.

Mom never looked up so she wouldn't spoil the practical joke to come.

Right above the visitor, Dora would peek through the stair banister. Watching carefully, Dora would bide her time, waiting for the perfect moment. She would wait while the visitor settled in, leaned back and relaxed, and became most vulnerable.

Then, at just the right moment, Dora would leap up onto the stair banister and slide down. She would shriek the entire way down, her fur sticking out wildly, her yowl as terrifying as ever a cat could be. For her finale, she would land on the sofa back, right behind the visitor.

Most visitors would leap to their feet, screaming in terror. Most would then beat a hasty retreat, muttering about dangerous animals. Mom would offer apologies and nods of agreement to the shaken visitor's protests as she showed them the door.

Mom never began laughing hysterically until after the offended guest's departure. Then Dora always got a treat, though I was certain it wasn't for the treat that she performed her hair-raising trick. I am convinced that Dora enjoyed the whole thing just as much as Mom did. Mom hooted and hollered with laughter while Dora took a long, leisurely victory bath.

And, every once in a while when the first shock wore off, the guest would join in the laughter, recognizing a wonderful and perfect practical joke when she experienced one. Those few special guests became close friends for life. Dora and Mom recognized a good sport when they met one.

Dora and Mom. Two of a kind.

— Karen M. Leet —

92

The Cocoa Diet

The way to get on with a cat is to treat it
as an equal — or even better,
as the superior it knows itself to be.
~Elizabeth Peters

We should have known life with Cocoa would be different when he refused to eat anything but mixed vegetables. Every morning, we had to take frozen vegetables out of the freezer and cook him a plate, or else he would not eat. In our experience, this was unusual behavior for a kitten. None of the other cats had done anything like this. If only we had known what was to come.

You see, Cocoa was a thief. A food thief. Nothing was safe. Thankfully, Cocoa did learn to eat both dry and wet food. The dry food was left out all day. He would stick his head in the bowl as I poured, getting the food on his head as well as in the bowl and on the floor.

Wet food was a once-a-day treat. Cocoa's portion was never enough. Every morning, I stood between him and the other cat while they ate. Cocoa always finished first. If I wasn't standing between them, he would rush to the other plate and push the other cat off to finish what she left behind. So, I stood there between the two plates every morning. Eventually, Cocoa learned he had to sit and wait until the other cat left of her own free will. Only once she was away from her plate could he eat her leftovers.

If Cocoa only stole cat food, I would be telling a different story.

But Cocoa stole everything. I'm serious. I think he left raw onion and chocolate alone. Grapes and olives he tried to eat but could not conquer. Everything else was fair game.

Cocoa got great pleasure from stealing. He even had tricks to go with it. There was the time he twisted his head as far as he could to snatch a pancake off a plate. He regularly stretched his body to reach the top of the island, moving his paws across to see what he could grab. When no one was standing nearby, he jumped on the island or stove to see what morsel he could find. On the stove, he had pots to play with. He licked many pots clean, which we washed again later.

Nothing was a deterrent. If bread was in plastic, Cocoa ate through the plastic. It did not matter to him. He wanted the bread.

One night, I woke up to a loud thudding coming from the back hall. Cocoa was in the process of taking a one-pound box of butter down the stairs. He had gotten it off the island, through the kitchen, and almost down to the basement before I woke up. Had I stayed asleep, he would have gotten it to the basement, where I'm sure he would have tried to eat all four sticks. Through a combination of using his claws, rolling, and throwing, Cocoa almost got away with stealing the butter. At least, that is how I figured he got as far as he did. There were claw marks and holes in the box.

Then there was the garbage. For the longest time, our trash had a partially open top. Cocoa would reach in and pull out what he wanted: meat wrappers, chicken bones, avocado shells, and cantaloupe guts. He loved the stringy and seedy parts of a cantaloupe. Eventually, we got a trash can with a different top. Its two sides pushed down when throwing something away and then popped up once done. Essentially, the garbage was always closed — until Cocoa jumped on it and fell in.

If something fell on the floor, Cocoa was there to eat it. Cheese was a favorite. Cooked pieces of sausage and tomatoes were also worthy of investigation — although truly anything falling to the floor was worth a look.

Duck sausage was something else, though. When a piece of duck sausage fell off a piece of pizza, he moved the fastest I had ever seen. Until that day, little did I know how much he loved duck sausage.

The refrigerator was Cocoa's regular hangout. Every time someone opened the door, he ran from where he was to look inside. One day, a grocery-store rotisserie chicken fell out of the refrigerator, and the lid popped off. Right before him sat a chicken, all for him. I figure Cocoa spent the rest of his life waiting for that to happen again.

I know cats aren't supposed to do well with milk, but Cocoa loved dairy products. More than just cheese and butter. Every morning, he demanded the remaining milk from my cereal. He would sit and wait, somehow knowing when I'd eaten my last bite. Depending on where I was sitting, he would then either shove his head in the bowl or meow while turning in circles until I gave him what he wanted.

He also went after ice cream and cottage cheese. One day, he ate a slice of pear because it was with the cottage cheese he wanted.

As much as Cocoa ate everything, he could be picky. He preferred sour-cream-and-onion potato chips over barbecue. When a gluten-free, eggless pancake was accidentally made, he became more distressed than I had ever seen him. These were not the pancakes he knew and loved, although he was happy to eat gluten-free, toaster-pastry dough.

Tuna gave Cocoa two benefits. Not only did he love tuna (especially in oil), but he was able to have fun dragging the can around with his tongue, licking up every last speck. Many times, we stepped on that can after he abandoned it, not knowing where he'd finished it off.

Even though we all tried to stop his stealing, our only successful answer was to hide everything. We had to cool banana bread and other baked goods in the microwave. Other things were hidden in the oven. Groceries had to be put away immediately.

The funny thing is, despite all he did and ate, Cocoa didn't gain weight and rarely got sick in his almost eighteen years. There was something to be said for that Cocoa diet.

— Kate Dorsey —

93

The Princesses and Their Peas

To eat is a necessity, but to eat intelligently is an art.
~François de la Rochefoucauld

Like many kids, when I was a little girl, I was a picky eater. Getting me to eat my vegetables was an epic challenge. I hated all of them except cucumbers — peeled and sliced, of course.

I had a special hatred for peas. They were my nemesis. Just their appearance on my plate could incite a meltdown. I was normally a compliant child, but this was the exception. No amount of cajoling, disguising, or bargaining could make me eat those peas.

One thing I did love was Campbell's alphabet soup. I ate it for lunch regularly, creating words with the pasta letters. Unfortunately, there were peas in the soup, so I had to extract them every time I ate it.

We were a cat family, always adopting the strays who found us. Lily was one such cat. She came to us one fall, starving and desperate. She enthusiastically gobbled the moist food we provided several times a day. That is, until one day when we fed her Gourmet Mix. She enthusiastically ate as usual, but when she finished, we noticed something left in the bottom of the bowl. Upon closer examination, we discovered she had picked out all the peas and left them behind, just like I did. Even though she was quite hungry, she just couldn't stomach those peas.

From that point on, Lily and I were the subject of oft-repeated family stories about the princesses and their peas.

—Donna L. Roberts—

94

Diagnosis: Naughty Cat

*Cat people are different to the extent that they
generally are not conformists. How could they
be with a cat running their lives?*
~Louis J. Camuti

I had everything arranged for an introductory Zoom call with my new therapist. The sofa pillows were propped just so, and my laptop was poised atop a stack of cookbooks with a Bible thrown in for good measure. A box of tissues stood ready. I had previewed my video image and tilted the screen to sharpen my jawline.

As I hovered the cursor over the meeting link, I pondered the chances of creating an intimate connection via computer. With the stress of the COVID lockdown, many people were seeking counseling, and virtual appointments were the only option available. But, wow, did it feel awkward.

When Susan popped up on the screen, we exchanged greetings and slowly began to segue into this "new-normal" session. Her hair was pulled back, her glasses serious. She radiated competency. Would I be able to reveal intimate secrets to her? The not-so-nice parts of myself? My gut roiled, and my fists clenched.

Just then, Sam swaggered into the room. Oh, perfect. Any virtual meetings seemed to light a fire under my cat's furry rump. That's why, just before the meeting, I had ensured that he was sleeping like an angel. My apprehension ratcheted up to an eleven on a scale of ten. Nearby, I sensed Sam gearing up for trouble.

Susan was sharing her qualifications and background. "I spent many years working in prisons," she said. My inner wimp cowered.

"I see from your questionnaire that you want to address your issues with setting boundaries," she continued.

"Absolutely," I replied. "I have a problem saying 'no' and really meaning it."

Just then, Sam buried his talons deep into the couch leg.

"No!" I blurted out. Susan blinked and made a note.

Focus, focus, I thought.

Sam continued his resurfacing project, fine-tuning the jagged threads jutting from the sofa. I grabbed the box of tissues and batted at him.

"Sam!"

Susan looked concerned and made another note, probably along the lines of "imaginary friend."

Next, Sam reared back in preparation for a friendly feline love bite.

"Back, back, back!" I hissed, wielding the flowered box like a sword.

The cat lunged out of reach, and Susan was treated to a compelling view of my arm flailing about madly. She was surely jotting down, "Possible drug flashbacks." Should I hit the video icon and temporarily go to audio only?

"Can I ask what you're doing?" Susan remained composed, although I detected a telltale quiver of her lips.

Sam's teeth found purchase, and I hurled the near-empty box at him as he skittered away. It glanced harmlessly off the aforementioned rump.

"My cat…," I began lamely.

"Ah, say no more."

As she nodded, Susan's delicate earrings glimmered, and her eyes softened behind the stern frames. A few tendrils of hair had escaped from her ponytail.

"Dogs have masters. Cats have servants. Right?" she asked.

"I've got that T-shirt," I admitted, and we laughed. My heart sang, and my fingers unfurled. Maybe, just maybe, this was going to work.

"Next week, let's begin delving into your boundary issues," Susan said. "I think we both know where we need to start."

And that's when Sam jumped on my lap and turned his best side to the camera.

— Kim Johnson McGuire —

95

Bill and Bindi

Cats have personalities.
~T.S. Eliot

Bill is not my cat. He is my neighbors' cat. When the neighbors are away skiing, hiking, surfing, and doing the outdoorsy things that young couples with good bodies do, they pay me, a sedentary playwright, to pet-sit Bill the cat and their big yellow dog named Bindi.

Bill and Bindi live under the same roof but are not natural companions. Bill seems to put up with Bindi in the way one tolerates that visiting relative who brings up religion and politics at family dinners.

The first time, the neighbor explained that my job would involve the simple tasks of feeding Bill and Bindi morning and evening, and taking Bindi, older and suffering some hip stiffness, for slow walks around the block. I was to use the green, clove-scented poo bags tied into the leash handle.

"Watch out for Bill," said my neighbor. "That cat likes to sneak out if you're not careful. Whatever you do, don't let Bill outside. He will try to get out. But there are coyotes. And cars. And that one mail truck that goes too fast."

The first of our walks was on a foggy morning the day after Thanksgiving. Bindi, who sleeps in a big metal crate on a messy nest of quilts, was happy to be sprung. As I clipped on his leash, I didn't see Bill, whom I assumed was probably sleeping beyond the pet gate in a back bedroom.

Then I opened the front door and—whoosh!—there went a skinny gray-and-white cat past my legs, out the door and into the bushes.

Yipes. An escape artist. I tried "Here, kitty, kitty" and other entreaties. Ignored. I broke into a light sweat. Bindi urgently needed relief, however, so off we went on the slow, sniff-everything walk up the block, with me scanning every lawn and tree for that cat.

Two houses down, Bindi paused and looked over her shoulder. Sure enough, there was Bill, slinking onto another neighbor's porch, watching us with a maddening nonchalance.

I talked to Bindi about this. "What's Bill up to? What do you think?" Bindi sniffed a mound of fallen acorns and snuffled into a pile of raked-up leaves. We walked on. And Bill followed, from a distance, always hugging closely to the walls and porches of each house as Bindi and I stayed near the curb.

Every ten yards or so, Bindi would stop and look around, and there Bill would be—by the front steps of a red-brick ranch house or peeking around the corner of somebody's garage. At the entrance to the alley, Bill did a little gallop toward some crows, and they fluttered up and away. At the end of the street, by the house fronted by a drooping palm tree, a mockingbird whistled a warning to its friends that a cat was approaching. At least that's how it sounded to me.

As we rounded the last stretch of the block, I lost sight of Bill. *Oh, dear. What if he's gone on a walkabout? What if he runs away, gets squashed by that mail truck, or wanders up to the light-rail tracks?* I posed the questions to Bindi, who had no answers. I wrote a script in my head about what to say to my neighbors about their missing cat.

Back on our side of the street, I looked at my neighbors' porch. There was Bill, sitting on the welcome mat at the door. How had he beat us home?

And thus, we repeated this walk twice a day for the next two weeks, with Bindi on the leash and Bill on the loose, but always close enough to watch over his dog housemate and me. I stopped freaking out about Bill zooming out the door. He needed a walk, too, I figured. His job was watching Bindi, I thought. Watching me too, perhaps.

One afternoon, a fellow dog-walker I encountered asked, "Is that your cat? I've seen him following you on the walks. I've never seen a cat do that."

Bill did lots of things I've never seen cats do. He would sit on the hearthstone and stare at the dark fireplace for thirty minutes at a time. Then he'd scale the fireplace bricks and paw at some invisible spirit in a sooty corner. He'd sit and gaze out the French doors onto the patio for long stretches, as if yearning to travel to a place only cats can imagine.

He kept his distance from me. My neighbors gave me permission to watch Netflix on their giant TV, so some evenings I'd linger after feeding the pets and binge on episodes of *The Crown*. Bill ignored me. He would nap inside Bindi's crate until the dog would look at me as if to say, "I'm tired, and there's a trespasser." Then I'd shoo the cat out of Bindi's bed, and Bill would hop the gate leading to the hall and go bed down for the night on somebody else's bed. This ritual seemed familiar to these two.

In the mornings, if I didn't stick around after dishing out their breakfast, I discovered that Bindi would try to eat Bill's cat food, so I started putting Bill's bowl on the counter, out of reach, and hanging out until he'd eaten his fill.

Maybe Bill appreciated the gesture, because one night, as Princess Margaret was entertaining LBJ with a ribald story on *The Crown*, Bill hopped up on the sofa and sprawled out in my lap. I didn't move. He fell asleep and purred. I felt accepted.

The next morning, Bindi, Bill and I went for our last walk together. The mockingbirds sounded their alarm as we rounded the last corner. And, as always, Bill beat us back to the front door.

— Elaine Liner —

96

From Boring to Beaming

An animal's eyes have the power
to speak a great language.
~Martin Buber

We were three weeks into my Research Methods course. This university class that I taught met once a week for three hours in the evening. COVID fatigue and online learning while quarantined made the class more challenging.

It was a long stretch of time to fret over variables and data collection, especially when most students were working adults who had already put in a full day before our evening class. Many were active-duty military members who worked demanding shifts and even deployed to various locations during the term. Three of the students had newborns, two were caring for ill family members, and one had a family member move in during quarantine. Needless to say, my students had a lot of things competing for their time and attention.

While I try to keep students engaged, research methodology does not lend itself to lively discussions. The material is important and relevant to their studies, but it is often difficult and dry. Watching their tired faces on camera one night, I could tell they were becoming bored and frustrated, so I wrapped up the topic and asked for questions before we took a break. To my surprise, a hand went up. Maybe they were more engaged than it seemed! When I signaled for the student to take the mic, I anticipated a question about applying quantitative versus qualitative methodologies to their proposals. Instead, I got an unexpected question.

"So, we were talking together in the chat, and we were wondering... When you lean down every so often, are you petting one of your cats?"

I sighed, realizing that they were not engaged in my lecture, but instead were distracted.

Clearly, they had read my instructor bio and knew that I was a rescue mom with a ragtag brood of furry rascals in my home.

"No, I'm just adjusting the temperature on my space heater, but good guess. I am usually petting one cat or another."

The students' faces fell, and I realized they were disappointed in my rather mundane response. I wondered if the break would refresh them enough to hang on for the rest of the evening's class. I was just about to call for the break when my senior black cat jumped into my lap, her face perfectly centered on camera as if to say, "Here I am!"

Suddenly, thirty-six expressions changed. Grins broke out all over, and the chat box filled with ooohhhs and aaaahhhhs. One after another, students excitedly brought their beloved pets to the camera to show the class.

We spent our break that night laughing with delight and admiring each other's fur babies while sharing names, rescue stories and amusing anecdotes. Among the critters on camera was a cat named Kat, a few Pugs, two Great Dane brothers, and Laurel and Hardy the guinea pigs. Even camera-shy Larry the Lizard made a cameo appearance.

When I finally had to reconvene the lesson, many pets stayed curled up on laps and beside computers, and the smiles continued throughout the session. There was a new energy to the class, and the students seemed more willing to work through the challenging material.

After that night, we opened every class session with a check-in about our furry companions and the joy they had brought to our lives during the past week. And, somehow, the statistics, literature

My Very Good, Very Bad Cat |

reviews and data analyses — and even the quarantine — didn't seem quite so bad anymore.

—Donna L. Roberts—

97

The Magic of the LBC

The cat is, above all things, a dramatist.
~Margaret Benson

I recently inherited a new roommate: a little black cat. I say inherited because Rhiannon officially belongs to my son's girlfriend who moved in with us during the COVID-19 pandemic. Not long after, Rhiannon followed. It was just a few months after losing my own cat, Frankie, so I wasn't ready to adopt another one. No one could fill her paws, I believed. So, while I was open to another roommate, I kept an emotionally safe distance — until I discovered the magic of the LBC, or Little Black Cat.

My Frankie was one of a kind. She clearly had ties to the Norwegian Forest cat family, which I discovered by chance through Instagram. That explained her affinity for frigid weather. Reminiscent of the snow-capped mountains of her ancestors' country, her lustrous gold, black, and brown coat was punctuated with splashes of creamy white. The scruff encircling her expressive face rivaled that of the king of the jungle, growing even bushier and lion-like each winter. But her true enchantment arose from her fearless, independent, and free-spirited personality — scaling a tree in a flash and balancing on the peak of our roof.

I knew in my heart there would never be another Frankie. And while this was certainly true, a deeper truth unfolded as I got to know Rhiannon.

It took her some time to warm up to me — and, honestly, me to her. She started slowly, creeping into the kitchen during the wee hours of the morning when only I was awake. At first, she'd peek around the corner and then hurry down to the basement. Each day, she'd stay a few minutes more, tempted by the little bag of kitty treats I'd bought.

I soon discovered that while Rhiannon may have looked like a thousand other black cats, there was more to her than met the eye. Beneath the humble exterior of this LBC beat the heart of a surprisingly complex and colorful character.

For example, she drank water like a princess enjoying afternoon tea. She'd daintily dip one paw into the bowl, and gently lick the droplets from her pads. When entering the living room, she avoided the shag rug at all costs, artfully leaping from one chairback to another, as agile as a tightrope walker. And the constant motion of her sleek black tail was as expressive, rhythmic, and mesmerizing as an orchestra conductor's baton.

The more I noticed and appreciated her cute, little quirks, the more I realized how vastly I'd misjudged the bewitching powers of the Little Black Cat. Like the infamous LBD, or Little Black Dress, LBCs may seem plain and unadorned, but there's nothing basic about them.

That's what I've discovered about our LBC. She may not look flashy, but like the LBD her appeal is timeless. Charm, character, and individuality are more than a fashion statement; they're what make the purr-fectly simple LBC completely irresistible.

— Margrita Colabuno —

98

Harrowing Harness

There is no more intrepid explorer than a kitten.
~Jules Champfleury

Mumfurd is learning to go for a walk. This wouldn't be such a big deal if he wasn't an eight-month-old kitten with a flair for the dramatic. When we adopted him, our seventeen-year-old daughter Mireya was determined to take him on a walk. She enthusiastically bought him a cat harness and leash. She read about how to train him. She prepared herself mentally and emotionally.

But not even that could get her ready for Mumfurd's reaction. After carefully sizing the harness to make sure it did not restrict his movement in any way, shape, or form, she snapped it on him. He immediately collapsed on his side as if he'd been shot.

She quickly unhooked it and checked the harness over carefully. I checked it. It was perfectly fine. Not hanging loose, but by no means tight. So, we snapped it back on. He immediately collapsed on his side as if he'd been shot.

It became his trick. We'd wait until everyone was watching, we'd snap on the harness, and then… PLOP. He'd lie on the floor, twitching his tail (I liked to think of it as his version of death throes), and refused to get up until the harness was removed. This went on for a few days. But Mireya is a pretty determined person. She tried out a different harness. He still plopped over but got up and walked for a minute or two. Then he started to walk in his harness but wouldn't jump on anything without making a rather dramatic show of falling onto the floor.

This situation progressed until this Sunday when she put on a different harness. He'd worn it before, but it had gotten a little snug. Mireya figured out how to loosen it the rest of the way, and now he seemed to prefer it to the other, roomier one. At last, the moment had come. Mireya put the leash on Mumfurd, and they went outside.

I don't know if you've ever seen a kitten's eyes get as big as a pair of full moons. It's a sight to see. He stepped outside with his furry paws for the first time since we adopted him and immediately started chewing on grass.

There was a list of things I expected him to go for when he got outside, but going herbivore was not even in the top fifty.

For the rest of the day, Mumfurd went from a few ginger steps outside to going inside to yowling to go outside again where he'd walk a little farther. And, as of today, he's wearing his harness all around the house as if it is a magic cloak that gives him special powers.

Which, I suppose, it is.

— Winter D. Prosapio —

99

Shadow Perlmutter

Until one has loved an animal, a part of one's soul
remains unawakened.
~Anatole France

My library system had a strict no-library-cats policy, but Shadow Perlmutter didn't know anything about that. And if he had, I'm sure he would have disregarded it.

Shadow made his own rules. He lived down the block from the library and would wait patiently outside our building until the automatic doors opened. Then he'd saunter in like he owned the place.

He'd sit on the counter beside the sink in the circulation office until one of us turned on the faucet so he could enjoy a drink. He'd visit with the library director in her office. He'd tour the stacks. He'd keep us company at the circulation desk as we checked books in and out.

Eventually, he would settle into a comfy chair in the corner of the quiet reading room to doze.

Shadow Perlmutter became a valued member of the library community. For our patrons, especially children, a trip to the library wasn't complete without stopping by the quiet reading room to visit our unofficial Library Cat on "his" chair.

Occasionally, a patron would approach the circulation desk and exclaim, "There's a cat in the library!"

"That's Shadow Perlmutter," we'd say. "He's our feline patron."

"Isn't there a policy against cats in the library?" they'd ask.

Which meant that one of us would have to go get Shadow and

carry him outside. Within a few hours, of course, he would make his way back in, which was fine with us.

Librarians are notorious cat lovers. We enjoyed having Shadow around. We liked visiting with him, giving him head rubs and receiving a happy purr. We got a kick out of the fact that library-closing procedure at the end of the day now included "putting out the cat."

Then one day, we realized that Shadow had stopped coming to the library. We phoned the Perlmutters, expecting the worst. Not to worry, we were told. Shadow was alive and well, but we wouldn't be seeing him again.

The Perlmutters had moved away.

I recently spoke with Jon Perlmutter, Shadow's owner. He told me that when he lived in my town, Shadow hadn't just been our self-appointed library cat. He'd also befriended the students at the French school and served as the unofficial mascot of the Saint Joseph's University track team, which would take him along on their neighborhood runs, carrying him like a baton.

Jon reported that Shadow's social life continued in his new neighborhood. He would wait by the local church until the pastor's secretary let him into the building, where he would visit with the staff, attend services, or relax in a nest of pillows in a cardboard box under the secretary's desk.

When Shadow wasn't at church, you could find him with the kids at the neighborhood preschool or on the steps of the local co-op greeting shoppers.

When he returned home at the end of the day, Shadow couldn't tell his family about his adventures. But they became aware of them through their neighbors, who knew the Perlmutters as "Shadow's family" and filled them in on what their cat had been up to.

The Perlmutters knew their cat was popular, but they didn't realize just how popular until Shadow died, and "his" church decided to hold a memorial service for him. The Summit Presbyterian Church didn't normally hold memorial services for cats, but Shadow was special.

Over a hundred people showed up.

"I should be so lucky as to have a crowd like that turn up for me,"

Perlmutter told me. "There were a lot of sad people in that church. Folks were really grieving."

People from all walks of life, adults and children, stood up to share memories of how the cat had brightened their lives. Shadow wasn't just the Perlmutters' cat. He had belonged to an entire community.

"We've had beloved cats before," Jon told me. "But they were just cats, not neighborhood celebrities."

Everyone agreed that Shadow was a one-of-a-kind cat.

We never got another library cat. While our director, a cat lover, would welcome a "feline patron," she would never actually acquire a library cat in defiance of the policy set by our library system. Still, we lived in hope that another cat might wander in the door one day and make the library its home.

But it never happened. There was only one Shadow Perlmutter.

— Roz Warren —

The Perfect Gift

*There are few things in life more heartwarming
than to be welcomed by a cat.*
~Tay Hohoff

Christmas was approaching, and I had absolutely no idea what to get for my wife. As usual, I had left my holiday shopping until the last minute. I always had the feeling that the perfect gift would somehow pop up at the right time, although this didn't always happen. This year I didn't have any good ideas.

My spouse, Donna, was a planner. She often did her shopping a year in advance or whenever she saw an ideal gift or a wonderful item on sale. Unlike me, she loved to shop, so she would often have acquired a number of thoughtful gifts for everyone on the list long before Christmas rolled around.

Leave it to me to postpone things to the last few days. I was down to the last week before the holidays started and still didn't have a clue what to get. In my defense, I must add that we had just moved to Italy and were still unpacking. Donna was away attending a conference, so I had the rest of the week to work on the house and figure out what to get her as a Christmas gift before she got back.

My house companion while Donna was away was her cat, Princess, who was everything that her name implied. She came with the package when I married Donna, but she was still very much my wife's cat. She would allow me to feed her and brush her luxurious coat, but she really preferred to spend her time on Donna's lap, looking at me with disdain.

I was keeping Princess indoors in our new home until she became familiar with the place and then planned to slowly introduce her to the great outdoors. Princess had other ideas, and to my shock and horror, scampered out of the house as I was bringing in some groceries. By the time I had turned around and gone back out the door to look for her, she was gone.

Northern Italy is reasonably balmy even in the winter, so I wasn't worried that she would freeze. But we had just moved here, and it was the first time Princess had been outside. Besides being new and disorienting, it can also be a rough-and-tumble place for a cat to be, having to deal with the many feral cats that already live outdoors.

Donna would be back in a few days and it would ruin Christmas for both of us if Princess was not back by then, safe and sound. Donna had already excitedly told me over the phone that she had found several fun toys and delicious snacks for Princess as Christmas gifts. She couldn't wait to get back and wrap them up.

I was in big trouble. I had to find Princess — and fast. So, I made up a poster with her description and a hurried sketch of the cat that I personally drew because I couldn't find a photo of her anywhere. I was sure my wife had hundreds on her phone, but I didn't dare ask her for one. I didn't want her to know that her precious cat had escaped and vanished. It would ruin her time at the conference.

To make sure everyone in our small Italian town was looking for her, I made the description bilingual so that the locals understood everything I had written, and the Americans who worked on the nearby U.S. airbase would also understand. I offered a huge reward and plastered the posters everywhere I could think of.

Perhaps because my drawing and description were too vague, or because of the big reward offered, it wasn't long before folks in the area were arriving at my door with all kinds of feral cats. Though Princess wasn't among them, I could never turn away a hungry animal, so it wasn't long before a group of cats moved into our yard. I figured Donna would understand.

Donna's happy daily calls continued, as did my daily searches for Princess, which became more frantic by the hour. I still hadn't mentioned anything about the disappearance to my wife. I just couldn't bring myself to do it. It would destroy her.

Finally, the day came for my wife to return. I picked her up at the Venice airport but still didn't have the courage to tell her what had happened. I had held back the news for so long that it would now be even more horrific for her to find out. She excitedly showed me the gifts she had found for Princess as we drove home, while I silently racked my brain for a way to break the news to her.

As we drove up the driveway, she could see some of the feral cats munching kibble from bowls by the house. "Surprise!" I exclaimed as she looked wide-eyed at our new acquisitions. She was crying in an instant, but luckily for me, they were tears of joy! "Best Christmas gift ever," she uttered between sobs.

Just as I was about to break the bad news about Princess disappearing, who should appear walking up the driveway but her highness herself?

"Oh, my goodness, you spent the time to show her around the area and teach her to stay outside on her own. I knew you two would get along well while I was gone. Another fantastic Christmas gift," proclaimed my wife as she kissed me on the cheek before hurrying to scoop Princess into her arms and check out our new family of feral cats. I swear that Princess stuck her tongue out at me as she gazed at me with contempt.

So, that's how I managed to give two of the best Christmas gifts ever, all at the last minute.

— Sergio Del Bianco —

Writing Coach

What greater gift than the love of a cat.
~Charles Dickens

I write a sentence,
I write a word,
I write a joke you never heard.

I am a writer,
I wield a pen,
You may have heard of me now and then.

The hard truth for us,
Is that even when not on your own,
When you write, you write alone.

I am no exception,
But as a sliver of loneliness slips through the door,
So does Patch, and I fear no more.

He looks at me as if to say,
"What are you doing, human? I would like to do it, too."
He sidles next to me, and my fingers tap the keyboard anew.

His fluffy, fuzzy, silly self then sighs,
As if his life is complete,
Just lying there as he purrs so sweet.

He tolerates my hugs when I write something great,
He knows that I'm blocked when I stroke him steadily,
He helps me go to sleep most readily.

He sleeps beside me,
For the longest part of night,
And stays with me still when it's light.

He is my best friend,
He is always there,
He is a treasure, rare.

So, writers, I say to you,
It's a Charles Dickens approved fact:
Take my advice; you should get a cat.

—Abigail Metzger—

Meet Our Contributors

Kristi Adams loves sharing the humorous side of military life, including the family cat who views boarding as a personal invitation to Thunderdome. This is Tiki's second story in the *Chicken Soup for the Soul* series. Kristi fears there will be no living with him after this! Read more funny stories at www.kristiadamsmedia.com.

Monica Agnew-Kinnaman is 103 years old and served in an anti-aircraft artillery regiment in the British Army during WWII. She holds a doctorate in psychology and is the author of a non-fiction book about dog rescues, three children's books and numerous short stories.

Mary M. Alward lives in Ontario, Canada. She has had her short stories published in both print and online venues. Mary loves spending time with her family, gardening and reading. Currently, she is working on a series of children's books for young readers.

Valerie Archual is a children's author and travel writer, and is honored to be a contributor to the *Chicken Soup for the Soul* series. Aside from imagining stories and writing them down, she enjoys spending time with her family, including her cats whom she is constantly learning from! Learn more at www.valeriearchual.com.

Pamela Cali Bankston is the author of the *Frizzy Frieda* books, a middle-grade fiction series. Certified in Pediatrics, she practices as an R.N., is a columnist for *The Daily Star* newspaper, and has published, *"La Famiglia" Sicilian American Cookbook* and "Manchac Lighthouse," a short story in *Treasures Found in a Cedar Chest*.

Suzu Bell has been a cat lover since early childhood and has never been without a feline companion except for a few brief periods. She co-founded Kitty Safe Haven No-Kill Shelter, a 501(c)(3) charity, in southwest Missouri. She loves animals of all species, and as of this writing she provides foster care to twelve special kitties.

Cherrilynn Bisbano is an award-winning writer and speaker. Her topics include writing, leadership, and the Bible. She's an ordained minister and chaplain and served in the military. Cherrilynn lives with her son, Michael, Jr., and husband, Mike; she calls them her m&ms. She loves Christ, cats, coffee, and chocolate.

Vikki Burke has published several books, including *Some Days You Dance, Help! It's Dangerous Out Here*, and a daily devotional. She lives in Texas with her husband and their rescue Doberman, Belle. She enjoys her four grandchildren, oil painting, and genealogy. Vikki plans to publish a book about her ancestors.

Jill Burns lives in the mountains of West Virginia with her wonderful family. She's a retired piano teacher and performer. She enjoys writing, music, gardening, nature, and spending time with her grandchildren.

After graduating from art school, **Jack Byron** attempted a career as a freelance illustrator before working with dementia patients as an activity director at several facilities in California. He has also worked as a tattoo artist and had several of his art essays published in addition to his stories in the *Chicken Soup for the Soul* series.

Melanie Chartoff is a life-long stage, screen, voice, and now, virtual actor. She created roles on *Fridays, Seinfeld, Rugrats, Parker Lewis Can't Lose*, and *Weird Science*. Her book, *Odd Woman Out: Exposure in Essays and Stories* is rated 5 stars on Amazon and Barnes & Noble. She lives in Los Angeles, CA.

Annette M. Clayton has a master's degree in writing for children and young adults. Her book for kids ranges from silly to sweet. She is a proud mother of twin girls and an avid hiker. Learn more at www.annettemclayton.com and connect with her on Twitter @AnnetteMClayton.

Margrita Colabuno is a communications specialist, writing consultant, workshop facilitator, and holistic life coach who specializes in the healing power of expressive writing and daily journaling. She also writes an inspirational blog, "Good Vibrations," found on her website at manifestwithmargrita.com.

James Collins serves as the staff evangelist for Southwest Radio

Church and can be heard daily on over 350 Christian radio stations. He is a retired U.S. Army chaplain with multiple combat tours. He and his wife share their home with their three extraordinary children and a lifetime collection of books.

Pete Commander currently resides in Waco, TX and is a fourteen-year veteran of the Navy's Hospital Corp and Hospital Corpsman. He received a Master of Arts in international relations from St. Mary's University of San Antonio, TX. Pete, his wife Carolyn, and their son Terry are avid Texas Rangers and Houston Astro baseball fans. They have three cats at home.

Connie Cook is a retired RN living in Lynden, ON with her two black cats. The older one is now eighteen years old and the other is twelve. Connie admits to being a slave to them both. They know the treats are in the desk drawer and constantly edit her work by walking across the keyboard.

Toni Cordell graduated from high school reading at the fifth-grade level in the 1960s. She is an emerging writer and is enjoying having a voice and sharing stories. Her first self-published book is titled *Puppy on the Other Side of the Pound*.

Suzanne Cushman lives in Carmel-by-the-Sea, CA.

Sergio Del Bianco has a background in fine arts and psychology. He is an artist and writer interested in the intersection of art, psychology, and the humanities. He resides in Europe with his spouse and growing family of rescue animals. E-mail him at sergiodelbianco@yahoo.com or through twitter @DelBianco97.

John Dorroh has been writing all of his life. He completed his first novel when he was twelve. As a high school science teacher he wrote numerous articles for education magazines. He worked for three newspapers and has had over 300 poems published in approximately ninety journals. He is a Southerner living in the Midwest.

Kate Dorsey is a writer, blogger, and artist. Her work has been published in magazines as well as produced on the stage. She is currently working on a series of novels. Kate is also a quilt pattern designer. She designs patterns for her company, Kate's Kwilt Studio.

Janice R. Edwards received her BAT degree (with honors) in

1974. She taught English and journalism before working for Texaco. She wrote for *Image Magazine* until COVID caused it to fold. She has a weekly column in *Bulletin*, a local weekly paper. This is her tenth story published in the *Chicken Soup for the Soul* series.

Amanda Ellis is a writer of settler and indigenous descent. She has recently attended Sage Hill Writing Workshop and is a member of the Saskatchewan Writers' Guild. She does not live in Saskatchewan but enjoys rural vistas of cabbages as she wrangles ideas and her side hustle as a social justice warrior.

Darlene Ellis started writing when she retired from the Post Office. She also enjoys time outdoors and with family, friends, and of course — dogs and cats. Her love of cats and delight in reading cat stories in other *Chicken Soup for the Soul* books encouraged her to share Thumper's story.

Rachel Esser is a young writer from Calgary, Alberta. She is a new teacher and graduate of Mount Royal University, with a passion for creative writing. In her spare time Rachel enjoys writing educational rap songs and children's books, as well as adult fiction. This will be her first publication.

Kayla Fedeson is a television and media producer currently living and working in New York City. A graduate of Syracuse University, Kayla likes to spend her time traveling, writing, and honing her French and Spanish language skills. Kayla is a sports enthusiast and most recently has become enthralled with rock climbing.

Glenda Ferguson lives in Indiana with her husband Tim. Scruffy was loved by them both for several more years, but her favorite spot was anywhere Tim would sit. Glenda writes devotionals, nonfiction, and appears in other titles in the *Chicken Soup for the Soul* series.

Louise M. Foerster has always been — and always will be — a storyteller. A Bachelor of Arts in English and an MBA in marketing propelled her into marketing, consulting, and writing. Now a novelist, Louise lives with her family on the coastline of Connecticut. She enjoys encountering stories everywhere.

H.M. Forrest is the multi-award-winning author of *Dangerous Doorways are for Elfling Princes*. She has published numerous short stories and is currently writing new children's fantasy novels. She lives with her son and bearded dragon in sunny Arizona and enjoys going on new adventures with her son. Find her at www.hmforrest.com.

Stacia Friedman is a freelance writer who uses her own life for material, to the dismay of her family, friends and pets. She studied writing at Temple University and UCLA Extension. When not glued to her laptop, she expresses her creativity through watercolor painting. Learn more at www.StaciaFriedman.com.

James A. Gemmell can be found most summers walking one of the Caminos de Santiago in France or Spain. His other hobbies are writing, playing guitar, drawing/painting, golfing and collecting art.

Constance Gilbert retired from forty-five years of nursing and returned to her childhood dream of becoming a writer. She is an avid reader and loves to do in-depth Bible studies and, like a scribe, write her findings for future generations. Various anthologies have published her inspirational short stories. She encourages women to know they are not invisible in God's eyes.

Jeanna C. Godfrey received her Bachelor of Science degree from the University of Florida and a Doctor of Veterinary Medicine degree from Texas A&M University. After forty years of veterinary practice, she recently retired and enjoys traveling with her husband, reading, gardening, and crafting. She writes narrative nonfiction.

Beth Gooch and her husband Lester Goldsmith have volunteered with animal rescue groups near Memphis, TN for several years. Beth also writes fiction and is past director of Mid-South Christian Writers Conference. She's employed as a digital producer for an online newspaper and was formerly a newspaper copy editor.

Robert Grayson, an award-winning former daily newspaper reporter, writes books for young adults. Among his books are one on animal actors and one on animals in the military. He also writes magazine articles on professional sports stars. He and his wife have a fervent passion for rescuing and helping kittens and cats.

Anna Heaney is known as the Graney Nanny. She has been a visiting nurse for forty years. Anna has two wonderful children, a great husband, and, of course, the cat named Lady Ga-Ga!

Jennifer Heilman earned her undergraduate degree from Penn State University and has graduate degrees from Cleveland State University and Chatham University. She lives and works near the shores of Lake Erie and enjoys hiking, traveling, and spending time with family.

Brenda Hill writes stories about women in crisis who find joy by discovering the inner strength they sometimes forget they possess. Her novels have been published by imprints of Gale and Harlequin. She lives in Southern California with her rescued cats, although she doesn't tell them they rescued her. Learn more at www.brendahill.com.

Janet Hodges is retired and has loved animals all her life. She finds fulfillment in volunteering at a cat rescue center.

Kate Hodnett has been voted one of Louisiana's Best Emerging Poets for two consecutive years. She has been previously published in the *Chicken Soup for the Soul* series. For more of her writing, you can check out Kate Hodnett on YouTube, or shop at www.etsy.com/shop/theasterwitch or contact her via e-mail at khodnett1191@gmail.com.

Donna Hues holds a Master of Science in Education and retired from teaching high school art in 2013. Delving into history for her next mystery and trusting God for the characters and plot fill her time. She has self-published three novels in the *MNM Mystery Series* and won the 2018 Cascade Award for her devotion.

A.J. Hughes recently graduated, with honors, from Scottsdale Community College in Arizona. For nine years, she contributed to a small newspaper with a humorous column and is now a copywriter. She loves to hike and travel, and enjoys music, art, and her two cats. She's currently working on her first children's book.

David Hull is a retired teacher who lives in Holley, NY. He enjoys reading, writing, gardening, spending time with his cats, and watching too many reruns of *Star Trek*. E-mail him at Davidhull59@aol.com.

Brenda Jefferies is a freelance writer/editor living in Waterdown, Ontario with her husband, daughter, and assorted pets. She loves reading and writing, and champions several community literacy initiatives. She holds a Bachelor of Arts in English and French from McMaster University and is studying technical writing.

Lisa Kanarek is a Texas-based writer who writes about family, relationships, and acts of kindness. Her work has been published in *The New York Times*, *The Washington Post*, *Reader's Digest*, on CNBC and PBS's *Next Avenue*.

Janet Sheppard Kelleher earned a math degree from Sweet Briar College and enjoys hang gliding, skydiving, parasailing, hunting, and fishing. Look for *Big C, little ta-ta*, and her new memoir *But What If I Can? The Secret to Procuring Untapped Potential by Ignoring the Pros and Probing Your Past*. Learn more at www.facebook.com/JanetSheppardKelleher.

Deborah Kellogg teaches German at Normandale Community College in Bloomington, MN. She's been teaching for forty-plus years in both high school and college. She's been published in German and English and is a 2017 Fulbright recipient to Germany. She loves biking, travel and cooking, and lives in Eagan, MN with her family and six cats.

Andria Kennedy worked as a veterinary technician for over ten years before turning to her dream job of writing. She now happily splits her time between her freelance work — which mostly features animals, go figure — and working on speculative fiction. She lives in Virginia with her husband, three cats, and a Greyhound.

L.A. Kennedy writes short stories and creates works in polymer and papier mâché clay in her studio while supervised by three family cats: Tortie, Marble and Willy. Her ongoing project is refurbishing the inside and outside of the fixer-upper bought after losing the family home to a wildfire in 2018. E-mail her at elkaynca@aol.com.

Heidi Kling-Newnam received a doctorate in nursing from West Chester University. She works as a nurse practitioner in Pennsylvania. Heidi writes regularly and recently completed the first draft of her first book. Her work has appeared previously in the *Chicken Soup for the Soul* series.

Karen M. Leet enjoys writing from the bluegrass state of Kentucky. She's written a historical novel for kids, *Sarah's Courage*, as well as a nonfiction book about the Civil War in Kentucky, both from The History Press.

Elaine Liner lives, writes, and knits in Dallas, TX. Her novel, *2084: An American Parable*, is available online. Her play, *Finishing School*, can be optioned at Dramatic Publishing. Her latest play, *Dear Donald/Dear*

Hillary (*Their Secret Correspondence*), appeared at U.S. and Canadian fringe festivals in 2021. E-mail her at elaine@elaineliner.com.

Liana Mahoney is a teacher, poet, and children's book author from rural Upstate New York who has learned to multi-task with a black and white cat in her arms most of the time. She enjoys writing poetry, crafting, kayaking, and exploring outside, and fully intends to stay as curious as her cat no matter how old she gets.

David Martin's humor and political satire have appeared in many publications including *The New York Times*, the *Chicago Tribune* and *Smithsonian Magazine*. He has published several collections of his humor including *Dare to be Average* and *Screams and Whispers*, all of which are available online.

Margaret M. Marty, a life-long resident of Rock Creek in east central Minnesota, is a wife, mother, grandmother, and retired certified professional secretary. She is a guest writer for the *Pine City Pioneer*, has been published in seven editions of *The Talking Stick*, and three previous *Chicken Soup for the Soul* books.

Melanie Maxwell is the founder and publisher of *Smooth Jazz News*. She lives in San Diego, CA with two very spoiled rescue cats, Grey Boy and Lily. When Melanie travels to jazz festivals, she always makes sure that her little devils are well loved and taken care of by Denise Hovey, their cat nanny.

As a teenager, **Carol McCollister** dreamed of one day becoming an author. Her life of education, marriage, children, career, sailing, and singing did not allow time for her to pursue writing until she retired in Georgia to be near family. She is planning to spend her retirement writing mystery novels.

Mary McGrath writes from Naples, FL. Her credits include *Newsweek*, *Good Housekeeping*, *The Wall Street Journal*, and many other publications. Beyond writing, she is a published photographer, composer, and also teaches improv. Aside from the arts, she loves to swim, travel, and of course, laugh.

Kim Johnson McGuire received her Bachelor of Arts in Literature from the University of California, Santa Barbara. She has volunteered as a cat socializer for eighteen years. She works as a Pilates instructor and enjoys traveling and golfing. Kim and her two quirky cats live in Grover Beach, CA. E-mail her at kimmycat2@msn.com.

Beth McMurray writes and hikes in the San Francisco Bay Area.

Louisa Godissart McQuillen has published stories and poetry since childhood. She also has written five poetry chapbooks featuring nostalgia, nature and wildlife titled *When Seasons Change*, *Above the Evergreens*, *Hoofbeats*, *Come Fly with Me*, and *Tin Roof Tap*. Her chapbook is titled *Stories to Help You Sleep*. E-mail her at lzm4@psu.edu.

Abigail Metzger has been writing since the age of five; her first ever story was of a cat winning a pet show. Living with three cats of her own, her passion for cats and writing inevitably grew. When not writing or spending time with her felines, she enjoys illustrating, riding, painting, videography, and animation.

Robyn Milliken has her Master of Arts in Sociology. She lives in sunny Florida with her family. Robyn enjoys the beach, reading, spending time with family, daydreaming and writing.

Terilynn Mitchell is a registered veterinary nurse who has cared for unadoptable animals for over twenty-five years. She currently works as the surgical nurse for an organization that spays and neuters stray and community cats in Northern California. She is finishing a collection of rescue and hospice stories.

Sonia A. Moore has a bachelor's degree in information sciences. She has three sons, plus grandchildren and one great-grandson. She loves writing freelance and gardening. Art is also one of her greatest joys of life.

Ann Morrow is a writer, photographer, and animal advocate. She currently resides in South Dakota, along with her two mischievous cats and a trail-loving dog. Ann is a frequent contributor to the *Chicken Soup for the Soul* series and is currently working on a collection of humor essays to be published in late 2021.

Linda Yencha Nichols is a single mother of three and works as an in-home caregiver for the elderly. She enjoys writing, singing, and studying the paranormal, and hopes to one day write a book. Linda lives with two of her sons and her fiancé.

Anne Oliver, a native of West Virginia, holds bachelor's and master's degrees from the University of Georgia. She and her husband George reared three Army brats during his thirty-one years with the Army. (HOOAH!) She enjoys volunteering, reading, and is looking forward to more great adventures. E-mail her at armygr174@aol.com.

Loretta Olund lives in Prince George enjoying her time with her many pets, reading and writing. She has been published in *Chicken Soup for the Soul: I Can't Believe My Dog Did That* and in a short story collection by the SPCA.

Darlene Parnell has a master's degree in social work from Indiana University. She has a private practice in counseling and life coaching in Fishers, IN. She plans to continue writing inspirational books, stories, and poetry. E-mail her at darleneparnell@att.net or learn more at darleneparnellllcsw.com.

Nikesh Patel has been a physical therapist since 2000. He lives in Sugar Land, TX with his wife Priti and their two daughters Maiya and Jaida. Nikesh enjoys writing and loves taking his family on trips across the globe to visit new places.

Faith Paulsen's work appears in several *Chicken Soup for the Soul* books. Her poetry chapbook, *We Marry, We Bury, We Sing or We Weep*, was a runner-up in Moonstone Arts' Chapbook contest. Her writing has appeared in many venues including *One Art*, *Ghost City Press*, and *Book of Matches*. For kitten photos, visit www.faithpaulsenpoet.com/.

Laura Plummer is an American writer from Massachusetts whose work has been featured in a number of print and online publications. She is passionate about animals and frequently writes about her own beloved pets. Learn more at lauraplummer.me.

Melinda Pritzel received a B.A. in business/legal assistance from Avila University, Kansas City, MO. She enjoys photography and uses her photography skills, together with her love of animals and humor, to create greeting cards. You can find her cards at www.greetingcarduniverse.com/yowzers.

Winter D. Prosapio is a humor columnist, essayist, and novelist living in the Texas Hill Country. She is a frequent contributor to the *Chicken Soup of the Soul* series and believes cats have a complex inner monologue going on at all times.

Connie Kaseweter Pullen lives in rural Sandy, OR, near her five children and several grandchildren. She earned a B.A. degree, with honors, at the University of Portland in 2006, with a double major in psychology and sociology. Connie enjoys writing, photography and exploring nature. E-mail her at MyGrandmaPullen@aol.com.

Donna L. Roberts is a native Upstate New Yorker who lives and works in Europe. She is a university professor and holds a Ph.D. in psychology. Donna is an animal and human rights advocate and when she is researching or writing she can be found at her computer buried in rescue cats.

Janet Ramsdell Rockey is a freelance writer living in Florida with her family and two cats. Her writing dedication endures the long list of home improvements for her nearly 100-year-old bungalow, as well as feisty felines, who are useful distractions that inspire her fiction and nonfiction literary works.

Carolyn Byers Ruch is the author of two children's books and the founder of the Rise and Shine Movement, equipping adults to protect children from sexual abuse. She has seven adult children and two beloved grandchildren. Carolyn's two cats, Tilly and Yin, are her office buddies. She writes. They nap.

Rihab Sawah is a professor of physics. She co-authored *The Everything STEM Handbook* and *What's Your STEM*. To many who know her personally, Rihab is a poet and a writer. She loves to invite self-inquiry through stories and provokes deep reflections in her poetry. Rihab is also a Hatha Yoga teacher and practitioner.

Melanie Saxton is a writer based in Texas. Her six rescue pets are the inspiration for much of her work. She earned a degree in English and with the advent of an empty nest, is working on a later-in-life master's degree in digital media. Learn more at www.melaniesaxtonmedia.com.

Leslie C. Schneider grew up in Montana and currently lives in Denver, CO with her husband of over fifty years, Bill. Sons John and Bill live nearby as do four granddaughters and one grandson. Reading and writing have been Leslie's passions since childhood. In her spare time, she also makes Ukrainian eggs.

Judy Schwab is a semi-retired assistant librarian and in between those hours, she spends time with her hobbies of writing and photography. She's been writing verse since she was a teenager and has been published in *IDEALS* and *Good Old Days*, and has self-published three inspirational devotionals.

Paroma Sen has been writing stories since she was a child. She has a love for the written word that manifests with every poem and story she puts together. She is active on Medium and is a top writer in a few different categories on that platform.

Cassie Silva lives and works near Vancouver, BC. This is the fifth time her stories have appeared in the *Chicken Soup for the Soul* series. Trooper Silva enjoys chasing pinecones, squirrels, riding around on his mom's shoulders, and getting his own way. E-mail them both at cassiesilva@ymail.com.

M. Maureen Skahan is a member of the Carver Senior Center Writing Group. She won honorable mention in the Loudoun County Write-on Contest and has had several stories published in the Carver Center annual anthologies. A native of Richmond, VA she majored in Economics at the University of Richmond.

Billie Holladay Skelley received her bachelor's and master's degrees from the University of Wisconsin-Madison. A retired clinical nurse specialist, she is the mother of four and grandmother of two. Billie enjoys writing, and her work crosses several genres. She spends her non-writing time reading, gardening, and traveling.

Edwin F. Smith has been writing award-winning short stories, articles, and manuscripts for many years. Growing up in Bountiful, UT in the '50s and '60s provided a backdrop for wonderful memories and experiences in an era when everyone was a friend and entertainment was created from scratch.

Mary J. Staller is a member of the Florida Writers Association and cofounder of the Florida Gulf Coast Writers Circle. She has published short stories, a children's book and is currently working on a novel. Mary enjoys all things "beach" and takes her ukulele and notebook there to strum and find inspiration.

Diane Stark is a wife, mother, and freelance writer. She is a frequent contributor to the *Chicken Soup for the Soul* series. She loves to write about the important things in life: her family and her faith.

Lynn Tremblay lives in Ontario, Canada. She graduated from the University of Toronto in 2010 with an honour's degree in English literature and a minor in professional writing.

Naomi True studied dance and English, completing her post-graduate studies in 2004. As a mum of two and juggler of many roles, Naomi maintains her tenuous grasp on reality through writing, movement and sewing. She can be found drinking tea in the company of her midnight cat at doingmybestwithasmile.wordpress.com.

Esther Tucker is a registered nurse as well as a holistic health practitioner in a lovely little town called Murray, KY. She is the mother of five beautiful children and is owned by three cats. Writing poetry is one of Esther's passions; she is currently working on an autobiography.

Malcolm Twigg lives in Torquay, the spiritual home of Monty Python, which influences much of his writing. He won the 1995 Peter Pook Humorous Novel competition and was UK place winner on the L. Ron Hubbard Writers of the Future Contest the following year. He maintains a wide Indie publishing presence on various websites.

Writing coach **Roz Warren** writes for everyone from the *Funny Times* to *The New York Times* and has appeared on both the *Today Show* and *Morning Edition*. This is the fifteenth time her work has been included in the *Chicken Soup for the Soul* series. Roz loves to hear from readers. E-mail her at roSwarren@gmail.com.

Susan C. Willett is a writer and blogger whose award-winning stories, poems, and humor appear in print and online, including her website LifeWithDogsAndCats.com. She shares her home with four cats and three dogs — all rescues. Follow them all on Facebook and Twitter @WithDogsAndCats, and Instagram @LifeWithDogsAndCats.

Meet Amy Newmark

Amy Newmark is the bestselling author, editor-in-chief, and publisher of the *Chicken Soup for the Soul* book series. Since 2008, she has published 176 new books, most of them national bestsellers in the U.S. and Canada, more than doubling the number of Chicken Soup for the Soul titles in print today. She is also the author of *Simply Happy*, a crash course in Chicken Soup for the Soul advice and wisdom that is filled with easy-to-implement, practical tips for enjoying a better life.

Amy is credited with revitalizing the Chicken Soup for the Soul brand, which has been a publishing industry phenomenon since the first book came out in 1993. By compiling inspirational and aspirational true stories curated from ordinary people who have had extraordinary experiences, Amy has kept the twenty-eight-year-old Chicken Soup for the Soul brand fresh and relevant.

Amy graduated *magna cum laude* from Harvard University where she majored in Portuguese and minored in French. She then embarked on a three-decade career as a Wall Street analyst, a hedge fund manager, and a corporate executive in the technology field. She is a Chartered Financial Analyst.

Her return to literary pursuits was inevitable, as her honors thesis in college involved traveling throughout Brazil's impoverished northeast region, collecting stories from regular people. She is delighted to have come full circle in her writing career — from collecting stories "from the people" in Brazil as a twenty-year-old to, three decades later, collecting stories "from the people" for Chicken Soup for the Soul.

When Amy and her husband Bill, the CEO of Chicken Soup for the Soul, are not working, they are visiting their four grown children and their three grandchildren.

Follow Amy on Twitter @amynewmark. Listen to her free podcast — Chicken Soup for the Soul with Amy Newmark — on Apple, Google, or by using your favorite podcast app on your phone.

Thank You

We owe huge thanks to all our contributors and fans. We received thousands of submissions for this popular topic, and we spent months reading all of them. Our editors Crescent LoMonaco and Barbara LoMonaco read all of them and created the first manuscript with their favorites.

Susan Heim did the first round of editing, D'ette chose the perfect quotations to put at the beginning of each story, and Amy edited the stories and shaped the final manuscript.

As we finished our work, D'ette Corona continued to be Amy's right-hand woman in working with all our wonderful writers. Barbara LoMonaco, Kristiana Pastir, Mary Fisher, and Elaine Kimbler jumped in at the end to proof, proof, proof. And yes, there will always be typos anyway, so please feel free to let us know about them at webmaster@chickensoupforthesoul.com, and we will correct them in future printings.

The whole publishing team deserves a hand, including our Senior Director of Marketing Maureen Peltier, our Vice President of Production Victor Cataldo, and our graphic designer Daniel Zaccari, who turned our manuscript into this beautiful, inspirational book.

About
American Humane

American Humane is the country's first national humane organization, founded in 1877 and committed to ensuring the safety, welfare, and wellbeing of all animals. For more than 140 years, American Humane has been first to serve in promoting the welfare and safety of animals and strengthening the bond between animals and people. American Humane's initiatives are designed to help whenever and wherever animals are in need of rescue, shelter, protection, or security.

With remarkably effective programs and the highest efficiency ratio of any national humane group for the stewardship of donor dollars, the nonprofit has earned Charity Navigator's top "4-Star" rating, has been named a "Top-Rated Charity" by CharityWatch and a "Best Charity" by Consumer Reports, and achieved the prestigious "Gold Level" charity designation from GuideStar.

American Humane is first to serve animals around the world, striving to ensure their safety, welfare and humane treatment—from rescuing animals in disasters to ensuring that animals are humanely treated. One of its best-known programs is the "No Animals Were Harmed®" animals-in-entertainment certification, which appears during the end credits of films and TV shows, and today monitors some 1,000 productions yearly with an outstanding safety record.

American Humane's farm animal welfare program helps ensure

the humane treatment of nearly a billion farm animals, the largest animal welfare program of its kind. And recently, the historic nonprofit launched the American Humane Conservation program, an innovative initiative helping ensure the humane treatment of animals around the globe in zoos and aquariums.

Continuing its longstanding efforts to strengthen the healing power of the human-animal bond, American Humane pairs veterans struggling to cope with the invisible wounds of war with highly-trained service dogs, and spearheaded a groundbreaking clinical trial that provided for the first time scientific substantiation for the effectiveness of animal-assisted therapy (AAT) for children with cancer and their families.

To learn more about American Humane, visit americanhumane. org and follow them on Facebook, Instagram, and Twitter.

AMERICAN★HUMANE
FIRST TO SERVE°

Editor's Note: Chicken Soup for the Soul and American Humane have created *Humane Heroes*, a FREE new series of e-books and companion curricula for elementary, middle and high schoolers. Through 36 inspirational stories of animal rescue, rehabilitation, and humane conservation being performed at the world's leading zoological institutions, and 18 easy-to-follow lesson plans, *Humane Heroes* provides highly engaging free reading materials that also encourage young people to appreciate and protect Earth's disappearing species. To download the free e-books and learn about the program, please visit www.chickensoup.com/ah.

Sharing Happiness, Inspiration, and Hope

Real people sharing real stories, every day, all over the world. In 2007, *USA Today* named *Chicken Soup for the Soul* one of the five most memorable books in the last quarter-century. With over 100 million books sold to date in the U.S. and Canada alone, more than 250 titles in print, and translations into nearly fifty languages, "chicken soup for the soul®" is one of the world's best-known phrases.

Today, twenty-eight years after we first began sharing happiness, inspiration and hope through our books, we continue to delight our readers with new titles, but have also evolved beyond the bookshelves with super premium pet food, television shows, a podcast, video journalism from aplus.com, licensed products, and free movies and TV shows on our Popcornflix and Crackle apps. We are busy "changing your world one story at a time®." Thanks for reading!

Share with Us

We all have had Chicken Soup for the Soul moments in our lives. If you would like to share your story or poem with millions of people around the world, go to chickensoup. com and click on Submit Your Story. You may be able to help another reader and become a published author at the same time. Some of our past contributors have launched writing and speaking careers from the publication of their stories in our books!

We only accept story submissions via our website. They are no longer accepted via mail or fax. Visit our website, www.chickensoup. com, and click on Submit Your Story for our writing guidelines and a list of topics we are working on.

To contact us regarding other matters, please send us an e-mail through webmaster@chickensoupforthesoul.com, or fax or write us at:

Chicken Soup for the Soul
P.O. Box 700
Cos Cob, CT 06807-0700
Fax: 203-861-7194

One more note from your friends at Chicken Soup for the Soul: Occasionally, we receive an unsolicited book manuscript from one of our readers, and we would like to respectfully inform you that we do not accept unsolicited manuscripts, and we must discard the ones that appear.

Chicken Soup for the Soul

The Magic of Cats

101 Tales of Family, Friendship & Fun

Amy Newmark

Royalties from this book go to
AMERICAN·HUMANE
FIRST TO SERVE

Paperback: 978-1-61159-066-1
eBook: 978-1-61159-301-3

More heartwarming, fun stories

Chicken Soup for the Soul®

101 Tales of Canine Companionship

My Hilarious, Heroic, Human Dog

Amy Newmark

Royalties from this book go to
AMERICAN·HUMANE
FIRST TO SERVE™

Paperback: 978-1-61159-078-4
eBook: 978-1-61159-318-1

about our favorite family members

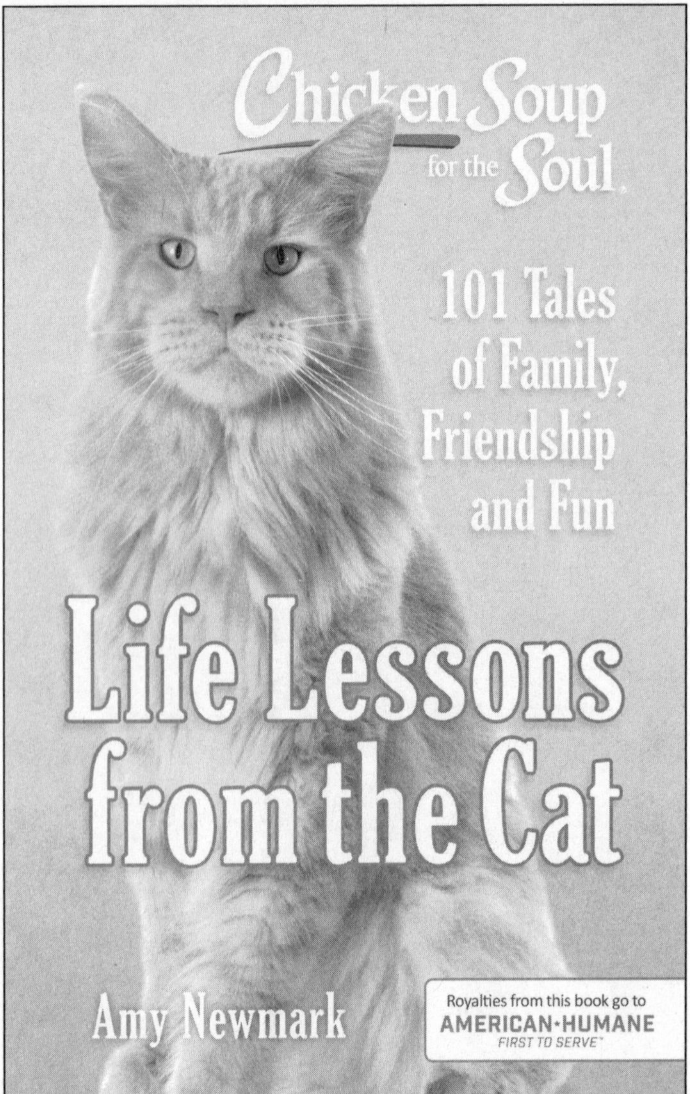

Chicken Soup for the Soul.

101 Tales
of Family,
Friendship
and Fun

Life Lessons
from the Cat

Amy Newmark

Royalties from this book go to
AMERICAN·HUMANE
FIRST TO SERVE

Paperback: 978-1-61159-989-3
eBook: 978-1-61159-289-4

More wisdom and inspiration

Chicken Soup for the Soul

Life Lessons from the Dog

101 Tales of Family, Friendship & Fun

Amy Newmark

Royalties from this book go to
AMERICAN·HUMANE
FIRST TO SERVE

Paperback: 978-1-61159-988-6
eBook: 978-1-61159-288-7

from our four-legged friends

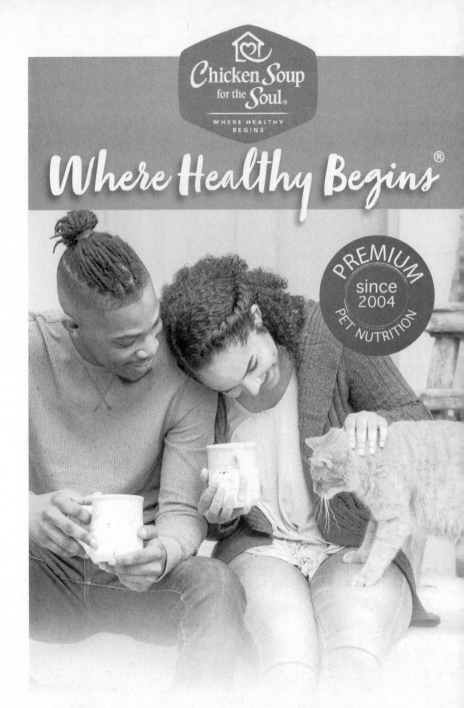

100% Satisfaction Guaranteed

Premium. Affordable. Nutrition.

✓ #1 Ingredient REAL meat or fish

✓ No wheat, corn or soy

✓ No by-product meals

✓ Made in the USA

www.chickensouppets.com | petsupport@chickensoupforthesoul.com

Changing lives one story at a time®
www.chickensoup.com